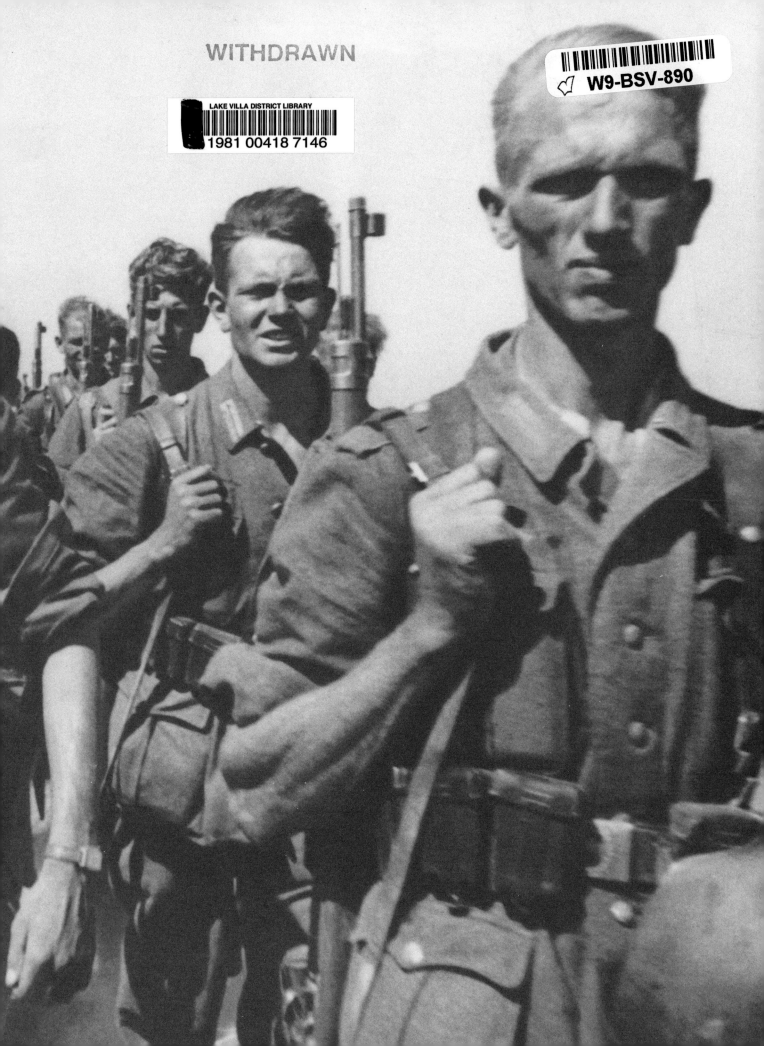

BARBAROSSA

THE FIRST 7 DAYS

BARBAROSSA

THE FIRST 7 DAYS

WILL FOWLER

CASEMATE
HAVERTOWN, PA

This edition first published in 2004 by

CASEMATE
2114 Darby Road
Havertown, PA 19083

Library of Congress Cataloging-in-Publication Data available.

ISBN 1-932033-23-8

Editorial and design by
Amber Books Ltd
Bradley's Close
74–77 White Lion Street
London N1 9PF
www.amberbooks.co.uk

Project Editor: Michael Spilling
Design: Jerry Williams
Picture Research: Natasha Jones
Maps: Peter Harper

Printed in Italy by Eurolitho S.p.A.

Contents

CHAPTER ONE

THE RISE OF A NEW ORDER

In the late 1930s Germans were full of
confidence. The country had emerged from the
shame of defeat in 1918 and was now a powerful
player on the world stage. Germans recognised
that the man who had made this possible was
Adolf Hitler, leader of the Nazi Party that now
controlled the country. He had reintroduced
military conscription and rearmament so
Germany's enemies – France and Britain – were
obliged to take her seriously.

EUROPE WAS BATHED IN LATE SUMMER SUNSHINE in 1939 as men
and women savoured the last weeks of a tense year of peace.
It would soon be wrecked and despoiled by over five years of
war – a war that would fundamentally change the character
of the continent forever.

Berliners escaped to the sandy foreshore of the Havel
lakes to the west of the city and others strolled in the cool
woodland of the Grunewald. On the Baltic coast Germans
basked in the sun and enjoyed the facilities of the *Kraft durch
Freude* (KdF, 'Strength through Joy') holiday resorts. Boys
were off at the *Hitler Jugend* and girls at *Bund Deutscher
Mädel* camps, vigorous environments in the healthy
outdoors that their parents had never enjoyed in the grim
1920s. The Germany enjoying what was now known as the
'*Führer*'s Weather' was a proud, powerful and confident
nation and not the humiliated, bankrupt, decadent post-war
republic based at the provincial spa town of Weimar, saddled

Left: At a Parteitag *(Party Day) rally at Nuremberg Adolf Hitler surveys
the massed ranks of the SA (*Sturmabteilung, Storm Detachment*) in
their distinctive brown uniforms. The SA helped him to power in 1933,
but afterwards its leaders were removed in the 'Night of the Long Knives'.*

with the debts of war reparations and guilt imposed by the Versailles Treaty.

In 1933 the *Nationalsozialistische Deutsche Arbeiterpartei* (NSDAP, National Socialist German Worker's Party or Nazi Party) had come to power led by a war veteran who had served on the Western Front. He caught the national mood of shame and anger and expressed both its resentment and a yearning for a better world, appealing to them with a vague but heady mixture of nationalism, racism and mysticism. In speeches and writings in the 1920s and 1930s he rolled anti-Semitism, contempt for democracy and hatred of Bolshevism into ranting outbursts that enraptured his audiences. The Communists were the enemies who had destroyed Germany in World War I and now plotted to corrupt and enslave Europe. Democracy had been responsible for two economic collapses that had impoverished hard working Germans. It was time for a new

Below: A Berlin policeman struggles to control an enraged crowd in the 1920s. Inflation had destroyed the value of the Mark *and radicalised even the middle classes – they would soon be attracted by the heady rhetoric of the Nazis and the Communists.*

THE RISE OF A NEW ORDER

order. The man who tapped this heady mixture of rage and resentment was an Austrian, a self-taught artist who had dodged a call up for military service in the Austro-Hungarian Army, but had volunteered for the German Army at the outbreak of war in 1914. His name was Adolf Hitler.

A CLASH OF IDEOLOGIES

However, his style of political movement had a powerful rival. After World War I, in which monarchies and capitalism had clashed in the most destructive war the world had ever seen, many Europeans saw in Communism a new movement for good and a belief in something greater than the individual, which would find echoes in twenty-first century religious fundamentalism. No sacrifice could be too great for the Comintern, the Communist International, a movement that knew no national borders. Communist sympathizers working as spies in Occupied Europe and Britain would give loyal and vital assistance to Moscow during the war. To conservatives in the 1930s the Comintern seemed sinister and threatening and for many Fascism with its nationalist agenda appeared an attractive alternative type of totalitarianism.

In Germany fear of Marxism and anti-Semitism was fuelled by the Jewish origins of revolutionaries like Leon Trotsky, born Lev Davidov Bronstein, and German-born Karl Marx, whose family had converted to Christianity from Judaism. After 1918 the *Dolchstosstheorie* ('stab in the back theory') had asserted that Germany had been destroyed from within by 'Jews, traitors and Social Democrats' and not defeated in the field of battle. Left-wing revolts in Germany were headed by the Bolshevik revolutionaries Rosa Luxemburg in Berlin and Kurt Eisner in Munich, both of whom were murdered in 1919 and subsequently portrayed as anti-German Jewish agitators.

Although there were German Communists, it was Hitler who would exert an almost hypnotic hold over Germany and its military and economic leaders for a period of 12 years, beginning with an exhilarating promise of a better future and ending in 1945 in ruins, disaster and a worse defeat than 1918. In the 1920s, however, nothing could seem as bad as the shame, inflation and poverty that gripped the once proud Imperial Germany.

In his drive for political power in the 1920s Hitler employed both the democratic process to exploit these grievances and also extra-legal methods. Based in one of the huge Munich beer halls, he attempted a *coup d'état* against the Bavarian state government on 9 November 1923. It failed and 19 men were killed. He was arrested and held in the comfort of Landsberg prison, where he received visitors and had time

NATIONAL SOCIALIST CAR PRODUCTION

The *Volkswagen*, which was originally to have been called the *Kdf Wagen*, was designed between 1933 and 1934 by Dr Ferdinand Porsche, then a designer at Daimler-Benz, Stuttgart. There are reports that Hitler laid down the design criteria for the robust hump-backed four-seater car. It was intended to be a low cost vehicle that would be affordable to ordinary workers who would buy it on a weekly subscription basis. Until this time the car had been a middle- and upper-class luxury. Hitler announced the project in 1935 and on 26 May 1938 laid the foundation stone for a factory at Fallersleben, near Brunswick, where the car would be built. More than 330,000 workers subscribed *Reichsmarks* 280 million for the car. Pilot models were built, but during the war the factory concentrated on the le Pkw Typ 62 and Typ 82 *Kübelwagen*, a 4 x 4 field car that was effectively a German Jeep. Some of the VW Beetles that were built during the war saw service in the German army as the 4 x 2 le Pkw Typ 82E/Typ 51 Limousine. After the war the British military government helped to get the factory working again to bring employment to the Germans. Production ended in West Germany but continued in the Volkswagen plant in Mexico, finding a ready market in the USA. The last 'Beetle', as the car came to be known, rolled off the VW production line in Mexico in June 2003.

to dictate his political testimony *Mein Kampf* (*My Struggle*). During the Weimar Republic in the 1920s the Nazi brown-shirted paramilitary group, the *Sturmabteilung* (SA, Storm Troops), headed by a former soldier Ernst Röhm, had fought street battles with the *Kommunistische Partei Deutschlands* (KPD, German Communist Party) and its paramilitary organization, the *Rotfrontkämpferbund* (RFB, Red Frontline Fighters' League).

The SA broke up the KPD meetings and intimidated rival politicians, but for Hitler the group would be dispensable. During the *Nacht der Langen Messe* ('Night of the Long Knives') or Blood Purge of 30 June 1934, Hitler used the *Schutzstaffel* SS or Protection Squad, founded as his personal bodyguard in 1929 with 280 men, to eliminate the leadership of the SA. The *Wehrmacht* resented Röhm's plans to take over the armed forces and absorb it into the SA and Hitler knew that he particularly needed the Army (*Heer*) more than the rabble-rousing SA.

THE NEW GERMANY

In the early 1930s, however, few could imagine that the Nazi government would become a monolithic organization with Hitler at the top, as the *Führer* or Leader, and eight layers of administration and control. From the top of the organization to its most junior members, the humble *Parteigenosse* (PG, Party Comrade), each man and woman was a proud *Nationalsozialistischer Deutscher* (NSD, or National Socialist German), a citizen of the Third Reich. It absorbed and penetrated every aspect of society in a policy called *Gleichshaltung* (Co-ordination of the Political Will),

Above: Flanked by senior Nazi party officers, Adolf Hitler takes the salute as columns of SA men march through the streets of old Nuremberg. The ritual, discipline and regalia appealed to many Germans who craved a world of order and security.

from trades unions to academic and professional societies. Perhaps the most bizarre and disturbing example of *Gleichshaltung* was the change to the badge of the *Deutsche Jägerschaft* (German Hunting Association). The original design, which drew on the old Christian myth of St Hubert, showed a stag's head with the Christian Cross set between the antlers. After 1933 the cross design changed to the Nazi *Hakenkreuz* ('crooked cross') or swastika. This decorative motif dated from the fourth century BC but, set at an angle, it was adopted by the Nazis and later, along with the eagle, became the German state symbol. To Nazi mystics it was an Aryan symbol, and their vision of Aryans – blonde, blue-eyed Nordics – stood at the top of the racial ladder.

> In the West the armies were too big for the country.
> In the East the country was too big for the armies.
>
> *Winston Churchill, 1931*

In 1933–4 Hitler came to power like a knight to the rescue; we thought nothing better could happen to Germany once we saw what he was doing to fight unemployment, corruption and so on.

Bernhard Schmitt

There had been numerous church and social youth movements in Germany for boys and girls in the inter-war period but under the Nazis they were absorbed into the *Hitler Jugend* (HJ, Hitler Youth) for boys or the *Bund Deutscher Mädel* (BdM, German Girls' League). From an organization with 100,000 members in 1932 the HJ had, with *Gleichshaltung*, increased 33 times within two years, making it the largest youth movement in the Western world.

In June 1935 the law was promulgated setting up the *Reichsarbeitsdienst* (RAD, State Labour Service). Between the ages of 19 and 25 all physically fit Germans were required to undertake work for six months. Huge construction projects as well as agricultural work were the remit of the RAD, which was in effect a toughening school for subsequent service in the armed forces.

The *Reichsautobahn* (state motorway) system in Germany, which had been started before the rise of the Nazis, had expanded rapidly after 1933. A total length of 6900km (4285 miles) was proposed and on 23 September 1933 Hitler broke ground on the stretch from Frankfurt to Darmstadt. By 15

Below: Girls of the Bund Deutscher Mädel *(BdM) – the German Girls' League – on a summer camp march. Though they enjoyed camping and outdoor activities the role of the BdM was to foster a politically sound setting for girls to prepare for marriage and motherhood.*

Above: Armed police surround an elderly Jewish shopkeeper following the destruction of Jewish property in Kristallnacht *in November 1938. It marked the beginning of repression that would end in the 1940s with deportation and the gas chambers of the concentration camps.*

December 1938 some 3000km (1863 miles) of *Reichsautobahn* had been completed. Most *Reichsautobahnen* were 24m (78ft 9in) wide and divided into two lanes each 7.5m (24ft 7in) wide. In the middle was a 5m (16ft 5in) grass strip with a 2m (6ft 6in) verge on the side of the road. The motorways, surfaced with concrete 20cm (7in) thick, were landscaped and special emphasis was given to bridge design. The construction programme was part of a larger operation to reduce unemployment in Germany and thousands of unemployed men were sent to the construction sites. Wages were low and the men were accommodated in barracks adjoining the motorways.

A BOOMING ECONOMY

This was part of a 'make work' programme that dramatically reduced unemployment in Germany, which totalled 5.4 million when the Nazis came to power in June 1933. The work programmes had in fact been put in place by the despised Weimar government, but the Nazis took the credit as they pushed the numbers of unemployed down rapidly. The unemployment figures dropped year by year and with their fall economic and national self-confidence increased.

> January 1934: 3.7 million unemployed
> January 1935: 2.9 million
> January 1936: 2.5 million
> January 1937: 1.8 million

A training and rearmament programme, which had been conducted in secret prior to June 1933, was made public and the tiny *Reichswehr* expanded into the *Wehrmacht*. Military

REICHSWEHR

Disarmament of the old Imperial Army after 1918 was actually an advantage since the new force was not cluttered with weapons and equipment that was becoming obsolete and so it could start with a clean slate. From 1919 to 1935 Germany's military forces were known as the *Reichswehr*. Following the Treaty of Versailles Germany was limited to an army of 100,000 men and a navy of 15,000, while an air force was forbidden.

The *Reichswehr* may have been small, but it was composed of experienced and dedicated soldiers who were keen to explore new ideas and tactics using tanks and aircraft. These men had been hand picked and would form the core of the *Wehrmacht* (Armed Forces) established in

1935. The staff officers fought 'war games' on map tables and sent soldiers and vehicles charging across training areas with 'tanks' that were civilian cars with fake armour made from cardboard. Even before the Nazis came to power the *Reichswehr* had established secret links with the Red Army: from 1924 tank crews were training in the USSR near the Karma River and from 1930 air-crews joined them. New secret armaments programmes were also under way using production facilities in neutral countries such as Sweden and Switzerland for cover. Hitler promised a programme of rearmament in a speech to generals on 3 February 1933. Conscription was introduced on 16 March 1935 and the force was renamed the *Wehrmacht*.

service was reintroduced in 1935 and a year later the army received new dress and field uniforms.

There was work in Nazi Germany but also organized leisure. The *NS Gemeinschaft Kraft durch Freude* (KdF, National Socialist Association of Strength through Joy) was a recreational organization designed to stimulate morale among workers. Headed by Robert Ley, a man notorious for his debauchery and anti-Semitism, KdF was based on the Italian Fascist scheme *Dopo Lavoro* and was first proposed as

Nach der Arbeit (After Work). It eventually became a huge leisure organization with two new cruise liners, holiday camps, cut price theatre tickets and the *Volkswagen* (the People's Car). The last of these was the only post-war survivor, living on as the familiar VW Beetle.

To outsiders Germany appeared extraordinarily dynamic and vigorous. Some foreign visitors, however, described the atmosphere as not being that of a nation at peace, but one on leave from World War I and preparing for World War II.

Yet there was an even darker side to Germany. In lurid scenes on the night of 10 May 1933, almost within days of coming to power, the Nazis instituted the *Bücherverbrennung*, the ritual destruction of books written by 'degenerate and Jewish littérateurs', which were hurled onto fires burning outside the libraries of German universities.

ANTI-SEMITISM

The first anti-Semitic laws were promulgated in September 1935, following a boycott of Jewish shops that had taken place two years earlier. Shops were daubed with swastikas and anti-Semitic slogans, and SA men stood guard outside to deter shoppers. In November 1935 a Law of Reich Citizenship defined who was a Jew or of mixed race (*Mischling*). By April 1938 all Jewish wealth had to be registered and in June all Jewish businesses had to be registered. From October all passports for Jews were stamped with the letter 'J'. *Kristallnacht* (Crystal Night, or Night of Broken Glass) in November saw the destruction of synagogues and Jewish shops and led to the imprisonment of more than 20,000 Jews. With the outbreak of war a curfew was imposed on Jews. The first deportations began in 1940 and in September 1941 all Jews were obliged to wear an identifying yellow cloth star.

Left: The poster for a film of the Berlin Olympics of 1936. There were superb stadia and the games ran with German efficiency. However the sporting success of the black American Jesse Owens contradicted the Nazi concept of racial superiority.

As soon as the Nazis came to power there were indicators of what was to come. The SA, police officials and even senior Nazis set up *Wilde Lager*, or *wilde KZ* (literally 'wild camps'), which were the first concentration camps. Most were closed down after the first rush of arrests had fallen off. The German public was informed that the camps were needed for the restoration of public order and security, and were legal under Article 48 of the Weimar Constitution. A law dated 28 February 1933 suspended clauses of the constitution and provided for dissenters to be taken into

Below: The Enigma encryption machine as used by the German armed forces and police for secure radio transmissions. Once letters had been encoded there were hundreds of millions of possible permutations and it seemed impossible to believe that it could be broken.

Schutzhaft (protective custody). In reality the camps offered SA men the opportunity to practice a little extortion and revenge against rivals and enemies.

REOCCUPYING THE RHINELAND

Within three years of taking power Hitler reinforced his popularity with Germans with the reoccupation of the Rhineland (*Rheinlandbesetzung*). It was his first foreign policy coup. The Rhineland was a strip of land about 60km (37 miles) long to the east of the River Rhine, including the cities of Cologne, Düsseldorf and Bonn and all the territory to the west. It had been demilitarized since 1918 as part of the Treaty of Versailles, a move ratified at the Locarno Pact. On 7 March 1936, in an operation code-named Winter Exercise, Hitler ordered about one division of German troops to enter the

ULTRA

Developed in 1923 by the German engineer Arthur Scherbius from a design by Dutchman H.A. Koch, the Enigma encryption machine had a keyboard that looked superficially like a typewriter and had originally been intended for the commercial market. The German Army and Navy saw its potential and bought it in 1929. In its simplest form, for every letter it sent there were hundreds of millions of possible solutions. The Germans firmly believed that it was completely secure. Unfortunately they forgot that the number of letters in the alphabet is finite, that no letter could stand for itself, and that the machine had no number keys, so figures had to be spelled out. Working from this the Poles began reading signals in 1932, the French intelligence services in 1938 and the British in February 1940. For the British, who set up a specialist code-breaking unit at Bletchley Park, the secrecy of the project was at such a high level that they classified it 'Ultra Secret', and so the project became ULTRA.

On 19 July 1941 Prime Minister Winston Churchill decided that intelligence derived from ULTRA would be passed to the Soviet High Command via the British Military Mission in Moscow. It would be attributed to 'a well-placed source in Berlin'. Next month, on the evening of 25 August, Churchill broadcast accusing the Germans of 'merciless butchery' in the East. ULTRA intercepts had picked up reports by the *Einsatzgruppen* to the SD headquarters in Berlin concerning the success of their *Aktionen* and the grim details had been passed to the Prime Minister. Speaking of their operations Churchill said, 'Since the Mongol invasions of Europe in the fourteenth century there has never been methodical, merciless butchery on such a scale. We are in the presence of a crime without a name.' He may have run the risk of compromising the ULTRA secret, but his anger at the monstrosity of the self satisfied reports by the *Einsatzgruppen* murderers compelled him to speak.

territory. He asserted that a Franco–Soviet pact had broken the Treaty of Locarno and this justified his breach of the Treaty of Versailles. He gambled on the pacifist sentiments in France and Britain and offered, as a sop for the breach of the Treaty of Versailles, to sign a 25-year non-aggression pact with France, Belgium and the Netherlands to be guaranteed by Britain and Italy. Many of Hitler's senior military advisers urged him not to enter the Rhineland, since they knew that the *Wehrmacht* could not survive a concerted attack by the British, Belgians and French. The successful gamble, however, convinced him that it was worth pushing the West for further concessions, while increasing his influence and hold over the armed forces.

Where before we seldom had a decent football to play with, the Hitler Youth provided us with decent sports equipment, and previously out-of-bounds gymnasiums, swimming pools and even stadiums were now open to us. Never in my life had I been on a real holiday – father was much too poor for such extravagance. Now under Hitler, for very little money, I could go to lovely camps in the mountains, by rivers or near the sea.

Henry Metelmann

OLYMPIC ACHIEVEMENTS

For the 1936 Berlin Olympic Games, Olympiad XI, the government spent the equivalent of over £15 million building nine arenas, including a magnificent stadium. On the opening day a crowd of 110,000 roared with delight when Hans Woellke won gold for Germany in the shotput. Wins by competitors from other countries, however, caused the disenchanted Hitler to leave the stadium; he was particularly offended when the black American athlete Jesse Owens won four gold medals for track and field events. Despite this the outcome of the games was a success for the new German government since they won the largest number of medals. Leni Riefenstahl's internationally acclaimed film of the events celebrated the stable, confident community that had staged the Olympiad.

On 12 March 1938 Hitler made his next territorial grab as the *Wehrmacht* launched Operation Otto, the code name for the *Anschluss* (union) with Germany, which required armed forces to enter Austria. This was named after Otto of Habsburg, the young pretender to the throne who was then in exile in Belgium, and operations to prevent his restoration were part of the cover story for armed intervention. In reality it was an invasion assisted by Austrian Nazis headed by the lawyer and politician Arthur Seyss-Inquart, who had been fomenting trouble and undermining the government of Chancellor Kurt Schuschnigg. Seyss-Inquart was a champion of Austrian *Anschluss* and involved with nationalist associations including the Austrian–German National League and the paramilitary *Steirischen Heimatschutzes* (Styrian Homeland Defence).

On 30 September 1938 Germany, Italy, France and Britain had signed the Munich Agreement that ceded the German-speaking Sudetenland of Czechoslovakia to Germany. In August Hitler had mobilized the army and threatened to attack the Czechs because of the alleged ill treatment of the Sudeten Germans. Chamberlain and Daladier, the British and French Prime Ministers, had a series of meetings in which they were pressurized by Hitler and in turn pressed the Czechs. At Munich a modified version of Hitler's demands was deemed acceptable to the Anglo–French leaders. Chamberlain's appeasement policy allowed Hitler to dominate his generals, who had believed that this time France and Britain would call the *Führer's* bluff. The British, however, had bought time to build up their armaments industry and prepare for the war that came a year later.

THE CHANGING FACE OF WARFARE

After the Munich Agreement, Britain, France and Poland, linked by the common threat of Nazi Germany, had begun work on breaking the signals produced by German Enigma code machines. This was a fast mechanical encryption system used in radio transmissions. The German armed forces were convinced that the ability to change settings on the machines made it completely secure.

In July 1936 war broke out in Spain between the Republicans, who looked to Europe and the USSR for assistance, and the Nationalists under General Franco, who were supported by Nazi Germany and Fascist Italy. For the Germans, Italians and Soviets the conflict gave the opportunity to test some of their theories about armoured warfare and air power. The USSR provided about 730 Vickers-type T-26s, along with some early BT tanks with the distinctive American Christie suspension, in support of the Republicans. The Germans shipped in PzKpfw I tanks and the Italians the little Fiat-Ansaldo CV 33 to back up the Nationalists.

On 29 October 1936 the Soviet General Pavlov, working with the Republicans, attempted a deep armoured raid with 50 tanks at Esquivias. He tried again in March 1937 near Guadalajara. Both attacks faltered through lack of support and logistic back up, and many commentators concluded that the tank should work at the pace of the infantry and not be used for deep raids.

In the USSR, meanwhile, a tank design team led by M.I. Koshkin, A.A. Morozov and N.A. Kucherenko was working

LEGION KONDOR

The Spanish Civil War had begun in July 1936 and the Germans initially deployed Ju 52 transports to lift Franco's 15,000 Spanish Legion troops from Morocco to Spain. As the war expanded so did the German commitment, until by its close in 1939 the 6000 air and tank crew and logistic personnel who had been rotated through the theatre had suffered 420 casualties killed in action. The German force known as the *Legion Kondor* (Condor Legion) wore a distinctive brown uniform. After they returned aboard a KDF cruise liner in the summer of 1939, a parade was organized in Berlin on 6 June in which they carried gold-coloured tablets bearing the names of the Legion dead. For the *Luftwaffe* the Spanish Civil War was an excellent proving ground for Ju 87 Stuka dive-bombing tactics and also gave the Bf 109 fighter pilots their first experience of air combat. On the ground German anti-aircraft gun crews discovered that the high velocity 8.8cm (3.46in) Flak was a highly effective anti-tank gun – it would remain so throughout World War II.

on preliminary plans for a medium tank to replace the BT series of fast tanks. This would use Christie suspension, broad tracks, angled armour and a powerful 76mm (3in) gun. Called the T-34, it would change armoured warfare forever.

The Germans in the *Legion Kondor* were learning valuable lessons about the limitations and effectiveness of air power. The most brutal demonstration was the attack on the undefended Basque town of Guernica on 26 April. To the world it appeared a wanton act. Nine aircraft dropped 7950kg (17,530lb) of bombs, which were in fact intended for military targets outside the town. Casualty figures are disputed (some sources state 100 and others 1600 were killed), but what was not disputed was the destruction of 71 per cent of the town. With the benefit of hindsight Guernica showed that tactical and later strategic bombing was a double-edged weapon, sometimes failing to hit the target and often producing adverse propaganda.

In March 1939 the Germans took over the whole of Czechoslovakia and were able to add the excellent indigenous Skoda LT-35 and Ceskomoravska Kolben Danek (CDK) LT Vz 38 tanks to their inventory of armoured vehicles. The Czechs had exported tanks to Sweden, Hungary, Yugoslavia, Latvia and even Afghanistan and Peru. The *Wehrmacht* received approximately 300 LT-35s and, with the designation PzKpfw (*PanzerKampfwagen*) 35(t), they were formed into a *Panzerdivision*. Two more divisions were made up from the excellent LT Vz 38, now designated PzKpfw 38(t). They would be a valuable addition to the light PzKpfw I and II and medium PzKpfw III tanks, as well as a small number of PzKpfw IV tanks, that made up the *Panzerdivisionen*.

'PEACE IN OUR TIME'

On 20 August 1939 Hitler sent a telegram to Joseph Stalin, the Soviet Union's head of state, to urge an agreement because of the 'worsening situation in Poland'. To many Germans contact with the sinister and destructive Soviet Union was at least a startling surprise, at worst a shocking betrayal. Three days later, as newsreel cameras rolled, the German–Soviet Non-Aggression Pact was signed in Moscow by the German Foreign Minister Joachim von Ribbentrop and Soviet Minister Vyacheslav Molotov, then they toasted the pact with champagne. Stalin appeared in the photographs of the ceremony smiling, glass in hand, in the background. From the outset the Russian Communists and their 'Bolshevik'

Below: Greeted by waving crowds German troops in full marching order enter Austria in March 1938. For many Austrians Anschluss – *Union with Germany – was welcome since its larger neighbour to the north was powerful and a leader in Europe in the 1930s.*

followers in Europe had been the Nazis' ultimate enemy. Now ordinary Nazis were confused, conservative Germans shocked and Communists across Europe, many of whom had fought Fascism in Spain, were equally shaken by the unexpected agreement. For other Germans there was a feeling of relief akin to that felt by the British when Prime Minister Neville Chamberlain returned from Munich in September 1938 and assured the public that they would enjoy 'peace in our time'.

The pact with Stalin meant they would not be fighting a war on two fronts, as had happened in World War I. A curious result of the pact was that some loyal Communists in France and Britain felt that they should now see Nazi Germany in a

Let us suppose that Hitler turns his weapons against the east and invades territories occupied by the Red Army. Under these conditions, partisans of the Fourth International, without changing in any way their attitude towards the Kremlin oligarchy, will advance to the forefront, as the most urgent task of the hour, the military resistance against Hitler. The workers will say: 'We cannot cede to Hitler the overthrowing of Stalin; that is *our own task*'.

Leon Trotsky
25 September 1939

more favourable light, and accordingly they would make little contribution to the Allied war effort until 22 June 1941. The German–Soviet Pact that was agreed in August 1939 may have shocked Nazis and severely tested the loyalty of Communists worldwide but it paved the way for the two countries' invasion of Poland in September. The pact ensured that:

1. Neither party would attack the other.
2. Should one of them become the object of belligerent action by a third power, the other party would in no manner lend its support to this third power.
3. Neither Germany nor the USSR would join any grouping of Powers whatsoever aimed directly or indirectly at the other party.

A secret protocol was attached to the pact, identifying spheres of interest in Poland and the Baltic: the USSR had claims on Finland, Estonia, Latvia and Lithuania, with the northern border of Lithuania as a diving line. In Poland Soviet influence would reach as far as the line of the rivers Narew, Vistula and San. Hitler, in a piece of brutal strategic pragmatism, had ensured that the USSR

Left: Pilots of Messerschmitt Bf 109C fighters of the Legion Kondor *receive a dawn briefing prior to operations in Spain. The Luftwaffe gained valuable experience with tactics and weapons' handling techniques in the Civil War.*

would not intervene to support the Poles. For France and Great Britain the attack on Poland was the final fatal move.

Committed to defending Poland in a treaty signed on 23 August 1939, Great Britain declared war on Nazi Germany at 11:00 on 3 September 1939 and France followed at 17:00. In Britain the public had tuned their radios into the Home Service and heard the Prime Minister Neville Chamberlain explain quietly that the British Government had requested that Germany should withdraw her troops from Poland. He ended the broadcast with resignation, 'No reply has been received from the German government and consequently a state of war now exists between Great Britain and Germany'.

The Polish armies, positioned close to the border in linear defences under a scheme designated Plan Z or 'West', could not have been worse sited to withstand a mechanized and armoured attack with well coordinated close air support. The Polish planners hoped that French and British forces in the West would attack Germany and so draw off some of the pressure. The flat wheat fields of Poland offered few natural obstacles on which to base a defence, but rivers like the Bzura, Narev, Bug and the Vistula were considerable barriers.

BLITZKRIEG

In *Fall Weiss* (Plan White), the attack on Poland on 1 September 1939, four German armies punched across Poland's borders and, in great curving thrusts, cut off the Polish armies deployed along the western frontier. In four

Above: The Czech designed PzKpfw 38(t) was armed with a 37mm (1.46in) cannon and two 7.92mm (0.312in) machine guns. It weighed 9400kg (9.25 tons) was a manoeuvrable vehicle with a top speed of 42km/h (26mph) and range of 250km (155 miles).

weeks the German armies, consisting of the Third and Fourth Armies of Army Group North under General Fedor von Bock and the Eighth, Tenth and Fourteenth Armies of Army Group South under General Gerd von Rundstedt, had defeated the Poles. This collapse, however, was accelerated by the invasion of eastern Poland by the Red Army on 17 September. Warsaw capitulated on 27 September and the last vestige of resistance ended by 5 October. The campaign had cost the Germans 8082 killed, 27,278 wounded and 5029 missing. The Poles lost 70,000 killed and 130,000 wounded.

The invading German and Soviet forces met at Brest-Litovsk, a Polish town on the confluence of the rivers Bug and Muchaviec. It was an opportunity for the two armies to see one another at close quarters. The Germans were not impressed. A veteran interviewed after the war recalled that, as a young artillery NCO, 'The Soviets made a right poor impression. The vehicles, above all the tanks, were – I must say – a collection of oily junk'.

Conventional defences, as adopted by the Poles, were layered with infantry in the front line in trenches and bunkers, artillery in depth to provide supporting fire, and mobile reserves in the rear ready to plug any gaps or halt enemy breakthroughs. The speed of the Polish defeat, though, stunned the Allies and neutrals. To describe it one journalist covering the war chose a phrase that is now used universally, *Blitzkrieg* ('lightning war'). Writing in 1940, Eugene Hadamovsky had called the operations a '*Blitzmarsch nach Warschau*' ('lightning march to Warsaw') and from this

---

PzKpfw 38(t)

Built by CKD in Czechoslovakia as the TNH/PS or the LT Vz 38 for the Czech Army, it was taken over by the Germans following the absorption of the country. The tank originally had a three-man crew, but by reducing the main ammunition load the Germans fitted a fourth crew member in as a loader to make operating the turret gun easier. The 38(t) saw action in Poland, France and the USSR, and then its chassis was used for a variety of SP (self propelled) guns. By 1942, when production stopped, about 1168 had been built for the Czech and German armies.

Above: Stalin smiles as Molotov, his Foreign Minister, signs the German–Soviet Non-Aggression Pact on 28 August 1939. The German Foreign Minister von Ribbentrop stands beside Stalin during the ceremony in Moscow. The signature cleared the way for both countries to divide Poland between them.

came the word *Blitzkrieg*. The Nazi propagandists were quick to appreciate its potential – it was new, dramatic and, for their enemies, frightening.

In the years that followed *Blitzkrieg* would be the winning tactical formula that would take German forces through these fixed defences to the gates of Moscow and Cairo. To work it required well trained and equipped soldiers in tanks and half track SdKfz 251 armoured personnel carriers (APCs) with fighters like the Messerschmitt Bf 109 and dive-bombers like Junkers Ju 87 Stuka working in close cooperation. Efficient radio communications enabled these forces to react quickly and seize and maintain the initiative.

At the outset of the offensive, conventional troops backed by towed artillery attacked the enemy along a wide front. Frontal attacks were the least favoured tactic since they hit the most strongly defended enemy areas, but they tied up his troops. Then at selected unexpected points, following a short but very intense air and artillery bombardment, the *Panzerdivisionen* (armoured divisions) attacked and broke through the enemy defences. These points of main effort, often a comparatively narrow front, received the

Schwerpunkt, literally 'the heavy blow'. Once the hole had been punched, more tanks and APCs poured through the gap, followed by infantry in trucks, and plunged deep into the enemy rear, headed by fast moving reconnaissance units that found gaps in defences or unguarded bridges. Speed kept the enemy off balance. The armoured divisions then began to hook to left and right to encircle their enemy in huge pockets.

Constant and ferocious air attacks prevented the enemy from moving men and vehicles and destroyed communications, HQs and depots. The dive-bombers acted as 'flying artillery' for the tank crews, able to keep pace with them as they advanced. Within the pockets the enemy forces were pounded by artillery as the conventional infantry, who were marching into action, closed the noose tighter around the trapped forces.

In the West the French and British governments watched stupefied as these tactics crushed Poland; they did nothing except send small patrols to probe the German border positions. The period was dubbed the *drôle de guerre, sitzkrieg* or, in the words of a US congressman, 'The Phoney War'.

SOVIET AMBITIONS

The Soviet leader Joseph Stalin had already established with Joachim von Ribbentrop that the Baltic states of Latvia, Lithuania and Estonia were in the Soviet sphere of influence. In October 1939 a 'mutual assistance pact' was agreed between the USSR and Latvia. In June 1940, while the world watched the German invasion of the West, the USSR effortlessly gathered up the three tiny Baltic states.

Finland, however, was a different customer. Stalin saw the proximity of the fortified Finnish border to Leningrad, the USSR's second city, as a threat. He offered a mutual assistance treaty and demanded that Finland cede the area known as the Karelian Isthmus to the USSR. Finland refused on both counts and on 30 November 1939 the Soviet Red Army invaded.

In the bitter winter 15 Finnish divisions inflicted a heavy defeat on 45 Soviet divisions, which had attacked overland and in three amphibious operations. At Suomussalmi in Karelia, outnumbered Finnish ski troops counter-attacked the Soviet 163rd and 44th Divisions on 5 January 1940 and destroyed them. The German staff officers watched the incompetent performance of the Soviet divisions and concluded that the USSR would be easy meat for their *Panzerdivisionen* and *Blitzkrieg* tactics.

Below: Men of the Waffen-SS *take cover during street fighting Socharzow in Poland in September 1939. The Army was initially dismissive of the* Waffen-SS *but it soon earned a fearsome reputation as a ruthless fighting organisation, particularly on the Eastern Front.*

Left: Soldiers of the 123rd Lenin Banner Infantry Division, one of the units that penetrated the Mannerheim Line in Finland. The younger man in the front on the right has the distinctive sleeve badge showing he is the division's political officer or Kommissar.

The poor performance of the Red Army was in part the result of Stalin's purges. In a frenzy of paranoia in 1938 Stalin ordered show trials to be held in Moscow, at which some 10,000 senior officers were accused of treachery. Almost all 'confessed', were found guilty, and were executed or sent to labour camps (*Gulags*) in Siberia. Among the many experienced and talented commanders lost by the Red Army was Marshal Mikhail Tukhachevskiy, the 'father' of the Soviet tank arm. He came from an aristocratic Russian family and as a second lieutenant had been captured in the fighting for Warsaw in 1915. Life in a German PoW camp may have radicalized him, since after the Revolution he embraced the tenets of Communism. Leon Trotsky, who was forming the Red Army, saw in Tukhachevskiy a man of talent and the former Tsarist officer proved an able commander. It was this association with Trotsky, who fell out with Stalin and was exiled in 1929, that led to Tukhachevskiy's own downfall, but his legacy would survive since he had laid the foundations for the development of the formidable T-34 tank. Many of the officers associated with him, and who had grasped the techniques of armoured warfare he propounded, would be released from the *Gulags* following the German attack on the Soviet Union. At all levels they would bring professionalism and sound military doctrine to the Red Army and redeem themselves in the eyes of the political leadership.

Despite heavy losses, early in 1940 the massively reinforced Soviet Northwest Front, composed of the Seventh and Thirteenth Armies under General Merestokov, punched through the Finnish defences of the Mannerheim Line. The little country was crushed by sheer weight of numbers. The Soviet Union eventually forced Baron Carl Mannerheim, the 72-year-old Finnish premier, to capitulate on 12 March 1940. The war had cost the Soviets 200,000 men, nearly 700 aircraft and 1600 tanks. The Finns lost 25,000 men.

Right: The superb German SdKfz 251 halftrack. It had a crew of two, carried 10 troops, was capable of 52km/h (32mph) on roads and had a range of 180km (112 miles). Some 22 different versions were produced for roles like HQ or radio communications.

SDKFZ 251 HALF TRACK

Design work on the superb SdKfz 251 half track that carried *Panzergrenadiere* into action began in 1935; by the time the Ausf D model was introduced in 1943 a total of 2650 had been built by Borgward and Hanomag. It was a well liked and versatile vehicle, although access to the engines was difficult. The SdKfz 251 was used as the platform for support weapons as well as a command vehicle and ambulance. It was the inspiration for the American M3 half track.

THE DRIVE TO THE WEST

France and Britain were preparing to send troops to assist the Finns when events elsewhere took a different turn. At 04:15 on 9 April 1940 the German invasion of Denmark and Norway, known as *Weserübung* (Weser Exercise), began as two German motorized brigade groups crossed the Danish border. Assisted by parachute and air landing attacks on the airfields at Ålborg in north Jutland and the key bridges between the islands, they quickly overwhelmed the country. Denmark was effectively a stepping stone for the German invasion of Norway.

The forces tasked with the Norwegian invasion, commanded by *Generaloberst* Niklaus von Falkenhorst, were divided into five groups: Group I landed at Narvik in the north, Group II at Trondheim, Group III at Bergen, Group IV at Kristiansand and Group V aimed at Oslo, the Norwegian capital, where they would be assisted by air landing forces. Southern Norway fell fairly rapidly, but at Narvik French, British and Norwegian forces fought the Germans to a draw, causing heavy naval losses. Only the

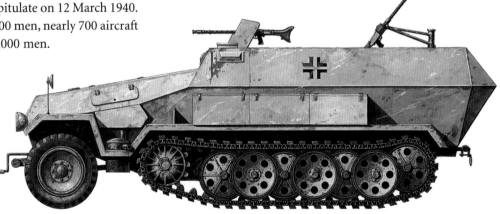

BMW R-75 MOTORCYCLE COMBINATION

The 750cc BMW R-75 *mit Seitenwagen* was a special military design motorcycle sidecar, of which 16,510 were built by Bayerische Motoren Werke AG, Munich, between 1940 and 1944. It had a crew of two or three and carried a spare wheel on the sidecar with panniers for the crew's kit and ammunition. An MG 34 or MG 42 machine gun could be bolted onto a bar on the sidecar giving the R-75 considerable and effective firepower.

The R-75 was used for front line liaison carrying senior officers to the front line as well as reconnaissance. Motorcycle reconnaissance troops in their full length rubberized coats and with goggles on their helmets were an enduring symbol of the *Blitzkrieg* in Europe and Russia. They may have looked impressive, but after a day's operations the soldiers could be pretty tired, since the bike had a helical sprung saddle instead of rear suspension.

Built on a tubular duplex cradle frame, the motorcycle's rear and sidecar wheels were driven via a four-speed and reverse gearbox, cardan shaft and cross shaft. It had a lockable differential and hydraulic brakes on driven wheels, mechanical brakes on the front wheel and a 'maintenance free' telescopic front fork. It was not the first motorbike to have telescopic front forks but was the first to adopt hydraulic damping in series production. The motorcycle was powered by a 746cc, 2.4-litre BMW R75 twin-cylinder, four-stroke petrol engine developing 26hp at 4400rpm, by today's standards a modest power ratio.

The all up weight was 420kg (926lb), rising to 670kg (1477lb) with the sidecar. The maximum road speed was 92km/h (57mph) with the sidecar and it had a road range of 340km (211 miles), although this could be extended to 800km (500 miles) with extra petrol jerrycans strapped to the sidecar. The low ratio gears on the BMW allowed it to travel almost anywhere and provided the best all terrain solution until lightweight 4 x 4 vehicles were successfully developed. In skilled hands both the BMW and the similarly specified Zündapp KS 750 were effective vehicles, but without thorough training they could be hazardous to rider and crew. They were also among the most complex military motorcycles ever produced. This and the cost were among the reasons why production ended before 1945.

In the extreme cold of the Eastern Front the exhaust for the BMW and Zündapp was modified with a high mounted single silencer and heat exchanger that provided a flow of warm air over the rider's feet and hands and into the sidecar. One of the original concepts for the R-75 and the Zündapp KS 750 was to tow light field guns for airborne forces, but it was found that the towbar weight lifted the front wheel off the ground. It did, however, operate with a simple two-wheel trailer.

---

attack on France in May saved the German airborne and mountain troops from defeat.

On 10 May 1940 *Fall Gelb* (Plan Yellow), the long awaited attack on France and the Low Countries, began with attacks by a new weapon, paratroops, and conventional foot-slogging infantry. The German operation began with air attacks on Dutch and Belgian airfields, and airborne assaults on the bridges at Moerdijk and Rotterdam and on the Dutch seat of government at The Hague. With the bridges in German hands the river line defences of 'Fortress Holland' were penetrated and, following a savage air attack on the city of Rotterdam, the Dutch capitulated on 14 May. The German 1st Parachute Regiment, an élite force, landed in ten gliders within the Belgian fort of Eben Emael, which protected the eastern border of the country, and neutralized it using revolutionary shaped charges.

In a pre-planned operation, British and French troops moved north into Belgium to halt the German attacks on the Netherlands and Belgium, not knowing that German tanks and mechanized infantry had worked their way through southern Belgium and Luxembourg, protected by the *Luftwaffe*. On the evening of 12 May they reached the east bank of the Meuse at Sedan.

General Heinz Guderian, commanding XIX Panzer Corps, knew that it was essential to keep the pressure on the French. Although his tanks were still reaching the river, with support from the Stukas of General Wolfram von Richthofen's VIII *Fliegerkorps* he committed his assault troops and crossed it the following day, seizing the adjoining high ground. By the evening, although still under intermittent artillery fire, German engineers had constructed

Right: A German motorcycle and SdKfz 222 armoured car reconnaissance platoon pauses in a French town. The BMW R-75 was capable of a maximum road speed of 92 km/h (57mph) with the sidecar and range of 340km (211 miles).

Above: Though obsolete by 1940, the PzKpfw I, a training vehicle with a modest twin machine gun armament, was retained in service for the invasion of France. A year later it was employed in Barbarossa but here the terrain was very different.

bridges that opened a door for the 1st, 5th and 10th Panzer divisions. To the north, at Monthermé, the XLI Panzer Corps under Reinhardt had established a bridgehead by 15 May and the 6th and 8th Panzer divisions began their drive to the sea. At Dinant and Onhaye the XV Panzer Corps had achieved a lodgement across the Meuse by the 14th. The reconnaissance troops of General Erwin Rommel's 7th Panzer Division had found an unguarded weir and manoeuvred their motorcycles carefully across the narrow walkway. The 5th Panzer Division joined the westward dash. To the north the XVI Panzer Corps under General Erich Höpner, actually part of Army Group B, swung left through Belgium into France.

PUSHED INTO THE SEA

By 16 May the German salient was between 20 and 40km (12–24 miles) deep. There had been a brief delay at Montcornet on 15 May when an armoured division

commanded by General de Gaulle attempted a counter-attack. The rivers Aisne and Somme covered the Germans' left flank as they pushed westwards. On 20 May the tanks and motorcyclists of the 2nd Panzer Division reached the sea at Noyelles; the sickle cut trap had been sprung and the French and British forces were trapped against the sea at Dunkirk.

The British Expeditionary Force (BEF), Belgian Army and French First Army were caught in a pocket on the Channel coast that included the port and resort town of Dunkirk. Initially the pocket, squeezed by tanks from Army Group A and infantry from Army Group B, reached from Gravelines on the coast in the west to beyond Ostend, across the Belgian border, in the east, and inland as far as Valenciennes.

Following Belgium's surrender on the 28th, however, it shrank rapidly to an area about 50km (31 miles) square.

Operation *Dynamo*, the naval evacuation by the Royal Navy of the BEF from Dunkirk and the beaches, began at 19:00 on 26 May and ended at 03:40 on 4 June. It involved more than a thousand vessels, including private pleasure craft, trawlers and smaller warships, such as Royal Navy destroyers. Some 338,000 British and French troops were evacuated to Britain, at the cost of six British and three French destroyers sunk and 19 damaged, as well as 56 other ships and 161 small craft sunk. In dogfights over Dunkirk the RAF lost more than a hundred fighters, but downed a similar number of *Luftwaffe* aircraft. It had only been possible because ULTRA had told the British that the Panzers would not crush the pocket on Hitler's orders.

On 20 May General Maxime Weygand replaced Gamelin and he redeployed the French 2nd, 6th, 7th and 10th Armies along the Somme. When the Germans launched *Fall Rot* (Case Red) on 5 June, the second phase of the attack on France, the French fought bravely but by now were severely weakened. When the 14th and 16th Panzer Corps were held, the OKW simply redeployed them and punched through further south. On the Channel coast the 5th and 7th Panzer divisions crossed the Seine at Rouen and reached Cherbourg and Brest on 19 June.

The French government left Paris, the capital was declared an open city and the Germans entered it on 14 June. Guderian's Panzer Group reached Pontarlier on the Swiss border on 17 June, trapping General Prételat's French Army Group 2 against the Maginot Line. On 22 June the French

Below: The PzKpfw II was armed with a 2cm (0.79in) cannon and one 7.92mm (0.312in) machine gun. It had a crew of three and remained in production until 1942. Thereafter the chassis was used for a range of self-propelled weapons mounts.

were forced to surrender and accept German terms in a railway carriage at Compiègne, 100km (62 miles) northeast of Paris. It was a symbolic revenge selected on Hitler's orders, since this was the same carriage in which the French Marshal Foch had accepted the surrender of German armies in November 1918.

ITALIAN SETBACKS

One of the beneficiaries of the German victory in France was Fascist Italy. Under Benito Mussolini, who styled himself '*Il Duce*', it had declared war on France and Britain on 10 June. Although its attacks on southern France had been ineffective, it still managed to grab some French territory after the fighting was over.

From its North African colony of Libya it now launched an attack on British-held Egypt on 13 September 1940. The operation was slow starting and, in a daring counter-attack, a hugely outnumbered British and Commonwealth force under General Sir Archibald Wavell drove the Italians out of Egypt and back into Libya. By early February 1941 the Italians had lost 20,000 men, 200 guns and 120 tanks to a force that was no more than 3000 men.

Not for the first time Germany realized it would have to bale out its unreliable ally. On 12 February the *Deutsches Afrika Korps* (DAK), or *Afrika Korps*, consisting of the 15th Panzer and 5th Light (later renamed 21st Panzer) Divisions, landed at Tripoli to assist the Italians in Africa. It was commanded by Lt General Erwin Rommel, an aggressive and energetic leader, who, even before his forces were fully up to strength, would elect to attack.

Some months earlier, on Monday 28 October 1940, Mussolini signalled Hitler, '*Führer, we are on the march*', and informed him that Italian troops in Albania had begun to attack Greece. A day later the two leaders met at the Brenner Pass and Hitler, though angry at the lack of consultation, offered Mussolini the assistance of German forces. The *Duce* declined, since he saw the Balkans as his sphere of influence. Launching their campaign in grim weather at 05:30, six Italian divisions of the Eleventh and Ninth Armies under General Visconti-Prasca had made some headway in four thrusts into the Greek mountains. Accompanied by Albanian troops and volunteers, they were ostensibly on a mission of 'liberation' for Albanians living in Greece. They faced four divisions of the

Greek First Army. Although on paper the Greeks appeared outnumbered, their divisions were larger at 18,500 strong, in contrast to the Italians at between 12,000 and 14,000. They also had more efficient light and medium artillery and more machine guns.

The Italian attacks were halted and then, on 4 November, the II Corps under Colonel Papadopoulos counter-attacked the Italian Eleventh Army under General Gelsos. The Greek Army of Macedonia inflicted a startling defeat on the élite Italian Julia Mountain Division. Greek forces recaptured border areas and forced the Italians out of Greece and across the border into Albania. By mid-November they had deployed 11 infantry divisions, two infantry brigades and one cavalry division against 15 Italian infantry divisions and one tank division. Mussolini's generals had warned him against launching an attack in this harsh terrain so late in the year. His Chief of Staff, Marshal Pietro Badoglio, resigned in protest and on 4 December his Under Secretary of State for War, General Ubaldo Soddu, recommended an armistice with the Greeks. On 23 February 1941 the Greek government under Alexandros Korizis accepted the offer of British military assistance. This was to be known as W Force, under Lt General Maitland Wilson, and consisted of 50,672 men from the New Zealand Division, together with the 6th and 7th Australian Divisions of the I Australian Corps under Lt General Blamey. In addition, armour and artillery support was to be drawn from the Middle East Command of General Wavell in Egypt. By 1 March the Greek forces were within striking distance of the Albanian capital Tirana, and three days later W Force began landing at Piraeus, the port of Athens.

Across the Mediterranean in North Africa, the Germans hit the British positions at Al Agheila on 24 March and, as the exhausted British forces fell back, this allowed the DAK to roam deep into the desert. Benghazi fell on 4 April, Derna on the 7th and Rommel had reached the Egyptian border by 25 April. The Italian and German forces, however, lacked the strength to take the port of Tobruk and, although under siege from 10 April, it held out for six months until relieved.

Hitler's plans for the invasion of the Soviet Union were well advanced when reports reached him in March 1941 that W Force was landing in Greece. He at once feared that his right flank would be insecure. Romania was now supplying Germany with the bulk of its fuel and oil requirements from

Left: In a scene that could have come out of the Franco–Prussian War, General Kurt von Briesen takes the salute for an artillery battery as it rides down one of the avenues radiating from the Arc de Triomphe in Paris on 14 June 1940.

the Ploesti oilfields and bombers based in a hostile Greece could easily reach Romania.

In 1939 Germany had imported 861,600 tonnes of oil from Romania. By 1940 this had risen to 1,196,000 tonnes, supplemented by 626,900 tonnes from the USSR that helped fuel the aircraft and tanks that crashed through Western Europe that spring. In the following year, with the invasion of the USSR, the total imported stood at a wartime record of 3,011,000 tonnes. The fastest and most effective way to prevent the threat of air attacks on Ploesti was to neutralize Greece. The original operation, in a directive issued by Hitler in 13 December 1940, called for the occupation of the Aegean coast and Salonika basin. In the end the Germans and their Italian allies would seize not only mainland Greece, but also the offshore islands.

THE BALKANS CAMPAIGN

A passive or cooperative Yugoslavia was necessary for German troops to move south. The Yugoslav government in Belgrade was strong-armed by the Germans and Italians into joining the Tripartite Pact on 25 March. Two days later, however, encouraged by the British Foreign Office, Serbian officers in the Air Force led a *coup d'état* against the government of Prince Paul, rejecting the pact and setting up a government of national unity under General Dusan Simovic, with the 17-year-old Prince Peter as monarch.

Hitler was enraged. To him the pact was perfectly reasonable – Yugoslavia would offer German troops free passage to attack Greece and in exchange she would be able to seize the Greek province of Salonika. He ordered an air attack, aptly named Operation Punishment, against the unprotected Yugoslav capital, Belgrade. At 05:10 on Easter Sunday (6 April) *Luftflotte* IV under General Löhr attacked airfields in Yugoslavia. Flying in three waves, 484 bombers and dive-bombers with 250 fighter escorts hit Belgrade in a succession of 20-minute attacks. The figures reported killed in what was a supposedly open city vary considerably from 5000 to 17,000, but it is certain that the attacks panicked the young king and his government into flight. The Yugoslav Army plan of operations, 'R-41', like that adopted by Poland

---

STURZKAMPFFLUGZEUG – STUKA

The Junkers Ju 87 *Sturzkampfflugzeug* ('diving war plane') or Stuka was a formidable weapon in the armoury of the *Luftwaffe*. Against hardened targets the Stuka would carry a single SC-500 bomb, while for field defences and soft targets a typical bomb load would be one SC-250 under the fuselage and four SC-50s under the wings. What made the Stuka so effective was its accuracy. A trained pilot could deliver 50 per cent of his ordnance within 25m (82ft) of the centre of the target. When approaching a target Stukas would adopt a *Ketten*, a three-aircraft formation, at about 4570m (15,000ft), cruising at 241km/h (150mph). Larger formations would be made up of several *Ketten* with an interval of 274m (900ft) between each formation. The maximum formation was usually a *Gruppe* of 30 bombers. Against smaller targets the aircraft would move into echelon, but for area targets like harbours the pilots in the *Ketten* would simply tip the nose of their bomber down and dive from their formation.

The signal for the attack was given by the formation leader beginning his dive at an angle of 80°. Pilots would deploy the dive brakes so that the bomber gained speed only gradually until, below 2438m (8000ft), it reached its maximum speed at 563km/h (350mph). A dive from about 4572m (15,000ft) to a release altitude of 914m (3000ft) took about 30 seconds and during this time the pilot controlled the aircraft to keep the target in the centre of the reflector sight. A horn sounded four seconds before the Ju 87 passed the pull-out altitude that had been entered into the altimeter. It stopped at the release height and the pilot then pressed a button on the control column. This returned the elevator trim tab to neutral and the aircraft began to pull out. At the same moment the main bomb was swung forward on its hinged arm, clear of the propeller, and released along with the secondary ordnance. For some pilots the terrible strain of the G forces in the dive caused involuntary defecation or vomiting. The sound of a diving aircraft is frightening, but to add to the terror of their attacks Stuka pilots fitted a wind-driven siren that earned them the nickname *Jericho-Trompeten* (Trumpets of Jericho).

Pilots were not the only people to feel the strain of flying in the Ju 87. When the glamorous blonde German screen idol Olga Tschechowa 'baptized' a Stuka by taking a stomach-churning flight in the dive-bomber, she staggered from the cockpit on landing, green-faced and close to vomiting. A socially embarrassing scene was saved by the quick thinking of the squadron commander, who spun round and barked out the order, 'Squadron about turn – a song: one, two, three ...'

Left: Junkers Ju 87 'Stuka' dive bombers move into line abreast formation prior to an attack. The scream of the engines supplemented by the noise of a wind driven siren made an attack by Stukas terrifying for men with even the strongest nerves.

Nis and turned to attack Belgrade, driving through the Yugoslav Sixth Army, which was holding the Morava valley. The XIV *Panzer Korps* reached Skopje on 8 April. The German Twelfth Army attacked Thrace, detaching the XL Panzer Corps westward through the Vardar region of southern Yugoslavia that led to Macedonia and the Monastir Gap. On 10 April it linked up with Italian forces on Lake Ohrid and moved into positions where it could attack Greece from the north.

Luftwaffe bombers based in Bulgaria attacked Piraeus and hit the SS *Clan Fraser*, a freighter loaded with ammunition for the British Expeditionary Force. The ensuing explosion wrecked the port.

On 12 April German and Italian forces moved towards Greece. The Italian V, VI and XI Corps were backed by *Luftflotte* IV, which attacked the Yugoslav Seventh Army columns and troop concentrations around the Ljubljana area. The Italians encountered little resistance from the enemy, who were attempting to withdraw to the southeast. Around 30,000 Yugoslav troops concentrated near Delnice, waiting for the Italians so they could make their surrender. In a daring coup, Belgrade was captured on 13 April by motorcycle reconnaissance troops of the *Waffen-SS* Division *Das Reich*, part of the 2nd *SS-Infantrie-Division*.

The final drive of the campaign was on the historic city of Sarajevo. General von Weichs was aware that the mountainous terrain in the area would be ideal for waging a prolonged campaign. The Germans had been delayed by bad weather and poor roads, and if the Yugoslavs offered more resistance in the mountains fighting could last for months. The 2nd Army was reorganized into two pursuit groups to maintain the pressure on the Yugoslavs. Under command of the recently arrived LII Infantry Corps HQ, the western group consisted of four infantry divisions within XLIX Corps and LI Corps, as well as

in 1939, played into German hands. It called for defence of the entire length of the border and almost the whole army, 27 divisions, would be tied up. The only offensive operation envisaged was with Greek forces on the Albanian border against the Italians.

On land the German Second Army under General Freiherr von Weichs attacked from Austria, while General von Kleist's *Panzergruppe* 1, which had been earmarked for an attack on Thrace in Greece, pushed towards Belgrade from Bulgaria. In brief fighting the *Panzergruppen* smashed the right wing of the Yugoslav Fifth Army. A day later it took the 14th Panzer Division. The eastern force under *Panzergruppe* 1 was made up of six divisions, with the the 8th Panzer Division leading the drive towards Sarajevo from the east. *Luftflotte* IV was entrusted with neutralizing the anticipated enemy troop concentrations in the Mostar–Sarajevo sector.

By the evening of 13 April, as the 14th Panzer Division approached Sarajevo, reports reached the Germans of fighting between Serbs and Croats in Mostar. German aircraft were diverted to aid their Croat allies and attack the Serb positions. By next day fighting between these groups had spread to the whole of Dalmatia. On 15 April both pursuit groups of the Second Army were closing in on Sarajevo. As two *Panzerdivisionen* entered simultaneously from east and west, the Yugoslav Second Army, which had its headquarters in the city, capitulated. Just four days after the fall of Belgrade, an unconditional surrender was signed by the Yugoslavs at 21:00 on Thursday 17 April.

The German attack on Greece that began on 8 April was to be just as quick and ruthless. The Twelfth Army under General Wilhem von List pierced the Greek defences in Thrace and on 9 April the 2nd Panzer Division under General Veiel took Salonika. However poor roads, bad weather and, crucially, hard fighting by the Greek armies and British Expeditionary Force imposed delays on the Germans.

INTO GREECE

The Greek Second Army holding the Metaxas Line, which ran from the Aegean to the border with Yugoslavia and protected northern Greece and Salonika, was outflanked by attacks through Yugoslavia. Frontal attacks on the line by the XVIII *Gebirgsjäger* Corps had met with extremely tough resistance, even after three days of attacks supported by artillery and dive-bombers. The intensity of the fighting can be gauged by the fact that in the Rupul Gorge the German 125th Infantry Regiment suffered such heavy casualties that it was rendered combat ineffective. Trapped and bombarded, the Greek Second Army was finally forced to surrender on 9 April and the Germans released them after the soldiers had been disarmed.

By the morning of 10 April the 40th Panzer Corps had pushed through the Monastir Gap from Yugoslavia. The first contact with W Force took place the next day when a *Waffen-*

SS reconnaissance unit entered Vevi but was halted by Australian troops holding ground covering the pass to the south. It took a day to build up a picture of the enemy position and then at dusk the *Waffen-SS* attacked and broke through the defile. On the morning of 14 April the spearheads of the the 9th Panzer Division reached Kozani and established a bridgehead across the Aliakmon river. This, however, brought them to the Aliakmon Line, which was defended by W Force, and for three days the Panzer division was stalled in front of these well sited positions.

Right: Firing 15cm (6in) sFH 37(t) howitzers, Waffen-SS gunners bombard a British position in Greece; in the background are the snow covered peaks of Mount Olympus. The Czech guns, built and designed by Skoda, fired a 42kg (92lb) shell to a range of 15,100 metres (9 miles).

To the west the Greek First Army, which had fought heroically in Albania, was now at risk of being cut off by the rapid advance of German armour via Florina and by the British withdrawal to the Aliakmon Line. From 13 April the Greeks began to pull back towards the Pindus Mountains. At Kastoria Pass they encountered the advance guard of the German 73rd Infantry Division and fought hard for a day to break through.

On 19 April the *Waffen-SS* Regiment 1, which had reached Grevena, was ordered to move on a southeast axis towards Yannina in order to cut off the Greek First Army, grouped as the Army of Epirus and Army of Macedonia. A day later at the Metsovon Pass, high in the Pindus Mountains, Greek and German forces clashed in a desperate battle. Realizing that further fighting would only cause unnecessary losses, the Greek commander surrendered his forces. On Hitler's orders this was kept secret from the Italians and, in recognition of their valour, the officers were permitted to keep their side arms. The soldiers were disarmed and permitted to return home. Mussolini, however, insisted that the 1st Army should

also surrender to the Italians, with whom the Greeks had fought for a further two days. On 23 April the Greek commander signed a second surrender agreement that included the Italians.

Also on 19 April the Greeks agreed that W Force should be evacuated. The same day men of the German XVIII *Gebirgsjäger* Corps entered Larisa, capturing the airfield and British supply dumps. Ten truckloads of rations and fuel allowed the mountain troops to keep up their advance. At the port of Volos, which fell on 21 April, the Germans again seized large quantities of petrol, oil and lubricants (POL). These captures were invaluable for the Germans, since their supply lines were restricted by bad roads, demolitions and poor weather. They had even used Greek fishing vessels and lighters to ferry stores along the Aegean coast.

THERMOPYLAE REVISITED

In a fighting withdrawal the men of W Force held the Germans at Thermopylae, where German air reconnaissance had confirmed that a defensive line was under construction. On 22 April tanks and vehicles from the 5th Panzer Division, part of the XVIII Corps under General Böhme, attempted to bounce the Thermopylae position but were halted by fire from well camouflaged artillery and single tanks. The following day men of the German 6th *Gebirgsjäger* Division outflanked the position by working their way through difficult terrain to the west, in conjunction with another outflanking manoeuvre through Molos, where they encountered strong resistance. On the night of 24/25 April, however, W Force withdrew from the

Right: A patriotic and sentimental Italian postcard entitled L'Eroico Sacrificio – 'Heroic Sacrifice' – shows a wounded Italian officer in Africa at the moment when he falls manning a machine gun. Italian officers and soldiers would increasingly be called on to make heroic sacrifices in Russia and North Africa.

Thermopylae position. This action and access to ULTRA decrypts allowed the British to second guess the German moves. Under Operation Demon they were able to evacuate not only many of their men, but also King George II of Greece, who flew out to Crete. *Luftwaffe* reports said that British troops were being evacuated from Salamis, 20 large and 15 small ships were in Piraeus, and four large and 31 smaller vessels in Khalkis. All the ports were reported to be well protected by AA batteries. The evacuation of W Force was completed by 28 April. For the operation the Royal Navy

Above: The tough Ju 52 transport had a crew of three with 18 troops or 12 stretchers. Powered by three 830hp BMW 132T-2 engines it had maximum speed at 1400m (4,590ft) of 286 km/h (178mph) and the normal range was 1500km (930 miles).

had provided six cruisers and 19 destroyers as well as numerous transports. Two destroyers and four transports were sunk and the bulk of the troops evacuated to Crete.

German forces had reached Athens the previous day and the German love affair with ancient Greece was given a new character as Army photographers recorded the moment when the *Reichskriegsflagge* was run up a flagstaff on the Acropolis. In an act of symbolic resistance it would be torn down on the night of 30/31 May – one of the first of many acts of active and passive resistance during the occupation.

The campaign in Greece and Yugoslavia was a triumph for the German tactics of coordinating tanks, mechanized infantry and dive-bombers. Their casualties were 2559 killed, 5820 wounded and 3169 missing. The British, who had committed 75,000 to the campaign, lost 12,000 men and all their heavy equipment. Some 6298 Yugoslav officers and 337,864 NCOs and soldiers of Serbian extraction were taken prisoner. The Germans released Slovenian, Croatian and Macedonian prisoners. The Greeks, who were fully mobilized, lost 223,000 men.

'PLAN MERCURY'

The culmination of the Balkans campaign, *Fall Merkur* (Plan Mercury), the German attack on the island of Crete from 20 May 1941, was a unique operation. The Germans committed 13,000 paratroops of the 7th Airborne Division under Leutnant-General Kurt Student and 9000 men of the 5th *Gebirgsjäger* Division under Major-General Julius Ringel, with Colonel-General Alexander Lohr in overall command. They were supported by 500 fighters and bombers, together with 500 transports and 80 gliders.

The 35,000 British and Commonwealth forces on Crete were commanded by General Freyberg, who was familiar with German plans through ULTRA intercepts. Once the Germans had seized the airfield at Maleme, however, and

could fly in reinforcements the British and Commonwealth forces were pushed back and Freyberg knew that he would not win the battle. It would prove a terribly costly victory for the Germans, who lost 220 aircraft destroyed and 150 damaged. Some 6000 German paratroops were killed or wounded and 2000 were reported missing – the 7th Air Division suffered 50 per cent casualties. Allied losses were 3600 killed or wounded and 12,000 taken prisoner, some on the southern beaches of the island while waiting to be evacuated by the Royal Navy.

So severe were the losses on Crete that the Germans never attempted a major airborne operation again. Hitler declared to Student that, 'the day of the paratrooper is over. The parachute arm is a surprise weapon and without the element of surprise there can be no future for airborne forces.' With these words he condemned this superb force to a ground role where it would fight with distinction throughout the war.

JUNKERS JU 52/3M

The rugged *'Tante Ju'* (Auntie Junkers), with its distinctive corrugated fuselage, was the transport workhorse for the *Luftwaffe* throughout the war. A total of 4850 were built and ironically the largest operator of the type after the Germans was the USSR, which had more than 80 captured or repaired aircraft. The USAAF had one Ju 52, to which they gave the designation C-79, and the RAF had two. It was aboard Ju 52s that German paratroops were carried to Crete in the assault in 1941. Later on the Eastern Front it would be used for resupply and casualty evacuation, notably in the hopeless struggle to keep the Sixth Army supplied in Stalingrad in 1942–3.

Left: German paratroops in a captured British Landing Craft Assault approach the beached and wrecked cruiser HMS York *in Suda Bay, Crete in 1941. The* York *had been crippled by Italian explosive-laden speedboats. The Royal Navy suffered heavy casualties during evacuation operations.*

The campaign in the Balkans had been swift and victorious. It was another demonstration of the ruthless efficiency of the German war machine. However this campaign, forced on the Germans by Italian adventurism, had delayed the attack on the USSR by a critical five weeks. It had been scheduled for 15 May 1941 but owing to the diversions in the Balkans it would not now be launched until 22 June. If it had run to its original schedule the mud and snow of the winter would not have stopped the Panzers outside Moscow, since they would still have had more than a months' good going.

The *Duce* had set in train a course of events that would lose the war not only for Fascist Italy but also for Nazi Germany, changing the political boundaries of Europe for the next fifty years.

Below: Afrika Korps anti-tank gunners fire their 8.8cm (3.46in) gun off its carriage at Eighth Army armour in North Africa. The 'Eighty Eight' was a formidable anti-aircraft gun as well as being one of the most effective anti-tank guns of World War II.

The attack on the USSR was less than a week away when, in the intense summer heat of North Africa, the *Afrika Korps* survived Operation Battleaxe, mounted by General Wavell on 15 June, just as they had fought out Operation Brevity the previous month. Both British attacks had been intended to relieve the besieged port of Tobruk. In the spring of 1941 the German press was full of the exploits of the *Afrika Korps* and its energetic commander, but Africa would soon be eclipsed by war in the Soviet Union.

AWAITING THE STORM

Between 10 February 1940 and 22 June 1941 the USSR had conscientiously implemented the terms of the German–Soviet agreement signed in the aftermath of the defeat of Poland. It supplied 1.5 million tons of grain (rye, oats and wheat), cotton, 1 million tons of mineral oil, 2700kg (2.65 tons) of platinum and large quantities of strategic ores, such as manganese and chrome. The fuel and grain had been an important support for the Germans in their operations against the West in 1940. They were, however, slow payers and although goods worth *Reichmarks* (RM) 467 million had been supplied to the USSR, on the day it invaded Nazi Germany owed its enemy RM239 million.

To Stalin, who was always suspicious of the West, assisting Germany in the destruction of the Franco–British capitalist forces may have been compensation enough. Incredibly, the USSR and Germany were sending freight trains across the bridge over the River Bug at Brest-Litovsk into the early hours of 22 June 1941. Heinrich Eikmeier, part of the crew of an 8.8cm (3.45in) Flak gun, saw the 18:00 German train cross the bridge the previous evening: 'At six o'clock a goods

---

OKW

The *Oberkommando der Wehrmacht* (OKW, High Command of the Armed Forces), the tri-service command set up by Hitler on 4 February 1938 to replace the old *Reichskriegsministerium* (War Ministry), was divided into four departments. These were the *Wehrmachtführungsamt* (WFA) responsible for operations, headed by General Wilhelm Keitel; *Amt/Ausland Abwehr* responsible for foreign intelligence; *Wirtschafts-und Rüstungsamt* responsible for supply; and *Amtsgruppe Allgemeine Wehrmachtangelegenheiten* for general purposes. The structure of the organization changed three times between 1934–8, 1938–41 and 1941–5.

It must never be forgotten that the present rulers of Russia are blood-stained criminals, that here we have the dregs of humanity which, favoured by the circumstances of a tragic moment, overran a great State, degraded and extirpated millions of educated people out of sheer blood-lust, and that now for nearly 10 years they have ruled with such a savage tyranny as was never known before … It must not be forgotten that the international Jew, who is today the absolute master of Russia, does not look upon Germany as an ally but as a State condemned to the same doom as Russia.

Adolf Hitler
Mein Kampf, 1924–6

---

train loaded with either wheat or coal passed over the Bug river to Russia. We could not understand the point of delivering up these locomotive crews as victims. Actually we were somewhat uncertain over whether it was right or wrong. Was it going to be war or not?' At 02:00 Rudolf Gschöpf, the divisional chaplain with the 45th Infantry Division, heard a Soviet train as it crossed the four-span bridge into German-controlled western Poland. In less than two hours the two trading partners would be mortal enemies.

At Suwalki airbase in Poland Leutnant Heinz Knoke, a Messerschmitt Bf 109 fighter pilot with *Luftflotte* II, noted in his diary that orders had come through for the scheduled Berlin–Moscow airliner to be shot down. His commanding officer and a wing man took off to execute this cold-blooded mission. 'But', Knoke noted with regret, 'they failed to intercept the Douglas'.

At 04:00 the Soviet ambassador in Berlin, Vladimir Dekanozov, was summoned to the German Foreign Ministry in Wilhelmstrasse and informed that German forces had entered Soviet territory in response to a long list of 'border violations', which, it was claimed, 'systematically dismantled German–Soviet cooperation'. The memorandum prepared under Hitler's direction did not end with a declaration of war but with less precise words: 'Unfortunately, because of these unfriendly and provocative actions on the part of the Soviet Union, the German Government is obliged to meet the threat with all available military means'.

Right: An Afrika Korps MG34 machine gun crew in a rocky position. The MG34 was the world's first general-purpose machine gun that could be mounted on a tripod for long range engagements or with its tripod as a light machine gun used in the assault.

CHAPTER TWO

SEARCH FOR *LEBENSRAUM*

The German attack on the Soviet Union
was underpinned by a hatred of Communism
which was seen as a sinister international
organisation controlled in Moscow and a desire
to expand into new territory in the East.
The East was seen as an area that would yield up
raw materials, free labour and vast agricultural
lands; its capture would allow a new type
of colonial expansion and ensure the survival
of Nazi Germany.

THE GERMAN WAR WITH THE SOVIET UNION had long been predicted. For Hitler the *Drang nach Osten* ('drive on the east') would give the Germans *Lebensraum* ('living space'). He believed that Germany was overpopulated and needed more land to support the population. Poland and Russia were the new territories where *Lebensraum* could become a reality. In *Mein Kampf* he had written, 'If the Urals, with its immeasurable treasure of raw materials, Siberia, with its rich forests, and the Ukraine, with its limitless grain fields, were to lie in Germany, this country under National Socialist leadership would swim with plenty'.

France had just been defeated and the *Luftwaffe* was locked in combat with the RAF in daylight bombing operations in the Battle of Britain when, on 21 July 1940, Hitler mooted the idea of an attack on the USSR at a planning conference. Present were *Generalfeldmarschall* Walther von Brauchitsch

Left: Hitler, flanked by Generalfeldmarshalls *Keitel and Ritter von Leeb, studies a situation map. In the background is Hitler's* Luftwaffe *adjutant Nikolaus von Below. Hitler's untrained and haphazard approach to operations in the East was summarized by General Halder as 'patchwork'.*

for the Army, *Generaloberst* Hans Jeschonnek representing Goering and the *Luftwaffe*, Grand Admiral Erich Raeder for the *Kriegsmarine* with *Generalfeldmarschall* Wilhelm Keitel and *Generaloberst* Alfred Jodl for the OKW.

In Hitler's view Britain would be starved by the U-Boat campaign that was interdicting the supply of food and fuel to the island. Britain's only hope in Europe, he thought, was to induce the USSR to attack its treaty partner Germany. Hitler was suspicious of Stalin and the USSR and saw an attack as a pre-emptive strike that would remove this threat. Although

Below: This vision of Europe and the East was the product the minds of Nazi ideologues whose thoughts had drifted from the practical reality of military operations to a visionary fantasy which saw soldier-farmer colonists running estates in the conquered East.

LEBENSRAUM

For the Nazi ideologues the existence of an independent Poland was a block for *Lebensraum* ('living space') in the East, which in Hitler's geopolitics was essential for the expanding Third Reich. *Lebensraum* had originally been the slogan of German expansionism in the late nineteenth century, as Germany worked to create a colonial empire. In 1924, Hitler adopted the concept in his political testament *Mein Kampf*. He linked it with the racial theory of Aryan (Nordic German) superiority, and this pointed to Poland and Russia as the place where a new *Lebensraum* could be created, with the Slavs working for Aryan soldier farmers.

Right: Hitler and Generalfeldmarshall *von Brauchtisch. Though von Brauchtisch was an experienced and competent military officer, he was overawed by Hitler and would not stand up to him. Hitler, the ex-corporal, had no genuine respect for his generals.*

the United States was neutral, its sympathies were with Britain and he knew that in time it would be drawn into the world war. The aim would be to knock out the USSR by the end of 1941.

In some respects the attack would be like that by the Japanese on Pearl Harbor at the end of the year – both the USSR and USA had the industrial might and manpower to defeat their adversaries in a long war. The leaders of Germany and Japan thought that inflicting a serious defeat might remove the desire or capability to wage war, or buy time and territory. Neither considered that their adversary might desire an absolute revenge.

German soldiers who were privy to these secret plans and had a sense of history found themselves thinking of earlier invasions of the East by the Swedish King Carl XII in the eighteenth century and Napoleon I in the nineteenth. Both men were superb military leaders and innovators, yet both were defeated, Carl XII at Poltava in 1709 and Napoleon outside Moscow in 1812. The bitter winter was a key factor in the defeat of both invasions.

WAR ON TWO FRONTS

In August 1940 Keitel presented Hitler with a memorandum opposing the proposed two-front war. Hitler bluntly refuted the arguments and Keitel then tendered his resignation. As he later recalled, 'Hitler harshly rejected this: did he then have no right to inform me if in his view my judgement were wrong? He really would have to forbid his generals to go into a huff and ask to resign every time somebody lectured them, and in any case *he* had no chance of resigning his office either. He wanted it understood once and for all that it was nobody's right but his to relieve a person of his office if he saw fit, and until then that person would just have to put up with the job;

during the previous autumn, he said, he had had to tell Brauchitsch the same as well.' There would be no argument with the decision to attack the USSR and Keitel would become merely a messenger boy for Hitler, signing orders and passing on instructions.

The planners tasked with preparing for an attack on the USSR immediately identified that the Pripet Marshes would be a serious obstacle, forcing the attack into mobility corridors to the north and south. These heavily wooded marshes, formed in the Ice Age by a glacial lake in a basin of the Pripet river, covered about 270 square kilometres (105sq miles). Elevations ranged from about 100m (328ft) in the northeast to about 250m (820ft) in the south.

The fan shape of western Russia meant that, the further German forces penetrated eastwards, the more they would be more dispersed as the front became wider. An indication of the length of the front – 3000km (1,860 miles) – could be gauged by the fact that H-Hour, the dawn attack, was set for 03:05 in Army Group North's sector but would be at 03:15 further south in Army Group Centre. Down on the Romanian border, where the men of Army Group South would assemble, the attack would begin at 03:25.

The Soviet railway gauge was wider than the Europe standard and so all tracks would have to be converted to take German and European locomotives and rolling stock. The lines in what had been northeast Poland had not yet been converted by Soviet engineers following the seizure of the area in 1939 and so planners favoured this as an axis.

In 1940 the Panzers had used the excellent European roads to push westwards. From the borders of the Reich their tanks had to advance only 300km (186 miles) to reach the mouth of the Somme and cut off the northern French and British forces. Only three per cent of roads in the USSR, however were metalled: in summer the dirt tracks would became very dusty but in the spring thaw and autumn rains – a time the Russians called *rasputitsa* ('the season of no roads') – the dust would became deep muddy sloughs. This halted or slowed down men, horses and vehicles. It would be known by the Germans as the *Schlammperiode* and would significantly effect operations in the East between 1941 and 1944, stopping or slowing down Soviet as well as German offensives.

This meant that, even if there were virtually no resistance, the German armies would be forced to slow down to allow supplies like food and fuel to catch up with them. After advancing 300km into the USSR they would only have reached the city of Minsk, Smolensk would be a further 300km distant and, from their original start line, Moscow was 1000km (620 miles) beyond the distant horizon.

MAKING PLANS

Work on what would be the first plan to attack this vast country began on 29 July 1940. *Generalmajor* Erich Marcks, chief-of-staff of the Eighteenth Army based in Bromberg (now Bydgoszcz), West Prussia, was selected by General Franz Halder, the chief-of-staff of the OKH (*Oberkommando der Heeres*), to prepare a secret study for an attack on the Soviet Union. The Marcks plan envisaged the main weight of the attack being to the north of the Pripet Marshes with the Sixth and Fourth Armies launching converging attacks that would bypass Minsk in Byelorussia and link up at Smolensk. They would then jointly push for Moscow and the seat of Soviet government. The Eighteenth Army would attack through the Baltic states with Leningrad as its objective. To the south of the Pripet Marshes the Sixteenth Army would drive for Kiev and, once this city had been secured, would swing north to join the Sixth and Fourth Armies in the drive on Moscow. In the far south the Twelfth Army would attack into the Ukraine, although, like the Eighteenth Army to the north, this was not a major axis of attack.

At the OKW *Generaloberst* Jodl, head of the Operations Department, told his staff about the possible invasion on 29 July. The plan he tasked *Oberst* G.S. Lossberg to prepare placed the weight of the attack to the north of the Pripet Marshes because the rail links were better. To protect Romania and its oil fields, however, a thrust would be made south of the marshes into the Ukraine with a smaller subsidiary one across the Prut river towards Kishinev (now Chisinau).

The finished OKH plan that Halder presented to Hitler on 5 December placed the weight of the German attack in the north with two army groups attacking along three axes. The

---

BARBAROSSA

The invasion plans were originally code named *Fall Fritz* (Plan Fritz). On 18 December 1940, however, Hitler changed the name to *Unternehmen Barbarossa* (Operation Barbarossa). The Holy Roman Emperor Friedrich I (1123–1190), known as 'Red Beard', was leading the Third Crusade to the Holy Land when, crossing a stream in Asia Minor clad in full armour, he fell in and was drowned. A legend that grew up around him asserted that he had lived on and resided in a cave in the Kyffhäuser Hills in the geographical centre of Germany, awaiting the call of his country. It was a summer tradition for thousands of schoolchildren to hike to the 'Barbarossa Cave' and to see the marble statue of this heroic figure.

Having chosen this grandiloquent name Hitler assured General Franz Halder in 1940 that, 'When Barbarossa commences the world will hold its breath and make no comment'.

Rußlandlied
Von Alfred Heinz Jlling

Auf, Kamerad! Die Zeit ist reif —
Am Himmel steht ein Feuerschweif!
Laßt uns nicht länger warten.
Wir werfen die Propeller an! —
Die Infant'rie ruft: „Marsch voran!" —
Laßt uns nach Rußland starten!

    Der Führer ruft — drum, Schatz, ade!
    Zum Siege stürmt die Ost-Armee!
    Und schlägt das dreiste Russenpack,
    Wie sie geschlagen den Polack.
    Drum, Schatz, ade, drum, Schatz, ade!
    Zum Siege stürmt die Ost-Armee!

Das Heer der Feinde schreckt uns nicht;
Wir tuen eisern unsre Pflicht
Und werden nicht verzagen, —
Bevor der Feind am Boden liegt,
Von uns vernichtet und besiegt, —
Und wir den Lorbeer tragen!
    Der Führer ruft . . . usw.

Trifft mich die Kugel gar zu gut,
So lieg ich denn in meinem Blut
In Rußlands roter Erde. —
Doch weiter stürmt das graue Heer
Und treibt den Kosak vor sich her,
Gleichwohl, ob er sich wehrte!
    Der Führer ruft . . . usw.

northern would drive for Leningrad while in the centre two would converge on Smolensk. South of the marshes a major thrust would be directed from Poland into the Ukraine. Halder asserted that Moscow should be the main objective following major battles of encirclement around Minsk and Smolensk.

Hitler heard the OKH presentation and then proposed his plan for the invasion. The weight would be on the left flank with a heavy thrust towards Leningrad. South of the marshes, Kiev and the Ukraine would be objectives, but Moscow would not be a major priority.

On 18 December Hitler issued Directive 21: Operation Barbarossa. The directive was vague and reflected the terrific optimism that infected both the senior political and military leadership in Germany. There was a vast ignorance about the real strength of the Soviet armed forces and their equipment. The shock of encountering the first T-34/76 medium tanks with their tough armour and superb mobility in snow and mud would become one of the enduring tales of the first months of Barbarossa. German soldiers would recall the desperate shout of the infantry for '*Pak und Flak*' (anti-tank or anti-aircraft guns) to be deployed forward to engage the

Above: Rußlandlied *('The Russia Song') – a propaganda song composed by Alfred Jilling. The reality of the dry and dusty slog into the Soviet Union shows on the faces of the soldiers – few had time or energy to sing as they marched on rough roads.*

armour threat. However, the German forces were impressed by the quality and later the quantity of weapons, from small arms to mortars and artillery, that the Red Army deployed. They paid their adversaries the greatest compliment by first using captured weapons and then having them copied in the factories of the Third Reich.

TAKING ON THE 'STEAM ROLLER'
The ability of the USSR to sustain losses in men and equipment that would have produced a collapse of confidence and defeat in a European adversary seemed incomprehensible. The delay in mobilizing the vast army reserves until the war actually crashed over its borders was a tactical disaster for the USSR, but strategically a triumph. It meant that thousands of men were being called up and committed to battle progressively over the first two years of the war. In 1941 the 18- to 22-year-olds had just been called

Left: German forces in the East showing a typical mix of trucks, horse drawn wagons and marching infantry moving through a village. The road is still in good condition but with the onset of the autumn rains will turn into a muddy mush.

up and these inexperienced soldiers often bore the brunt of the German attacks. There was an immediate call up of the 23 to 36 age group, however, men who had completed training, and by as early as July 1941 some 5.3 million men were under arms. Worse still for the Germans, in the first years of the war in the East the USSR could lose huge tracts of land and major cities without affecting its ability to wage war – but all this was to be discovered by the Germans in the future.

The Germans had taken on the 'Russian Steam Roller', as the vast Soviet army had been nicknamed by the Allies in World War I. This time it would not collapse in revolution, corruption and incompetence as it had in 1917–18, but would with increasing competence roll westwards to crush them.

In 1940–1 the Germans were utterly convinced that they would win another lightning victory against an enemy who was poorly equipped and badly led, and regarded as less than human. They had after all defeated Denmark, Norway, France, Belgium, the Netherlands, Yugoslavia and Greece and driven the British from the mainland of Europe. This had been achieved at breakneck speeds and with minimal losses – they were entitled in their own eyes to see themselves as invincible.

More details of the plan had been confirmed. The German attack on the Soviet Union would be split between three *Heeresgruppen* (Army Groups). Army Group North under *Generalfeldmarschall* Ritter von Leeb consisted of seven divisions and three *Panzerdivisionen*. Army Group Centre under *Generalfeldmarschall* Fedor von Bock had 42 divisions and nine *Panzerdivisionen*. Army Group South under *Generalfeldmarschall* Gerd von Rundstedt consisted of 52 divisions, of which 15 were Romanian, two Hungarian and two Italian, plus five *Panzerdivisionen*.

Army Group North had its left flank on the Baltic and right on the town of Suwalki. The right flank of Army Group Centre was the centre of the Pripet Marshes, while Army Group South covered a huge front from the Pripet Marshes to the Black Sea.

> This land is endless, beneath an endless sky with roads trailing endlessly into an incalculable distance. Each village and town seems just like the one that preceded it. They all have the same women and children standing dumbly by the roadside, the same wells, the same farmsteads … If the column comes off the road and moves on a compass bearing across fields, we look like lost world circumnavigators seeking new coasts beyond these oceans.
>
> *Felix Lützkenorf*
> *Propaganda-Kompagnie, Waffen-SS, Ukraine, 1941*

The Army Groups were supported by nine lines of communications divisions, which would rebuild bridges and change the gauge of the Soviet railways. Optimistic German planners envisaged holding a line from Archangel in the north to Astrakhan in the south, the A–A line, by the onset of winter in 1941. The line ran east of Kazan and Kuybyshev and included Stalingrad.

From senior staff officers down to *Schütze* (Private) Benno Zeiser, a young German soldier under training as a driver, there was a confidence that the war would be short and victorious: 'The whole thing should be over in three or four weeks, they said; others were more cautious and gave it two or three months. There was even one who said it would take a whole year, but we laughed him right out. "Why, how long did the Poles take us, and how long to settle France, eh?"'

Helmut Ritgen, the Adjutant of 2nd Battalion 11th Panzer Regiment, confessed that he 'was most optimistic. At school I had been regarded as a good mathematician. So I tried to compute the duration of our campaign by the duration of the past campaigns in Poland and France in relation to the strength of the opposing forces, distances and other factors. My conclusion was that the war would be over at the end of July. Thus I set my wedding-day for

Left: Armed with an MP34 Steyr-Solothurn SMG, a German NCO, his helmet outline camouflaged with grass, scans the countryside. The MP34 probably came from stocks taken from the Austrian Police at the time of the Anschluss.

2 August. Unfortunately, I had failed to consider an unknown factor in my computation. So my fiancée had to wait two more years!'

On 23 June *Generalfeldmarschall* von Brauchitsch, commander in chief of the German Army, entered the offices of General Paulus, the *Oberquartiermeister* I (Deputy Chief of the General Staff for Operations), at the OKH headquarters in Angerburg (now Wegorzewo), East Prussia. Paulus briefed his boss on the day's events and then von Brauchitsch asked, 'Well, Paulus, how long will the campaign be?' Paulus paused and replied, 'I think six to eight weeks, sir.'

'Yes, Paulus, you may be right, we shall probably need six to eight weeks for finishing Russia.'

WINTER WEATHER CONDITIONS

Optimism and ignorance also featured in the assessment of the severity of the Russian winter. Men were woefully ill equipped and in the first winter received no cold weather uniforms while the lubricants in engines and grease in their

weapons thickened and froze. In the bitter winter of 1941–2 the German Army would suffer 133,620 frostbite casualties.

Though the tanks would be the cutting edge of the attacks, supported by *Panzergrenadiere* in SdKfz 251 half tracks, the bulk of German forces would advance at the same speed as Napoleon's *Grande Armée* when it entered Russia in 1812. Men marched and were backed up by horse-drawn wagons, guns and field kitchens known as *Gulaschkanonen*. The German Army deployed 750,000 horses for the attack on the Soviet Union. Of the 153 divisions in Barbarossa, 119 still contained horse-drawn vehicles.

In artillery regiments, though many horses towed the excellent German 10.5cm (4.13in) leFH 18 howitzer, they also towed a mixture of captured guns from earlier

Below: As larger German Army supply wagons move through a Ukrainian village their drivers watch as a fellow soldier struggles to extricate a horse from a deep pothole. The wagon is a simple Russian panje *with hay secured to the back for feed.*

NAPOLEON I

As German forces pushed deeper into the USSR, Stalin and his advisers realized that the appeal that would galvanize the population was to fight not a political but a patriotic war. World War II became the Great Patriotic War and Hitler was compared to Napoleon I. Towards the end of the War of the Third Coalition (1803–12), Napoleon had invaded Russia in June 1812 and driven deep into the country, initially winning battles against the Imperial Russian Army, although at some cost. At Borodino on 5–6 September he lost 43 generals, 110 colonels and 30,000 troops, but still claimed victory. The campaign so far had cost the French 150,000 men. A few months later, although he had captured Moscow, Napoleon was forced to withdraw from the city. At the Berezina ('Birch') river the Russians were avenged in a savage battle on 26–29 November that was the culmination of a withdrawal that cost the French 400,000 men, 175,000 horses, 1000 cannon, while the Russians lost 250,000, plus an estimated 50,000 Cossack irregulars. Between 1941 and 1945 many of the names of battles and generals from the war of 1812 would be used by Soviet planners for operations and campaigns.

During the planning phase for Barbarossa General Gunther von Blumentritt recalled that, 'In particular Napoleon's 1812 campaign was the subject of much study. Kluge read General de Caulaincourt's account of that campaign with the greatest attention: it revealed the difficulties of fighting, and even living in Russia ... we knew that we would soon be following in Napoleon's footsteps.'

campaigns including the Czech Skoda 105mm (4.13in) Model 1935 and French Schneider Model 1936. Soviet artillery would soon become part of the German inventory with the excellent 122mm (5in) M1938 howitzer being highly favoured, while captured 76.2mm (3in) M1936 anti-tank guns were critical in halting Soviet tanks like the T-34 and KV-1. The guns were later modified to accept German ammunition and became standard anti-tank guns in both the towed and self-propelled role.

Even those divisions equipped with trucks found that many of these were ex-French Army vehicles like the Peugeot DK5J, Renault AGC, Peugeot DMA and Citroën T45. Production had continued in French factories for the Wehrmacht with the big Latil TL7-RR being built between 1942 and 1943 to run on the railways in the USSR. German troops even used British vehicles captured in France in 1940.

While this was an excellent use of the spoils of war it was a logistic nightmare. Spare parts for this wide variety of vehicles were difficult to source and transport. Vehicles with only 4 x 2 drive and suspensions too frail for rutted Soviet roads would break down and the crews remain stranded waiting for repairs. In the summer of 1941 the rural population was initially curious and not unfriendly, but, as the partisan threat increased, broken down trucks were abandoned by their crews, who escaped on surviving serviceable vehicles. The *SS-Panzergrenadier Brigade 'Leibstandarte Adolf Hitler'* would begin the campaign with 2325 vehicles, of which 240 were captured. More than 1200 would break down quickly due to lack of spares.

In contrast, the Soviet advances from 1943 onwards would benefit from the huge numbers of US-built trucks and Jeeps supplied as part of the huge Lend-Lease Programme that also helped to equip the British and later French forces. US trucks were rugged and reliable and allowed stores and troops to keep pace with the advancing Soviet armour.

The terrain, however, would be tough on men as well as vehicles. On 20 March 1941 the commander of the Fourth Army, General von Kluge, directed that training should concentrate on hardening the soldiers. They needed to be tougher to cope with the inevitability of close combat and overcome their aversion to fighting at night. Soviet soldiers were not dismissed as an enemy but described as 'children of nature' who revelled in close combat, night fighting and operations in forests. HQ staffs would have to be prepared for attacks by partisans and Red Army soldiers cut off by fast moving operations.

From the outset of the war the men of the *Propaganda-Kompagnien* (PK, Propaganda Companies) would play an important role. Their film, photographs and reports would explain the war and report the victories in the East to the German people and those of occupied Western Europe.

RACE WAR

In the late 1930s the ministry of Dr Joseph Goebbels, *Reichsminister für Volkserklärung und Propaganda* (Public Enlightenment and Propaganda), compiled a list of reporters, photographers and cameramen who were suited as war correspondents. They attended an eight-week training

RUSSIA

SPECIAL KIEV

KIRPONOS

Pripet
Marshes

XXXX
5 POTAPOV

XXXX
6 MUZYCHENKO

XXXX
4 KOROBKOV

Pripet
Marshes

XXXX
26 PONEDELIN

XXXX
12 YAKOSHENKO

XXX
XIV

XXX
XV

XXX
XXVII

XXX
XV

Dniestr

XXX
Brest-Litovsk

XXX
XVI

XXX
XXVII

XXX
XLVI

XXX
XLVII

XXX
III

XXX
XXIX

XXX
XIV

Lvov

XXX
XVI

XXX
IX

XXX
XXIV

XXX
XII

XXX
XLVIII

XXX
IV

XXX
XVI

XXX
VII

XXX
LXIII

XXXX
1 VON KLEIST

XXX
VIII

XXX
XIII

XXX
XVII

XXX.
XLIV

XXX
LV

XXX
VI

XXX
XIII

XXXX
VON KLUGE

XXXX
2 GUDERIAN

XXXX
6 VON REICHENAU

XXX
IV

XXX
VII

Vistula

XXX
XLIX

XXX
LII

HU

(P O L A N D)

XXXX
17 STULPNAGEL

0

0

SOUTH

VON RUNDSTEDT

Super Man proposed in *Also sprach Zarathustra*, and a concept that had been adopted by the Nazis who saw themselves as Aryan 'super men'.

Following the attack, Benno Zeiser recalled his first encounter with Soviet prisoners: 'A broad earth-brown crocodile slowly shuffled down the road towards us. From it came a subdued hum, like a beehive. Prisoners of War, Russians, six deep. We couldn't see the end of the column. As they drew near the terrible stench which met us made us quite sick; it was like the biting stench of the lion house and the filthy odour of the monkey house at the same time.' Yet despite the racial and political conditioning the front-line soldiers quickly grew to respect their tough Soviet adversary and his and her robust and reliable weapons. The *Untermensch* quickly became the more familiar *Ivan* to German soldiers. Hitler characterized the coming war in the East as a *Rassenkampf* ('race war') fought between crude sub-human Slavs and superior Aryans. In a conference with senior officers in March 1941 he said, 'The war with Russia will be such that it cannot be conducted in a chivalrous fashion. This struggle is one of ideologies and racial differences and will be conducted with unprecedented, merciless and unrelenting harshness.'

EINSATZGRUPPEN

To carry out his savage orders, innocently named *Einsatzgruppen* (Task Forces) followed behind the army groups. They were structured as *Einsatzkommandos* with a staff designated as an *Einsatzstab*. There were four *Einsatzgruppen*, A, B, C and D under, respectively, *Gruppenführer* Franz Stahlecker, Artur Nebe, Otto Rasch and Otto Ohlendorf. The commanders of the *Einsatzgruppen* received their instructions from Bruno Streckenbach, deputy to *Obergruppenführer* Reinhard Heydrich, who was head of the SIPO (State and Criminal Police) and the SD (*Sicherheitsdienst*, Security Service), the intelligence branch of the SS. It was Streckenbach who in 1939 had conducted 'Action AB', the destruction of the Polish intelligentsia, and subsequently enjoyed a successful career in this field. The *Einsatzgruppen* were assigned to Army Groups North, Centre, South and the Eleventh Army and were staffed by men of the SIPO and SD. Their mission was to organize operations against 'individuals hostile to the

course covering war reporting techniques and military skills. Though many photographs were distributed through the Brussels-based SIPO agency photographers were individually credited. The photographers and reporters were described by Goebbels as 'cold-blooded and fearless', and newsreel film footage shot by PK cameramen showed their courage as it took German cinema audiences for the weekly *Wochenschau* film news right into the front line.

On Hitler's orders *Sondermeldungen* ('special announcements') from the OKW on the radio throughout Germany were to be preceded by the spectacular fanfare from Franz Liszt's symphonic poem *Les Préludes*. To German listeners this would become the 'Russian Fanfare'. In his diary Goebbels confided his excitement at making the first broadcast preceded by the 'Russian Fanfare', announcing the attack on the Soviet Union: 'The new fanfare sounds. Filled with power, booming and majestic. I read the Führer's proclamation to the German people over all stations. A solemn moment for me.'

The images and film that the PK photographers shot in the summer of 1941 confirmed the Nazi view of the Soviet Union. The grubby and exhausted Soviet soldiers with their shaved heads, cowed in captivity, were the *Untermenschen* ('sub-humans'). The word had been coined as the antithesis of Friedrich Nietzsche's concept of the *Übermensch*, the operations or otherwise showing resistance. The following regulations will apply … on capture they will be immediately separated from other prisoners on the field of battle … After they have been segregated they will be liquidated'.

The order was signed by Keitel and accepted by Halder and *Generalfeldmarschall* Walther von Brauchitsch, the Army Commander in Chief. However, to their credit they did issue an order stating that it was the duty of troops to fight and that there would be no time for special searches or mopping-up operations. No soldier would be permitted to act on his own; soldiers must always follow the commands of their officers.

At unit level in the army some commanding officers found the *Kommissar Erlass* repugnant and refused to disseminate the order. They were appalled by what they saw as a departure from the traditional values of the *Heer* (Army). One commanding officer read out the order, which was heard in 'deathly silence', and then reminded his officers of the Hague Convention on Land Warfare and its provisions on the treatment of prisoners. He concluded, 'Anyone who abuses prisoners and wounded I shall have court-martialled. Do you understand me, gentlemen?'

Hauptmann Klaus von Bismarck of Infantry Regiment 4 had determined that he would not shoot commissars because as a soldier and Christian he could not see why men of the *Wehrmacht* should despatch others simply because they had an alternative view of the world.

CRIME WITHOUT PUNISHMENT

However the execution of commissars was not only carried out by the *Einsatzgruppen* and the SS but also, despite the reservations of officers, by ordinary German soldiers. The 'Barbarossa Jurisdiction Decree' exempted soldiers from prosecution if they committed a crime against a Soviet citizen. In reality the war in the East would begin brutally and deteriorate into barbarism and these values would then be replicated in the West where, following the Allied landings at D-Day, German troops would execute prisoners, kill civilians and burn villages. Veterans, though, would concede these crimes were nothing compared to the scale of actions in the Soviet Union.

At Kiev some 33,000 Jewish men, women and children were taken outside the city to the ravine at Babi Yar on 29–30 September 1941 and machine-gunned to death by men of *Einsatzgruppe* C under *SS-Standartenführer* Paul Blobel. The *Einsatzgruppe* had put up posters in the city telling the Jewish citizens to report for resettlement. They were instructed to bring food and basic clothing. At Babi Yar they were killed in batches of 100. Veteran executioners reported that it was

DEATH OF A COMMISSAR

Peter Neumann, an NCO serving with the *Waffen-SS 5 Panzer-Division 'Wiking'*, witnessed the working of the *Kommissar Erlass* at the hands of a fellow NCO named Libesis.

'Quietly, casually, with deliberate movements, the corporal gets up and goes towards one of the commissars.

"Narodnii Komissar li voui?" ("You are a People's Commissar?")

"Da. Potchemoi?" ("Yes. Why?"), answers the man, surprised.

Libesis slowly takes his Mauser from its holster, loads it under the suddenly bulging eyes of the Russian, aims it at the shaved head and squeezes the trigger. There is now only one People's Commissar. A moment later, there are no People's Commissars at all. The first man slid to the ground, crying out, not knowing what had happened. The second tried to bolt. The bullet must have got him in the spinal column, for he rolled on the ground for quite some time, kicking with his legs in all directions but not moving his body. Then he went rigid once and for all.'

easier to kill the Jews, who stood patiently awaiting their death; the Roma were a problem because in their grief and terror they would not stay still and so presented harder targets. Some were not killed in the burst of fire and struggled to reach the surface through the mounds of smashed and bleeding bodies – those that were spotted were despatched by the men of the *Einsatzgruppe*. Children were thrown directly into the ravine.

In total the *Einsatzgruppen* would kill about two million people in Eastern Europe before the industrialized methods of the extermination camps took over. Many German soldiers had entered Soviet territory carrying personal cameras and became 'atrocity tourists' taking snapshots of hangings and shootings, many showing grinning Germans in the background. At Babi Yar *Feldmarschall* von Rundstedt issued orders that soldiers of Army Group South were not to watch or photograph the *Einsatzgruppe* in action, but did not order it to cease its operation.

Death could come in other ways. In a directive for the economic exploitation of the USSR, issued on 23 May 1941, *Reichsmarschall* Hermann Goering asserted that, as part of the programme, famine and the deaths of millions of Russians would be inevitable.

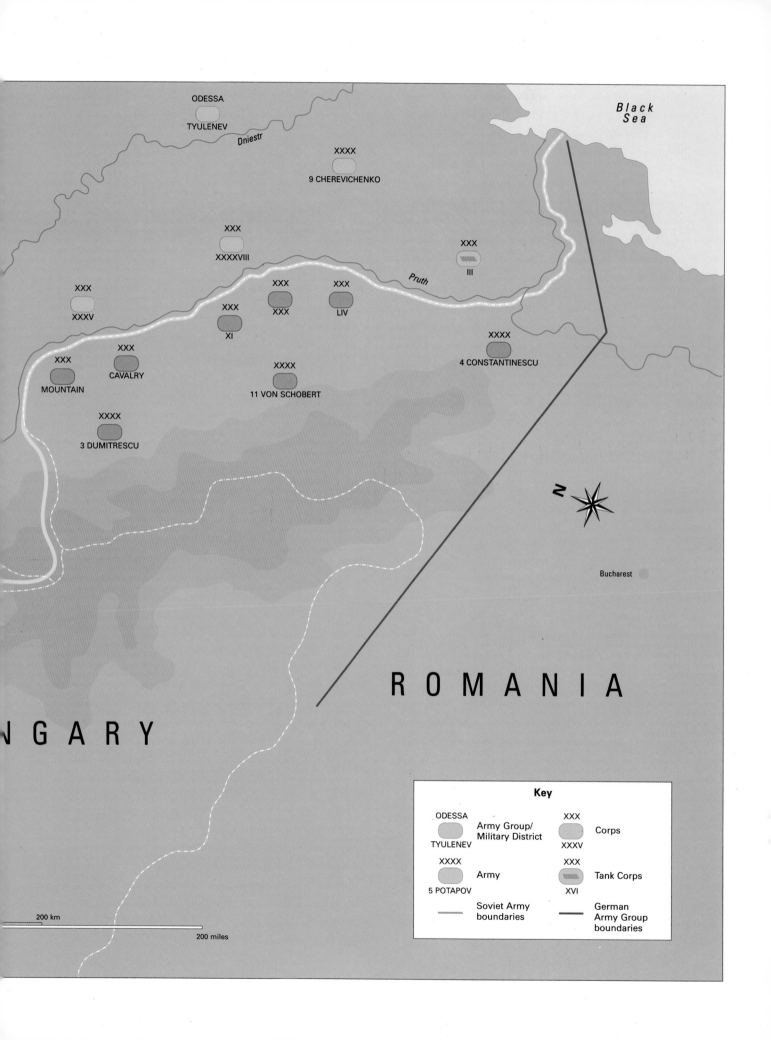

Black
Sea

ODESSA

TYULENEV

Dniestr

XXXX
9 CHEREVICHENKO

XXX
XXXXVIII

XXX
III

Pruth

XXX
XXXV

XXX
XXX

XXX
XXX

XXX
LIV

XXX
XI

XXX
CAVALRY

XXX
MOUNTAIN

XXXX
11 VON SCHOBERT

XXXX
4 CONSTANTINESCU

XXXX
3 DUMITRESCU

N

Bucharest

R O M A N I A

NGARY

200 km

200 miles

Key

ODESSA **[symbol]** TYULENEV	Army Group/ Military District	XXX **[symbol]** XXXV	Corps
XXXX **[symbol]** 5 POTAPOV	Army	XXX **[symbol]** XVI	Tank Corps
——	Soviet Army boundaries	——	German Army Group boundaries

The plan for the invasion of the Soviet Union prepared by Generalmajor *Erich Marcks* following a request from General *Franz Halder* of the OKH in July 1940. The 'Marcks Plan' envisaged heavy thrusts towards Moscow and Kiev with the Baltic and Black Sea flanks covered by lighter forces.

The OKH plan that evolved from the Marcks Plan saw the weight of the attack switched to Leningrad, with that directed at Moscow strengthened at the expense of the drive on Kiev. It was presented to Hitler on 5 December 1940.

Hitler's variant saw the weight of attacks move to the north with Leningrad the primary objective and Moscow as secondary. All the plans were constrained by the area of the Pripet Marshes that blocked a drive through Belorussia.

Above: Tired, dirty, smelly and demoralised Soviet PoWs are herded westwards. To the Germans in the summer of 1941 they looked a like a beaten army made up of beings from a lower order of humanity. These despised Slavs would however be the nemesis of the Third Reich.

Reich' – they were in fact to eliminate Communist officials, Jews and Roma. Dr Otto Rasch insisted that every man in his *Einsatzgruppe* should take part in the executions so that the individual could 'overcome himself'. This ensured a bond of collective guilt. However, when General Halder assembled army commanders at Orscha in December 1941 the generals were unanimous in their praise of the *Einsatzgruppen*: 'These people are worth their weight in gold to us. They guarantee the security of our rear communications and so save us calling upon troops for this purpose.'

'KOMMISSAR ERLASS'

The pressure on ordinary soldiers was ratcheted up when, on 6 June 1941, Hitler issued *Guidelines for the Conduct of the Troops in Russia*, which spelled out that:

1. Bolshevism is the mortal enemy of the National Socialist German people; Germany's struggle is directed against this destructive ideology and its carriers.

2. This struggle demands ruthless and energetic measures against Bolshevik agitators, guerrillas, saboteurs and Jews, and elimination of all resistance.

A specific order that became known as the *Kommissar Erlass*, and which stated that Soviet political officers or commissars attached to the Red Army were to be executed, was also issued on 6 June 1941. It explained, 'In the struggle against Bolshevism, we must not assume that the enemy's conduct will be based on principles of humanity or international law. Political officers have initiated barbaric, Asiatic methods of warfare. Consequently they will be dealt with immediately and with maximum severity. As a matter of principle they will be shot at once, whether captured during

Other Germans, however, agonized over what they saw. Infantryman Robert Rupp wrote home to his wife: 'Only rarely did I weep. Crying is no way out when you are standing amid these events. When I am back again with you and able to unwind in tranquillity, then we will need to cry a lot and you will be able to understand your husband. Here, there is no point in weeping, even when confronted with the saddest scenes … a feeling of human pathos and guilt is gradually awakened in everyone. A deep shame develops. Sometimes I am ashamed even to have been loved.' Rupp would die in the snow near Kashira on 4 December 1941.

Below: German Feldgendarmerie – Military Police – *armed with Erma EMP P08 submachine guns carry out a summary execution of a man near Smolensk. The* Feldgendarmerie *were also responsible for the more formal public hangings of captured or suspected partisans in occupied territories.*

THE COST

Six months earlier, as Berlin baked in the summer sun, Hitler sanctioned the attack in the East and at 13:00 on 21 June 1941 the OKW issued the codeword 'Dortmund', confirming that H-Hour would be at 03:30 on 22 June.

In the war that followed, out of a Soviet population of 194.1 million, an estimated 30 million men and women would serve in the armed forces and of these 11 million would be posted killed or missing, along with 6.7 million civilians. The Soviet army would lose around 6 million as prisoners, of whom only one in ten would return home.

The German armed forces, including the *Waffen-SS*, would lose 2,415,690 men killed and missing, 3,498,060 wounded and an unknown number captured.

As the last seconds ticked away on Sunday 22 June 1941, few Germans could imagine that they were about to embark on a war that would cause such misery to two nations.

CHAPTER THREE

SOVIET DISPOSITIONS

The Soviet Union under Stalin was ill prepared for the German attack but in 1941 it was re-equipping with new combat aircraft and tanks like the KV-1 and T-34. Over two years these weapons as well as improving Soviet tactics would shift the tactical initiative to the Russians. However, Stalin's reluctance to accept that Hitler would abrogate the German–Soviet Pact of 1939 initially led to terrible losses in men and materiel.

IN THE SPRING OF 1941 STALIN was receiving numerous indicators that German forces were massing on the Soviet–Polish border, but he chose to ignore them, secure perhaps in the belief that the German–Soviet Pact still held. He may not have wished to provoke Hitler or perhaps believed that the *Führer* would not start a war in the East while Britain remained undefeated in the West. War on two fronts had always been a recipe for disaster.

Among the indicators that Stalin ignored was the improvement and development of road and rail links from Germany through Eastern Europe leading to the borders of the Soviet Union. Known as the *Otto-Programme* – 'Otto' stood for *Ost* (East) – this had been initiated on 1 October 1940 and was completed on 10 May 1941 in preparation for the attack.

Left: A T-34/76A and two T-34/76B medium tanks captured by the Germans when their crews drove them into a swamp. The tanks appear undamaged but the turrets are aligned defensively. The Germans were completely unprepared for the T-34, which seemed almost invulnerable.

SOVIET INTELLIGENCE

In Tokyo Richard Sorge, a German Communist and agent of the Soviet Army intelligence service, the *Glavnoye Razvedyvatel'noye Upravleniye* (GRU, Central Intelligence Administration), learned about Barbarossa four months before the attack and warned the Russians.

In Germany the *Rote Kapelle* (Red Choir), the largest spy and resistance organization within Germany and Occupied Europe, had been passing information to Moscow since 1938. Even though it had officially stood down following the German–Soviet pact in August 1939, it too had warned Stalin. It was reactivated following the German invasion in 1941 and within a year had some 100 radio transmitters forwarding information to the USSR.

The driving force behind the operation was Leopold Trepper, a Polish Jew who based himself in Belgium and

Above: Richard Sorge, whose eccentric life style proved an effective cover for his work as an agent for the Soviet Union. Working in Tokyo as a journalist he became part of the German community in Japan and privy to military and diplomatic secrets.

made contact with dissident Germans. Trepper was also known as 'Gilbert' and, rather pretentiously, as 'Grand Chef'. The *Rote Kapelle*'s most important contacts were Harro Schulze-Boysen, a grandson of Admiral von Tirpitz who worked at the *Luftwaffe* HQ in Berlin, and Arvid Harnack, nephew of a celebrated theologian and whose wife Mildred was American. In August 1942 the *Abwehr* made 46 arrests, capturing radio operators and their equipment. The radios were then used by the SD to send false information. The members of the *Rote Kapelle* were interrogated brutally and all the men were hanged at Plötzensee prison in Berlin, while Mildred Harnack and the other women were guillotined. Trepper was arrested in France and interrogated, but managed to escape. Following the Liberation he was flown to

---

MASTER SPY

Richard Sorge was born in Baku in the Caucasus in 1895, the son of a German mining engineer working for the Imperial Russian Oil Company. Intriguingly he was also the grandson of a secretary to Karl Marx. When he was aged three the family returned to Germany. He served on the Western Front during World War I and was badly wounded. Between 1917 and 1918 he studied at the universities of Berlin, Kiel and Hamburg, and during this time he became a Communist and an active agent for the Comintern, the international Communist movement.

Working for a German news service he went to China and was based in Shanghai. He then went to Japan as a correspondent for the *Frankfurter Allgemeine Zeitung* in Tokyo. Tall, untidy and a heavy drinker, he became something of a character in the German community in Japan, particularly when he chose a flat in one of the slum districts of Tokyo. He joined the Nazi Party and this enhanced his cover. As Press Attaché at the German Embassy in Tokyo he was a confidant of General Eugen Ott, Hitler's envoy to the Emperor.

Sorge and his Japanese assistant were finally tracked down by the Japanese counter-intelligence organization and arrested in October 1941. It was reported that he was hanged in Tokyo on 7 November 1944. In 1964 the USSR awarded Sorge the posthumous decoration 'Hero of the Soviet Union' and issued a commemorative stamp showing the agent.

Moscow where he was accused of collaborating with his German captors and gaoled. After 10 years in prison he was released following Stalin's death and emigrated to Israel.

ULTRA INTELLIGENCE

In Switzerland the 'Lucy' spy ring operated by the Hungarian Sándor Rado, assisted by Rudolf Rössler, a Bavarian journalist with strong Protestant religious convictions, provided the most valuable information, including detailed high-grade material derived from ULTRA but filtered to it from the United Kingdom. The intelligence derived from decrypted signals passed to the 'Lucy' ring was reported to

have come from an agent named 'Werther'. Until details of the ULTRA operation were revealed in the 1970s, it was assumed that 'Werther' was a senior officer or officers deep inside the OKW and post-war German historians spent fruitless hours hazarding who this traitor might be. On 14 June 'Lucy' confirmed that an attack would be launched on the Soviet Union on 22 June.

Incredibly, this was not the first report concerning that day. As early as 25 April 1941 the German *Kriegsmarine* Attaché in Moscow sent a telegram to the *Oberkommando der Marine*, the Naval High Command, via the Foreign Office in Berlin. His message was electrifying: 'Rumours about impending German–Russian war greatly increased in scope. British Ambassador gives 22 June as date of beginning of war.'

Finally, if the Soviet leader had studied *Mein Kampf* he would have read Hitler's comment that 'Any alliance whose purpose is not the intention to wage war is senseless and useless'.

In London in mid-April British Prime Minister Winston Churchill contacted Sir Stafford Cripps, the British Ambassador in Moscow, with a message for Stalin: 'Following from me to M. Stalin, *provided it can be personally delivered by you*: "I have sure information from a trusted agent that when the Germans thought they had got Yugoslavia in the net – that is to say, after March 20 – they began to move three out of the five Panzer Divisions from Romania to southern Poland. The moment they heard of the Serbian revolution this movement was countermanded. Your Excellency will readily appreciate the significance of these facts".' Churchill was careful to conceal that this 'sure information from a trusted agent' came from ULTRA signals intercepts. It was top grade intelligence.

ORGANIZATION FOR WAR

Stalin thought there would be a war with Germany, but he had convinced himself that it would be in 1942. The historian and World War II veteran Dmitri Volkogonov expressed it

Left: A Russian anti-aircraft gunner with triple Maxim 1910 machine guns scans the sky. Since it is winter the guns are air-cooled and easier to handle without the corrugated metal jackets containing cooling water.

JOSEPH STALIN

Stalin, the Soviet leader who would dominate the war in the East, was born into a poor family in Gori, Georgia, on 21 December 1879. He was christened Joseph Vissarionovich Dzhugashvili. Between 1888 and 1894 he was obliged to learn Russian at the Gori church school, where he was known by his friends as 'Soso'. As a good student he won a scholarship to the Tbilisi Theological Seminary to study for the priesthood. He also read widely, however, including Karl Marx's *Das Kapital*, and became a Marxist. Leaving the seminary before graduating, he joined the Social-Democratic party in 1899 and worked as a propagandist among Tbilisi rail workers. Arrested in Batumi in 1902, he spent a year in prison before being exiled to Siberia, from where he escaped in 1904. On his return he married Yekaterina Svanidze, who died in 1910, the year he adopted the name 'Stalin' ('Steel Man'). A second wife, Nadezhda Alliluyeva, whom he married in 1919, committed suicide in 1932. Between 1902 and 1913 Stalin was arrested eight times, exiled seven times and escaped six times.

In the last years of Tsarist Russia Stalin was a follower rather than a leader. He supported the Bolshevik faction of the party and in 1907 robbed a Tbilisi bank to 'expropriate' funds. Lenin promoted him in the party by co-opting him into the Bolsheviks' Central Committee in 1912. The next year Stalin briefly edited the new party newspaper, *Pravda* (Truth).

After the March 1917 Revolution, Stalin returned to Petrograd (St Petersburg), and resumed the editorship of *Pravda*. Together with Lev Kamenev, he dominated party decisions before Lenin returned in April. The two advocated a policy of moderation and cooperation with the provisional government. As the Bolsheviks' expert on nationalism, Lenin chose him to head the Commissariat for Nationality Affairs. Together with Yakov Sverdlov and Leon Trotsky, he helped Lenin with emergency decisions in the first period of the Civil War, during which he served as a commander on several fronts. He was commissar for state control in 1919–23. As secretary-general of the party from 1922 he was able to build a power base, which he consolidated after Lenin's death in 1924 until, by his fiftieth birthday in 1929, he was sole leader of the Soviet Union.

Stalin reacted to lagging agricultural production in the late 1920s by a ruthless expropriation of grain from peasants in the Ukraine. When other crises threatened in late 1929, he expanded what had been a moderate collectivization programme into a nationwide offensive against the land-owning peasantry (*kulaks*). This caused mass starvation and the death

of about 60 million *kulaks*. The industrialization and electrification programmes in the 1930s were much more successful, raising the backward USSR to the rank of the industrial powers. Liberal and intellectual Western visitors were impressed and described the Soviet Union as 'the future'. This industrial base would prove critical in World War II, when Soviet women would build the weapons that helped defeat Nazi Germany.

Stalin's purges of any opposition, real or imagined, in the 1930s through executions and imprisonment in the *Gulags*, the slave labour camps operated by his secret police, the NKVD (*Narodnyi Kommissariat Vnutrennikh*, People's Commissariat for Internal Affairs), mark him as the greatest tyrant of the twentieth century, indeed as more murderous than Hitler.

Stalin participated in the Allies' conferences at Tehran (1943), Yalta and Potsdam (both in 1945). He obtained recognition of a Soviet sphere of influence in Eastern Europe, and after the war extended Communist control over the countries liberated by the Soviet armies. His single-minded determination to prevent another attack on the USSR resulted in the arms race and the Cold War.

During his last years he became increasingly paranoid and frail. In January 1953 he ordered the arrest of many Moscow doctors, mostly Jews, charging them with medical assassinations. The trials in the so-called Doctors' Plot were halted by his sudden death on 5 March 1953.

dramatically: 'Stalin was like God on earth. He alone said, "the war will not happen now" … It is likely that Stalin's deception over the outbreak of war was directly related to the earlier suppression of information he did not want to hear. What should not happen was therefore unlikely to occur.'

In 1941 the population of Stalin's USSR, including the newly-occupied Baltic territories, was about 190 million. It was made up of more than 170 different races speaking 140 different languages. Only 20 of these had populations in excess of half a million, however, and the dominant ethnic groups were the Russians and Ukrainians.

THE SOVIET ARMY

The Soviet Armed Forces consisted of five main elements: the Ground Forces (79.3 per cent), Navy (5.8 per cent), Air Force (11.5 per cent), National Air Defence and Armed Forces Support. The Ground Forces, by far the largest element, was subdivided into five main combat arms (Rifle Forces, Tank and Mechanized, Artillery, Cavalry and Air Assault Forces), as well as a number of technical and support elements responsible for railway, automotive, engineering, chemical, defence and signals operations.

The Soviet command referred to their infantry as Rifle Forces, reflecting an old Russian tradition that viewed riflemen (*streltsi*) as superior to mere infantry (*pyekhoty*). The Rifle Forces were the largest single element of the Red Army in June 1941, comprising 75 per cent of its line divisions. At the outbreak of war the Red Army had 303 divisions, of which 88 were in the process of formation and not entirely combat ready. There were four principal types of rifle division at the time: 178 basic rifle divisions, 18 mountain rifle divisions, 31 motor rifle divisions for the mechanized corps and two independent motorized rifle divisions.

The tank and mechanized forces actually amounted to only a tenth of the strength of the Red Army, but were instrumental in the final victory. In 1941 the mechanized forces were massive, comprising 29 mechanized corps, each of which, with two tank and one motor

Right: The Soviet T-26A-3 light tank armed with 37mm (1.45in) and 7.62mm (0.3in) machineguns. Though obsolete by 1941 the different marks of the T-26 were committed to battle against the Germans. The T26B was armed with a 45mm (1.8in) gun.

Most people loved him. It sounds strange, they loved him, respected him, revered him almost like a god and trusted him unconditionally. There was a feeling he was from a higher sphere. But there was also the anxiety that he might take something the wrong way.

Stephan Mikoyan, friend of Stalin's family

rifle division, was far larger than the *Panzerdivisionen* of the invading German army. Although on paper the Soviet Army had a formidable 28,000 armoured vehicles, in reality only about 2000 were available in European Russia.

The tanks, largely the T-26 infantry tanks and BT fast tank, have been dismissed as obsolete, but they were a match for the PzKpfw II and were well armed with a 45mm (1.8in) gun. The problem lay in poor maintenance and lack of spares. In 1941 44 per cent were broken down and required major repairs, while 26 per cent were beyond local repair. As Soviet tank forces pulled back they left a trail of broken down vehicles.

The Soviet artillery arm was to inflict between 60 per cent and 80 per cent of the casualties suffered by the *Ost Heer*, the German Army in the East. At the outset of the war each rifle division had two artillery regiments with 76mm (3in), 122mm (5.1in) and 152mm (6in) guns and howitzers. Although German gunners were disparaging of the technical ability of their opponents, whose fire was predictable and often directed only at front line positions, the infantry in those positions had a great respect for the weight of fire.

The Soviet cavalry arm, retained in part because of sentiment among old Communist leaders and soldiers, played no part in the early fighting but would expand later in the war.

For simplicity the formations of the army were often grouped ethnically, with Russian officers and commissars. Russian was the language of

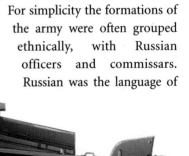

command and instruction. This concentration of ethnic groups produced the varied combat performance in World War II. Some men felt almost no loyalty to Moscow and were happy to surrender to the Germans, whom they saw as liberators. Others grimly fought to the death.

Russian society was also heavily regimented and controlled by the Communist Party, with young men and women receiving medical and military training in the *Osoaviakhim* organization. This meant that men were in effect pre-trained before they were conscripted. On 27 June 1941 members of the *Komsomol* (League of Communist Youth) were mobilized as 'political soldiers'. They would prove formidable enemies in the Partisan war behind German lines.

NATURAL OBSTACLES

During 1941 the German troop strengths began to change on the Soviet–German border. In early March 1941 there were 34 divisions in the East, by 23 April this figure had risen to 59. By 5 June there were 100 divisions in the East. In a staggering example of naive wishful thinking, Stalin, who was a brutal schemer, thought the Germans would issue a formal declaration of war. The Soviet thinking was that, following a declaration of war, the size and intensity of the attack would be limited and this would allow the USSR time to mobilize its reserves. There was therefore a thin skin of frontier troops but few reserves to block any German penetrations.

Behind them were the old pre-1939 border defences known by the grandiloquent title of the *Liniastalina* (Stalin Line). From the north these reinforced concrete bunkers followed natural obstacles such as Lake Peipus, the Velikaya and Dniepr rivers, the eastern and southern edge of the Pripet Marshes, across the northern Ukraine to the river Dniestr in the south. Although the Soviets never developed the sophisticated defences built by the Germans for the West Wall and Atlantic Wall, they were formidable builders of well camouflaged field defences and could dig in very quickly once they had seized ground.

An example of the ability of Soviet soldiers to build effective field defences was demonstrated in late June 1941 after the 4th Armoured Division had suffered heavy losses at the hands of the German *Panzergruppen*. The survivors withdrew into the huge virgin forest of Bialowieza, where,

Left: Soviet T-38 amphibious tanks pass Lenin's Mausoleum in massed formation on the May Day Parade in 1938. The lightly armed T-38 plavaiushchiva (amphibious tank) entered service in 1936 and was still on the strength of the Red Army in 1941.

ARMS AND THE MAN

In summer the ordinary Soviet soldiers dressed in khaki brown pullover, *gymnastiorka* shirt and matching reinforced *sharovri* trousers. They had ankle boots and puttees and wrapped strips of cloth around their feet in place of socks. Their helmets were either the M1936 or M1940, a modified version of the Swiss Army helmet, although some soldiers still had the M1916 'Adrian' helmet based on the French design. The popular khaki drill side cap (*pilotka*) had entered service. In 1941 most soldiers were armed with the Moisin Nagant 7.62mm M1891/30 rifle. Fitted with telescopic sights, the Moisin Nagant was a very effective sniper's weapon. Snipers dressed in camouflaged uniforms, some of them women, would plague German forces later in the war. The robust PPs-H-41 submachine-gun was entering service and was under trial with selected units. The water-cooled Maxim M1910 belt-fed medium machine gun, although heavy, was a reliable weapon, while the drum-fed DP light machine gun designed in 1928 was the section weapon. Captured examples of the elegant Tokarev SVT-40 self loading rifle were used by the Germans and later copied by the Walther design team as the Gew 43. Soviet soldiers were trained to dig in fast and construct robust field fortifications and their entrenching tools doubled as weapons in close combat.

Left: German Gebirgstruppen (Mountain Troops) *officers examine captured Russian Tokarev SVT-40 self-loading rifles. These much prized weapons, capable of single shot or fully automatic fire, were chosen by many German soldiers in preference to their issue rifle.*

dug in deep inside the woods, they used swampy ground as an obstacle and cleared cover at ankle height. Bunkers were sited to give all round protection, but with cover to the front so that when men of the 78th Infantry Division walked past the bunkers they were engaged from the rear. Red Army soldiers had trained for forest fighting, whereas German soldiers had been excluded from the jealously-protected woodlands of the Reich. By the close of fighting on 29 June the division had killed 600 and taken 1140 prisoners, against its own losses of 114 killed and 125 wounded.

About 2500 fortified posts had been constructed along the 1939 border with Germany, yet all but a thousand were armed with nothing more than machine guns. The Mobilization Plan (MP-41) approved by Stalin in February 1941 called for new construction to be accelerated. Between late February and early March the Supreme Military Council of the Red Army met in Moscow. G.I. Kulik, Deputy Commissar for Armaments, B.M. Shaposhnikov, Deputy Commissar for Fortified Areas, and Politburo member A.A. Zhdanov urged that the *Liniastalina* should be stripped to upgrade the new border defences. They were opposed by Zhukov and Defence Commissar Timoshenko.

FORTIFICATIONS

On the border, German officers on reconnaissance patrols and in forward observation posts (OPs) noted that trenches had been dug about 800 to 1000m (875–1100 yards) behind the border. Through their 6 x 30 service binoculars and artillery scissor telescopes they could not see any barbed wire or anti-tank obstacles in some areas, although elsewhere the NKVD border troops had constructed observation towers from local timber, with bunkers positioned around them.

When Barbarossa was only a few days old, *Leutnant* Hans-Ulrich Rudel, a youthful Stuka pilot who would end the war as one of the *Luftwaffe's* most highly decorated pilots, saw the Soviet defences from his cockpit: 'On my first sortie I notice the countless fortifications along the frontier. The fieldworks run deep into Russia for many hundreds of miles. They are partly positions under construction. We fly over half-completed airfields; here a concrete runway is just being built; there a few aircraft are already standing on an aerodrome.'

On 13 June the Soviet authorities in the Baltic states of Estonia,

Right: The tough and incredibly patient Soviet streltsi (rifleman), *here armed with a Moisin Nagant M1891/30 rifle and its fearsome spike bayonet with its triangular cross section. He wears the summer uniform of a* pilotka *cap and* gymnastiorka *shirt.*

Latvia and Lithuania arrested 50,000 potential enemies who might assist the Germans. The next day Soviet newspapers denied that Germany was about to attack, but on 15 June German higher formation commanders were told the date and time of the impending attack on the USSR and armoured formations began to move up under cover of the short summer nights.

Finland began a secret mobilization on the 17 June, calling up reservists up to the age of 44. Even though Germany had offered no support during the Winter War, since it was an ally of the USSR, the Finns were now being cultivated as potential allies. They agreed to seal off the northern Soviet port of Murmansk and to attack in the southeast in the Lake Ladoga area near Leningrad.

Right: 'Hedgehogs' anti-tank obstacles were first developed by the Czechs before the war, positioned to block an approach to Kiev in late summer 1941. For speedy construction or lack of nuts and bolts they have been secured together with concrete.

In a demonstration of naïve optimism, Stalin left Moscow for his summer vacation on 18 June.

COMBAT READINESS

Deserters from the German forces filtered across the border on 19 June and warned the Soviet forces of the impending attack. In Soviet army slang they were 'tongues' – men who might offer intelligence willingly or under duress following capture by a fighting patrol. One of these was a young

THE FORTRESS OF BREST-LITOVSK

A unique fortified position that would play a significant part in the opening days of the German offensive had fallen into Soviet hands as a result of the division of Poland in 1939. Straddling islands at the confluence of the rivers Western Bug and Mukhavets (Muchaviec in Polish), the fortress was built in the mid-nineteenth century at what was then known as Brest-Litovsk, on the former site of the ancient settlement on the islands. The project had been suggested by Russian military engineer Delovan in 1799 and worked out by the fortification engineers K. Opermann, Maletzki and A. Feldmann, who identified four defended zones. Their plan was adopted in 1830.

The central zone, the Citadel, was built on the site of the old commercial centre of the town, and then extended to the right branch of the Mukhavets. The southern (*Volyn*) fortification was built on the site of Brest Castle, which was pulled down during the construction of the *Volyn* fortification. The northern (*Kobryn*) fortification was built on the site of the Kobryn district of Brest, where previously there were public buildings and private houses. Finally the western (*Terespol*) fortification was being built alongside the western branch of the Bug, where there were many religious buildings. Some of these were reconstructed while others were incorporated into the garrison. The *Terespol*, *Kobryn* and *Volyn* fortifications protected the Citadel. The external defensive line of the fortress was formed by earthwork ramparts 10m (32ft 9in) high, with brick casemates that covered the canals and bridges.

The first stone was laid on 1 June 1836 and the fort became effective in 1842. The total area enclosed is 4 sq km (1.5 sq miles) and the defences are 6.4km (4 miles) long. The best-protected part of the fortress, the Citadel, consisted of two-storey barracks about two km (1.2 miles) long in the form of a curve. Its walls are about two metres (65ft 6in) thick and its 500 casemates could accommodate 12,000 troops with ammunition and rations. The Officers' Club was on the Citadel together with the church of St Nikolas, which was built on the highest part of the Central Island. The Citadel was connected with the outer fortifications by gated bridges. *Volyn* was linked to the Citadel by the Tsar Gate and to the mainland by the South Gate. Although the defences were improved between 1911 and 1914 and a second line of forts was built 6 to 7km (3.7–4.3 miles) away, the scheme remained unfinished at the beginning of World War I. In August 1915 the Russian headquarters evacuated the garrison and some of the defences were demolished.

In 1918 the White Palace in the fortress was the location for the signature of the Brest Peace Treaty, which took Russia out of the war with Imperial Germany. Following the Riga Peace Treaty of 1921 the western part of Belorussia, including Brest-Litovsk, became part of the newly created country of Poland. In fighting during September 1939 part of the Citadel was ruined and the buildings of the White Palace and the engineering administration were damaged. After the defeat of Poland it was used for quartering troops of the Red Army. In June 1941 the fortress was to be the site of a battle that ranks alongside the defence of the Alamo and Dien Bien Phu, although for many years it was unrecorded in Soviet military histories.

BT-7 FAST TANK

The Soviet BT, or *Bystrokhodnii Tank* ('fast tank'), used the suspension developed by the American inventor J. Walter Christie. The design began with the BT-2 and development went through the BT-5, climaxing with the BT-7.

Variants of the BT-7 included the BT-7A, a close support vehicle mounting the 76.2mm (3in) regimental howitzer in a larger turret and two DT machine guns. It was intended to support cavalry tank formations, carried 50 rounds of main ammunition and was slightly heavier than the BT-7. The OP-7 was a flame-thrower version that had the fuel cell for the projector in an armoured pannier on the right side of the hull. The BT-7 (V), or BT-7TU, was the commander's model, fitted with the turret of the BT-5 (V) and equipped with a radio and frame antenna; later models, however, had a whip antenna that made them a less obvious target in action against other tanks.

The thin armour made them easy meat for German anti-tank gun crews. As the crews attempted to escape, the open twin turret hatches reminded the German soldiers of the ears of Walt Disney's cartoon character Mickey Mouse.

attack would be launched on 22 June and had seen artillery positions being readied. Colonel Blokin passed this information to General Pavlov of the Western Special Military District. A Lithuanian deserter meanwhile told the staff of the 5th Rifle Division that the attack would be at 04:00. As late as 02:20 on 22 June the Soviet Fourth Army Command finished debriefing a deserter who said the attack was coming in less than two hours.

Finally Moscow issued orders for all Western Military Districts to be brought up to combat readiness: 'During the night of 6/22/1941, the defensive positions of the fortified zones on the national border are to be occupied inconspicuously. Before the dawn of 6/22/1941, all airfields, including the attached troop locations, will be camouflaged. All units are to be on combat readiness. The troops are to be dispersed and camouflaged. Air defences are to be brought to combat readiness. All measures will be taken to black out cities and installations. No other measures are to be taken without special approval.' At 02:32 the troops were instructed that 'No provocations will be made, which could lead to complications… meet a surprise German attack with all forces available.'

MILITARY DISTRICTS

The Soviet forces were grouped in three army groups known as Military Districts. This designation would soon be changed to the more combative title 'Front', and with it new commanders selected not for political reliability but for military competence. They were able to draw upon huge reserves and within six months 300 new divisions would be mobilized.

On the Baltic the Soviet forces consisted of 24 divisions, of which four were armoured. The armies of the three Baltic states had been formed into three separate rifle corps of the Red Army. They had kept their uniforms but with Soviet insignia. Moscow had purged the officers, who had been executed,

German soldier and Communist named Korpik, who slipped away from his unit's concentration area in Poland and crossed into the USSR on Saturday 21 June to warn the NKVD border guards of the impending attack. Writing of the incident after the war Nikita Khrushchev, a Commissar during the war and the future leader of the USSR, reported that on Stalin's orders Korpik was shot as an *agent provocateur*, although this may be part of the de-Stalinization myths.

Korpik was not the only named soldier to cross the border that day. Alfred Liskow, who was picked up in the Western Special Military District at 21:00, said he had heard officers saying the

Right: The BT-7 fast tank had armour protection of between 6 and 13mm (0.24 to 0.51in), a top speed on roads of 86km/h (53.41mph) and was armed with a 45mm (1.8in) gun and two 7.92mm (0.3in) machine guns.

dismissed or transported, often with their families, and Soviet officers and commissars had taken control of these formations.

In the west, opposite the Pripet Marshes, there were 30 divisions, including eight armoured. Around Kiev were 58 divisions, 16 of which were armoured, while to the south on the Romanian border were 12 divisions, including four armoured. Although the numbers might look impressive, the divisions were not deployed to fight a defensive campaign. Many were spread to a depth of 32 to 480km (200–300 miles) from the border.

POLITICS AND PATRIOTIC FERVOUR

On 29 June, a week into the German invasion, the gravest measures were announced against rumourmongers, panic-spreaders and cowards. Political discipline was tightened and commissars' powers were increased to parity with those of military commanders. The loss of weapons became a most

Opinion in the German Army frequently represented the Russian soldier as being discontented with the Soviet system [but] the Russian infantry defended the Stalin Line with great tenacity, and the further we penetrated into Russia the greater was our astonishment at their powers of resistance, their sniping ability and excellent defensive tactics. Very soon we had to admit that we were up against a different adversary from the one we had expected.

Gruppenführer Max Simon
SS-Panzerdivision 'Totenkopf'

Below: Kiev reservists listen to an announcement made by the Soviet Informburo *on the national radio on 22 June 1941. They have just learned about the German invasion. The tanks of* Generalfeldmarschall *Ewald von Kleist's* Panzergruppe 1 *would soon reach the city.*

serious offence. Special field general courts martial, consisting of military, NKVD officers and commissars, were set up on the withdrawal routes and throughout the rear areas. Particular suspicion was attached to any soldier without a tunic and papers, since this often denoted a commissar who, knowing his fate if captured, had shed his jacket with its distinctive insignia.

The NKVD wore distinctive khaki brown tunics, blue-grey trousers and peaked caps with a green crown. Later in the war the NKVD would expand from 15 rifle divisions to 53 divisions and 28 brigades – about a tenth of the total of Red Army rifle divisions. One of their roles would be as 'blocking detachments' behind the front line, collecting stragglers and executing men attempting to retreat.

Soviet military operations and philosophy were constrained by politics. This was obvious to all commanders, who were shadowed by Communist Party commissars. These were a creation of the Bolsheviks during the Civil War, their function then being to ensure political reliability from Red Army officers who might be inclined to switch allegiance to the White Russians. They operated with battalion sized and larger formations, while the junior grade political officer or *Politruk* served with smaller formations.

Commissars wore the same uniforms as line officers of the appropriate arm of service, but with different insignia. Their collar patches lacked the usual officer's gold trim, and instead of the gold and red rank chevrons they wore on each forearm an embroidered red star with gold hammer and sickle. During World War II some commissars, like Nikita Khrushchev at Stalingrad in 1942, would give support and aid to the officers and men under their charge. Others would blindly insist that orders must be obeyed and if the commander failed to fulfil his assigned mission he would be executed. For this reason, from the outset of the war Soviet soldiers were ordered forward in repeated human wave attacks, even when the first had been smashed by German firepower.

Below: In the spring of 1942 Soviet soldiers and officers, some veterans of heavy fighting, enjoy front line entertainment from a Red Army singer, violinist and guitarist. These soldiers are Russians but many men were conscripted from states within Soviet Central Asia.

'URRAH, URRAH'

For German soldiers, the long roar of 'Urrah, Urrah' and the sight of lines of men with fixed bayonets executing attacks that dated from another century was awe-inspiring – despite their ghastly losses, the Soviet commanders appeared to have an unlimited supply of armed and uniformed, if ill-trained, men. Some Soviet veterans recalled that only one in three men were issued with weapons prior to these suicidal human wave attacks. Those who were unarmed were told to pick up weapons on the battlefield from men who had been killed or wounded. German soldiers watched as successive waves would climb over the bodies of their comrades in order to close with the enemy.

Even though the MG34 machine guns had raked the lines of brown uniformed soldiers, some were not hit and as individuals continued the lone attack on the enemy position. The propagandists put this down to a mixture of vodka and Marxist exhortation – to German soldiers it was awesome.

Above: Waving his Tokarev TT-33 7.62mm (0.3in) automatic pistol, in what is certainly a posed propaganda picture, a Soviet officer urges his troops into the attack. Leadership by example could be costly, but often counted highly in the brutal fighting on the Eastern Front.

Early in the campaign Helmut Pole, a 3.7cm (1.45in) Pak anti-tank gunner, recalled that his crew had knocked out an obsolescent T-26: 'There was a Russian hanging in the turret who continued to shoot at us from above with a pistol as we approached. He was dangling inside without legs, having lost them when the tank was hit. Despite this, he still shot at us with his pistol.'

German soldiers believed that a Soviet light tank in the fortress at Brest had been knocked out and the crew killed. When the officers of a divisional HQ assembled in the fortress the turret began to traverse and the machine gun align on them. The tank was fired on and when the German infantry examined it they found that, although three of the crew had been dead for seven days and were beginning to decompose, one badly wounded man had survived. Without food or water, he had waited in the stinking interior of the tank to strike his last blow for Russia against a high-value target.

Some German historians assert that the attack on the USSR was inevitable because the Soviet Union intended to attack Europe. This is true in part since, as well as the Baltic states, the USSR had already seized the Romanian province of Bessarabia on the Black Sea and this had pushed its borders closer to the vital oil wells at Ploesti. More significantly Marshall Zhukov, who was aware of the increasing strength of German troop concentrations on the borders in 1941, had suggested a spoiling attack against Army Group South, but had been overruled by Stalin. When German forces penetrated the Soviet Union they became aware that the Red Army was not prepared for attack, but rather for defence.

THE 'POISON PAWN'

Both Stalin and Zhukov knew that the men of the West Special Military District, which included the weakened Bialystok salient opposite Army Group North and Centre, were desperately vulnerable if the Germans attacked. Their commander, General D.G. Pavlov, and his front line subordinates had become aware of the German moves and made their own preparations as well as sending warnings to Moscow. Pavlov may well have suspected that he and his men were, in chess terminology, to be Stalin's 'poison pawn', a small piece that could be sacrificed as part of a larger plan.

Post-war historians have surmised that Stalin, Zhukov and Timoshenko thought that, provided the West Special Military District fought, they could buy time for the USSR to

Left: Dressed in his winter uniform, a Soviet rifleman holds a Tokarev TT-33 rifle. He has a simple pack and an entrenching tool slung from his belt – the small shovel could be used in close combat as an axe as well as for digging trenches.

mobilize and set up defence in depth. In Stalin's paranoid world, however, Pavlov must not know his fate in case this alerted the Germans. Before the German attack Zhukov had managed to withdraw artillery, armour and bridging units from the salient for notional training exercises in the rear. It is possible that Pavlov may have complained that he and his troops were betrayed. Such an action would explain his fate – along with his chief of staff he died from a bullet to the head in the tiled execution cellars of the NKVD in July 1941.

Following the initial attack in June, Pavlov, who had lost communications with many of his headquarters and consequently lacked a clear picture of the way the battle was shaping, inadvertently assisted the Germans. He ordered forces in the Minsk area forward to reinforce the Third and Tenth Armies in the Bialystok salient, where he knew the Soviet forces were threatened with envelopment by German infantry who were advancing on foot. However, Pavlov was unaware of the deep mechanized attacks by Generals Herman Hoth and Heinz Guderian, which would close deep in his rear. The point at which the pincers would close would be Minsk – now left without defenders on Pavlov's orders.

BUYING TIME

The sacrifice of the poison pawn, however, along with obsolescent tanks and aircraft in the frontier battles, bought time for industrial plant and munitions factories to be evacuated to the Urals and for the formidable mobilization machinery of the USSR to build new armies.

The German armoured thrusts might have cut off and surrounded the Soviet forces in 1941, but in fact they always lacked the manpower to seal them and eliminate them completely. Consequently the phenomena of 'floating pockets' was created. These groups would either drift eastwards in an attempt to link up with larger Soviet formations or would turn into partisan groups. Either outcome was unsatisfactory for German commanders who

> As I handed them [mobilization papers] around I noticed how nervous the family became. I was astonished when men and wives began to weep. At the time, I thought them cowards. But I could never foresee how brutal and awful this war was to become.
>
> *Vladimir Kalesnik, student*

> The enemy's surprise attack found my units unprepared. We were not organized for action. A large part of the troops was in the garrisons or on practice ranges. The troops were all set for a peaceful life. That is how the enemy found us. He simply drove straight through us, he smashed us, and he has now taken Bobruysk and Minsk. We had no warning. The order alerting the frontier units arrived much too late. We had no idea.
>
> General D.G. Pavlov
> (according to General A. Yeremenko)

until the summer of 1941 had enjoyed clear victories.

This was to be in the future. On Sunday 22 June, after being informed of the attack, Winston Churchill broadcast to the United Kingdom. Speaking about Communism, of which he had long been an enemy, he said, 'I will unsay not a word that I have spoken about it. But all this fades away before the spectacle which is now unfolding.' He insisted that 'any man or state who fights against Nazidom will have our aid. Any man or state who marches with Hitler is our foe … We have but one aim and one irrevocable purpose. We are resolved to destroy Hitler and every vestige of the Nazi regime … The Russian danger is therefore our danger and the danger of the United States, just as the cause of any Russian fighting for his hearth and home is the cause of free men and free peoples in every quarter of the globe.'

When Churchill's youthful Private Secretary John Colville asked him how such a committed anti-Communist could bring himself to support the Soviet Union, the Prime Minister growled, 'I have only one purpose – the destruction of Hitler, and my life is much simplified thereby. If Hitler invaded Hell, I would make at least a favourable reference to the Devil in the House of Commons.'

Below: On a wet afternoon the Head of the Political Department of the Twenty First Army, Leonid I. Sokolov, talks to a group of soldiers near the town of Serafimovich. Kommissars were tasked with motivating troops and officers as well as monitoring performance of officers.

CHAPTER FOUR

'ALL HELL BROKE LOOSE!'

The German air and artillery bombardment of the Soviet frontline positions and airfields that exploded at 03:15 on 22 June hit as many identified targets as possible. Intelligence was incomplete, however, and though the Soviet forces were still in peacetime locations with little camouflage or protection some bombers and fighters survived. On the border the NKVD guards in their bunkers and border posts fought with considerable ferocity, even though they were outgunned and outnumbered.

THE GERMANS COMMITTED NEARLY 2000 aircraft to Barbarossa grouped in three air fleets, *Luftflotte* I under *Generaloberst* Alfred Keller supporting Army Group North, *Luftflotte* II under *Generalfeldmarschall* Albert Kesselring backing Army Group Centre, and *Luftflotte* IV under *Generaloberst* Alexander Löhr backing Army Group South. In the far north *Luftflotte* V under *Generaloberst* Hans-Jurgen Stumpff would support the mountain troops in their attack from Norway towards Murmansk.

As early as 1940 Polish and Jewish forced labour had been used to construct more than a hundred airfields and fifty dispersal strips in eastern Poland. Jan Szcepanink and Dominik Strug, two Polish labourers, recalled the building programme and asserted that 'Everybody knew, they knew that this was preparation for war against Russia.'

Left: A battery of 15 cm (5.9in) K18 howitzers in action. They could fire a 43kg (94.6lb) shell to a maximum range of 24,825m (27,060yds). The crews obviously do not expect any Soviet counter-battery fire and have not dug in the guns.

The grey dawn comes earlier here than in Germany. The birds began to chirp, a cuckoo called. There – precisely at 03:15 hours – the German artillery suddenly began to fire. A rumbling filled the air.

Ludwig Thalmaier
Geschützkompanie, *Infantry Regiment 63*

The exact breakdown of the *Luftwaffe* forces committed to the attack on the USSR totalled 1945 aircraft, of which 1280 were actually serviceable. These comprised 510 bombers, 290 dive-bombers, 440 single- and 40 twin-engined fighters and 120 long range reconnaissance aircraft. Hitler was shocked when *Luftwaffe* intelligence officers estimated that the

Voyenno Vozdushnye Sily (V-VS, Red Air Force) was at least 4000 aircraft strong. Actually the estimates were out by at least 50 per cent and the *Luftwaffe* had located only 30 per cent of the Red Air Force airfields and formations in European Russia. The *Luftwaffe*, however, was confident that what it lacked in numbers was more than compensated for by the experience of its pilots and the quality of the aircraft deployed. The Red Air Force training was regarded as crude, and in many cases the tactics adopted by Soviet pilots were unimaginative.

Below: Dressed in working fatigues a Luftwaffe *ground crew use muscle power to haul a bomb into the bomb bay of a Heinkel He 111. The He 111 was one of the mainstay bombers of the* Luftwaffe, *serving for the duration of the war.*

MESSERSCHMITT BF 109F-2

Almost two-thirds of the *Luftwaffe* fighter squadrons that participated in the opening attacks of Barbarossa were equipped with the Bf 109F. It also served with the *Afrika Korps* in North Africa. Its operational career was relatively brief, being replaced by the Bf 109G in 1942. The Bf 109F was then passed to allied formations, including the Hungarians and Croats. In the West it redressed the ascendancy gained by the RAF's new Spitfire Vs operating over northern France and the Channel.

During the planning phase of Barbarossa there was a dispute between the *Heer* and *Luftwaffe* – the Army wanted to attack at dawn, but the *Luftwaffe* needed to take off in darkness to be in position to attack Soviet Air Force bases at dawn. The Army wanted the ground attack aircraft to neutralize enemy positions but feared that the pre-dawn take-off would alert the Soviet forces on the border. Kesselring summed up the dilemma from the perspective of a squadron commander, 'My *Geschwader*, to get into formation and attack in force, need daylight. If the Army persists in marching in darkness, it will be a whole hour before we can be over the enemy's airfields, and by then the birds will have flown.'

The solution was to deploy 20 to 30 selected He 111 and Do 17 bomber crews from *Kampfgeschwader* (KGs) 2, 3 and 53. They took off before dawn and, flying in formations of three aircraft at 5000m (16,400ft), beyond sight or sound, crossed into the USSR. At 03:30 they would dive to attack selected airfields on the border. KG 53 hit airfields in Byelorussia between Bialystok and Minsk. Dorniers from KG 2 attacked airfields at Grodno (now Hrodna) and Vilnius, while KG 3's targets were between Brest and Kobrin.

Although the German aircraft would use cannon and machine gun fire in ground strafing as well as various sizes of free-fall bombs or *Spreng Cylindrische* (SC-50, SC-250 and SC-500), a new weapon, *Spreng Dickwand* SD-2 fragmentation bombs, was employed for the initial surprise attack. The Allies nicknamed them 'Butterfly Bombs', but *Luftwaffe* crews knew them as 'Devil's eggs'. Weighing 2kg (4.4lb), they had a spring-loaded casing that deployed like wings when they were dropped, slowing them down in flight. They could explode on impact or in flight after a time delay, and produced a blast radius of 12m (39ft). A Bf 109 or Junkers Ju 87 could carry 96, while the larger Junkers Ju 88 or

Dornier Do 17 carried 360. They were very effective against soft skinned targets and aircraft – a direct hit was the equivalent of a medium AA shell. Unfortunately they sometimes stuck in bomb racks, exploding there, or they would fall off as the aircraft came into land, presenting *Luftwaffe* ground crews with extra hazards. Later in the war SD-2s were carried in containers that opened after they had fallen clear of the aircraft, so becoming the world's first cluster bomb unit (CBU).

AIR RECONNAISSANCE

The attacks were not the first penetration of Soviet airspace. Long range, high altitude reconnaissance operations under the direction of *Oberstleutnant* Rowehl had been conducted by special He 111 and Do 215B2 bombers with pressurized cockpits flying at an altitude of 9000m (29,500ft). The four squadrons that made up the Rowehl *Geschwader* began photographing troop positions and key points such as bridges and roads. The area north of the Black Sea coast was photographed by a squadron operating from Budapest. The 'Special Squadron for High-Altitude Flying', from Cracow and Budapest, covered the area between Minsk and Kiev, flying special versions of the Junkers Ju 88P.

As far back as 21 September 1940 selected German staff officers were aware of these plans. Major Karl Wilhelm Thilo, working in the OKH headquarters at Fontainebleau in France, noted in his diary: 'On the order of the Führer, Russia is to be photographed from the air up to 300 kilometres beyond its borders; preparations for invasion. I myself have to work on a mission for the German Military Attaché in Moscow to reconnoitre routes and communications for three spearheads.'

This air reconnaissance was critical because, unlike Western Europe, the Germans possessed few accurate maps of the area into which they would be attacking and especially needed to locate and photograph the airfields. The Soviet

At four o'clock this morning, without declaration of war, and without any claims being made on the Soviet Union, German troops attacked our country, attacking our frontier in many places, and bombed Zhitomir, Kiev, Sevastopol, Kaunas and some other places from the air. There are over 200 dead or wounded. Similar air and artillery attacks have also been made from Romanian and Finnish territory.

Vyacheslav Molotov, Soviet Foreign Minister
Broadcast to the USSR, 12:00, 22 June 1941

POLIKARPOV U-2VS (PO-2)

First flown in January 1928, more than 13,000 had been built by June 1941. Though it was used primarily for training and liaison, it pioneered night raids. A number of captured aircraft were flown by ex-Soviet Air Force volunteer personnel for the *Luftwaffe* in night attacks in the Eastern Front. Production continued into the mid-1950s in eastern Europe.

leadership may have been aware of these aerial reconnaissance missions but chose to ignore them, lest their complaints be seen as provocation. There was one disaster when, only two days before Barbarossa, an aircraft developed engine trouble and landed in the Minsk area, but the crew destroyed the aircraft before they were captured.

Now, in the pre-dawn darkness of 22 June, Colonel Nikolai Yeryomin of the Soviet 41st Rifle Division near Lvov heard: 'The hollow rumble of many aircraft engines, swelling and then dying down again, vibrating over the camp, approaching from the west and sinking in the east. There was no doubt that they were warplanes, and heavy bombers at that …'.

SOVIET VULNERABILITY

On the first day of Barbarossa the *Luftwaffe* scored the biggest victory in the history of air combat. No fewer than 1811 Soviet aircraft were destroyed in the 66 frontier airfields against a German loss of 35. Of the Soviet aircraft 322 fell to fighters and flak, and 1489 were destroyed on the ground. The attacks divided into two phases with medium bombers hitting the airfields, followed by fighters and dive-bombers attacking headquarters, barracks and gun positions.

The air raids penetrated deep into the Soviet Union, hitting airfields, marshalling yards and ports as far afield as Kronstadt near Leningrad, Izmayil in Bessarabia and Sevastopol in the Crimea. By 26 June the number of airfields attacked had risen to 123.

The Soviet forces in the western USSR were particularly vulnerable to these interdiction attacks owing to their primitive communications network. Telephone and landline links were operated by the Peoples' Commissariat for Communications, a civilian organization. The NKVD manned a secure high-frequency (HF) net that used landlines for voice and telegraph. Shortly after the war began the HF net was handed over to senior military commanders. By 10:00 on 22 June, however, all telephone and telegraph communications with the three air divisions in western Russia had been completely severed. The scale of the collapse was indicated by the signal from the commander of the 3rd Army Air Force to his district command, 'I request that you report where the 122nd and 127th Fighter Regiments have been transferred and give us their call signs and wave lengths. I request that you reinforce us with fighters for the fight against the air enemy.'

Having gained air superiority the *Luftwaffe* tactical bombers attacked road and rail communications, destroyed headquarters and could even hit small targets like bunkers and trench lines. As in the campaigns of 1939 and 1940, these attacks severed the links between front line troops and their headquarters, causing a paralysis that could be exploited by mechanized forces. In Kovel, the Soviet General Fedyuninsky recalled the chaos, 'Railway junctions and lines of communication were being destroyed by German planes and diversionary groups. There was a shortage of wireless sets at army headquarters, nor did any of us know how to use them … Orders and instructions were slow in arriving and sometimes did not arrive at all.'

Four hours after the first attacks the first situation report from the Soviet Third Army HQ in Grodno reached the Chief of Staff of the Western Special Military District: 'From 04:00 hours, there were aviation raids of three to five aircraft each every 20 to 30 minutes. Grodno, Sopotskin and especially army headquarters were bombed. At 07:15 hours Grodno was bombed by 16 aircraft at an altitude of 1000 metres. Dombrovo and Novy Drogun are burning. There are fires in Grodno. From 04:30–07:00 hours there were four raids against the Novy Dvor airfield by groups of 13 to 15 aircraft. Losses: two men were seriously and six lightly wounded. At 05:00 hours the Sokulka airfield was subjected to enemy bombing and machine gunfire. Two men were killed and eight wounded.'

Surprisingly, not all the Soviet forward airfields had been neutralized and *Hauptmann* Herbert Pabst of *Stukageschwader* 77 watched as six twin-engined bombers delivered an attack on the airfield. As they turned away three Bf 109 fighters closed with the formation: 'As the first one fired, thin threads of smoke seemed to join it to the bomber. Turning ponderously to the side, the big bird flashed silver, then plunged vertically downwards with its engines

Right: Smoke streams from a multitude of burning targets as a Red Air Force Ilyushin DB-3F bomber puts in one of the rare attacks during the opening days of Barbarossa. Crude Soviet tactics made their bombers very vulnerable to German fighter attacks or flak.

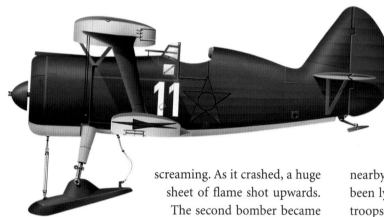

Left: The Soviet Air Force Polikarpov I-15 had a top speed at sea level of 366km/h (227mph) and its maximum range was 880km (547 miles). It was armed with four 7.62mm (0.3in) ShKAS MG, with provision for 100kg (220lb) of bombs or six underwing RS 82 rockets.

screaming. As it crashed, a huge sheet of flame shot upwards. The second bomber became a glare of red, exploded as it dived, and only the bits came floating down like autumnal leaves. The third turned over backwards on fire. A similar fate befell the rest, the last falling in a village and burning for an hour. Six columns of smoke rose from the horizon.'

Kesselring watched the destruction of the Red Air Force in the first few days of the campaign. 'It seemed almost criminal to me that they should use formations which were so ridiculous from the point of view of aerial tactics, and machines obviously incapable of getting out of trouble in the air … "This is the massacre of the innocents", I thought.'

The chaos and confusion of the air attacks was captured by Konstantin Simonov, a poet working as a war correspondent with the Red Army: 'Half an hour after I arrived the Germans discovered our assembly from the air and began to machine-gun the wood. Waves of aircraft flew, one after the other, at intervals of about 20 minutes. We lay down, pressing our heads against the gaunt trees. The trees were not very dense, so it was easy to shoot at us from the air … Finally, after three o'clock, a flight of Il-15s [Soviet fighter bombers] flew over. We jumped up elated because our own planes had turned up at last. But they gave us a good shower of lead and several men nearby were wounded – all of them in the foot. They had been lying in line.' The aircraft returned to strafe their own troops who, enraged, opened fire on them. Simonov reports that the half-burned body of a pilot was recovered and the soldiers thought he was German. This is unlikely but gives a feeling of the terror and confusion of the time.

SOVIET FIGHTBACK

What Red Air Force pilots lacked in combat experience they made up for with aggression. On the first day of the fighting the guns jammed on the I-16 fighter flown by Second Lieutenant D.V. Kokorev as he attacked a Bf 110 twin-engined *Zerstörer* fighter. The Soviet pilot put his fighter into a sharp turn and rammed his opponent – both aircraft were destroyed.

Although the I-153 and I-15 biplanes and the I-16 Ratas were slower than the German Bf 109 and 110 fighters, they were very manoeuvrable. One Bf 110 *Zerstörer* pilot had a PK cameraman in the rear gunner's position filming as he chased a Soviet fighter – he eventually downed his opponent but only after a fast hedge-hopping chase in which the Russian pilot performed some superb evasive flying.

Lt Schiess of JG 53 recalled, 'They would let us get almost into aiming position, then bring their machines around a full 180 degrees, till both aircraft were firing at each other head-on.' Three Soviet fighter pilots, Junior Lieutenants Zhukov, Sdorpwzew and Kharitonov, all based near Leningrad, became the first men in the Red Air Force to be awarded the title 'Hero of the Soviet Union' for their attempts to halt *Luftwaffe* attacks.

Two days into the war Soviet bombers enjoyed some success when they made a night sortie against shipping in the harbour at Klaipeda (known to the Germans as Memel),

POLIKARPOV I-153

First flown in 1938, the I-153 saw action in Finland and against the Japanese in the summer of 1939. It was outclassed by *Luftwaffe* fighters in the opening months of Barbarossa and by 1943 survivors had been relegated to second line duties. About 20 captured aircraft were used by the Finns. Heinz-Ulrich Rudel, a highly experienced *Luftwaffe* pilot, would say of the I-15 and the I-16 Rata, 'They are no serious match for our Messerschmitts, but they are easy to manoeuvre and of course a great deal faster than the Stukas. Consequently we cannot afford entirely to ignore them.'

Right: A loose formation of Luftwaffe *Junkers Ju 87 'Stuka' divebombers approach a target. The lack of effective Soviet air defence and fighter protection allowed the slow flying German bombers to operate freely. They could deliver bombs with considerable accuracy on suprisingly small targets.*

dropping 50 mines. On the night of 9/10 August the first of two attacks on Berlin was launched by either Ilyushin Il-4 or Petlyakov Pe-8 bombers, which took off on a 2400km (1500 mile) round trip from airfields on the Estonian islands of Dagö (now Hiiumaa) and Ösel (now Saaremaa). Of the five aircraft on the first operation two were intercepted and shot down, two failed to find the target, but one reached the capital and dropped its bombs on a city suburb.

In the closing months of the war, as their airfields once again came within range of the Third Reich's capital, there would be many more raids by the Red Air Force.

I could see our shell bursts clearly from our observation post, as well as the oily black and yellow smoke that rose from them. The unpleasant peppery smell of burned gunpowder soon filled the air as our guns continued to fire round after round. After 15 minutes we lifted our fire, and the soft pop-pop-pop of flares being fired replaced it as red lit up the sky and the infantry went on the attack.

Oberleutnant Siegfried Knappe
87th Infantry division, Army Group Centre

Left: A German Army artillery observer uses 'donkey ear' stereoscopic binoculars to study a distant target. Corn has been used to camouflage the tripod since the observer would be a target for snipers – the binoculars could be used from the cover of a trench or bunker.

through the wires. The tiny bomb drops out of this silence and immediately their engines begin to purr again.'

More ominously, General Halder confided to his diary a conversation with *Generalmajor* Hoffmann von Waldau of the *Luftwaffe*: 'The air force has greatly underestimated the enemy's numerical strength. It is quite evident that the Russians initially had more than 8000 planes. Half of this number has probably already been shot down or destroyed on the ground, so numerically we are now equal with the Russians.'

'ALL HELL BROKE LOOSE!'

The air attack was supported by a massive artillery bombardment. In mid-June the prospect of an impending attack became obvious to German gunners on the Soviet border as they carried ammunition up to gun pits. Initially this work had been undertaken in disguise in farm labourers' clothes with shells stacked in agricultural carts under brushwood. Earlier in the month the artillery battery in which *Oberleutnant* Siegfried Knappe was serving had arrived in East Prussia. The battery commander invited his officers to conduct a map exercise to 'determine the best positions for our guns in the event of an attack on Russia.'

In Army Group Centre, Heinrich Eikmeier and his 8.8cm (3.45in) Flak crew on the river Bug watched as field telephone lines were laid up to their pit during the evening of 21 June. Before dawn the next day the gunners were further disconcerted to watch several generals and other senior officers arrive in the vicinity of the position: 'We were told our gun would provide the signal to open fire. It was controlled by stopwatch, exactly when the time was determined. When we fired, numerous other guns, both left

One of the recurrent features of the war in the East would be the night-time nuisance raids by Polikarpov Po-2 biplane bombers. Early in the campaign *Luftwaffe* pilot Heinz-Ulrich Rudel recalled 'We are frequently subjected to raids by small aircraft at night with the object of disturbing our sleep and interrupting our supplies. Their evident successes are few. We get a taste of it at Lepel. Some of my colleagues sleeping under canvas in a wood are casualties. Whenever the "wire crates", as we call the little wire-braced biplanes, observe a light they drop their small shrapnel bombs. They do this everywhere, even in the front line. Often they shut off their engines so as to make it difficult to locate them and go into a glide; then all we can hear is the wind humming

Right: Luftwaffe anti-aircraft gunners fire a 2cm (0.8in) Flak 38 gun against a ground target. This excellent gun had a cyclic rate of 450 rounds per minute and fired a 0.3kg (0.66lb) HE shell from a 20 round box magazine.

NEBELWERFER

For the men of Army Group Centre there was another shock – for the first time Soviet and German forces heard the howl of salvoes of rockets as six-barrelled 15cm (5.9in) NbW 41 *Nebelwerfer* ('smoke projector') rocket launchers went into action. The *Nebelwerfer* weighed 540kg (1190lb) in action, could be elevated from -5.5 to +45 degrees, traversed through 24 degrees, had a range of 6700m (4.16 miles) and a 2.5kg (5.51lb) warhead. It was mounted on a modified version of the 3.7cm Pak 35/36 carriage. The tubes had to be fired one at a time, taking ten seconds to complete, in order to prevent the weapon overturning. Although inaccurate, it could be reloaded in 90 seconds and was very manoeuvrable.

Unusually the rockets were designed with the solid fuel motor mounted at the front and venting through a ring of 26 angled venturi about two-thirds from the nose of the projectile. Although the *Nebelwerfer* could fire smoke, the name was actually a cover and the high explosive warhead in the base of the rocket produced a massive blast effect. By the end of World War II the Germans had 150 *Werferregimenter*, in part because the rounds were much more cost effective than a 10.5cm leFH 18 shell – rockets came in at RM 3350 and shells at RM 16,400.

Right: The crew of a 21cm (8.26in) Mrs 18 throw their weight behind the rammer as they load a huge 113kg (249lb) shell. The powerful howitzer had a range of 18,700m (11.5 miles). It had an ingenious recoil system that produced a stable firing platform.

Artillery Regiment 20 joined the barrage, *Kanonier* Werner Adamczyk recalled, 'Standing next to the gun, one could feel the powerful burst of the propellant's explosion vibrating through the whole body. The shock wave of the explosion was so powerful that one had to keep one's mouth wide open to equalize the pressure exerted upon the eardrums – an unopened mouth could cause the eardrums to be damaged.'

While waiting for the attack to begin, infantryman Ernst Glasner in Army Group Centre noted in his diary, 'Involuntarily we counted the seconds. Then a shot tore through the stillness of this summer Sunday on the new Eastern Front. At the same moment a thundering, roaring and whining in the air. The artillery had begun.'

As the German infantry advanced the artillery shifted their fire to targets deeper inside Russia. However, for the infantry section from Regiment 67 commanded by *Gefreiter* (Corporal) Kredel, the fire was not lifted quickly enough and shells fell in what would now be called 'friendly fire', wounding German infantry.

RUSSIA MOBILIZES

Five days after the air attacks and artillery barrages had ripped into western Russia, the English language *Moscow News* published a classic cartoon by Kukryniksky. It showed a Soviet soldier levelling his rifle and bayonet at a rat-like Hitler, his benign mask thrown aside, emerging gun in hand through the tattered remains of the German–Soviet Non-Aggression Pact. The cartoon bore the slogan 'Wipe Fascism off the face of the Earth!'

The inside pages had features on mobilization for war but little information about the German advances. Incredibly, on the sports page at the back there was a story about summer season climbing in the Caucasus, including an expedition to Mount El'brus – at 5641m (18,510ft) the highest mountain in Europe. Few could imagine that on 23 August 1942, at the high-water mark of German expansion, *Gebirgsjäger* would climb this mountain and plant the Swastika at its summit.

and right would open up. Then the war would break out.'

Kanonier (Gunner) Gerhard Frey noted that, punctually at 03:15, the first fire mission crashed out into the silent dawn and then, 'All hell broke loose! It was a barrage unlike anything we had heard before. Left and right of us flashed the muzzles of countless cannon, and soon the flickering flames of the first fires on the other side of the Bug became apparent. Men there were experiencing this awful onslaught of fire in the middle of peacetime!'

As the 10.5cm (4.1in) le FH18 guns of

Right: The Nebelwerfer 41 *multi-barreled rocket launcher was a formidable weapon. Because the warhead was located at the rear of the rocket it exploded just above ground level with a considerable anti-personnel effect. The light carriage made it easy to manoeuvre.*

CHAPTER FIVE

ARMY GROUP NORTH

In June 1941 the soldiers of Army Group North were seen as liberators by the peoples of the Baltic states of Latvia, Lithuania and Estonia. Though the Soviet forces fought hard and launched some startling counter-attacks, the Germans were assisted by civilians and welcomed with flowers and food. The ugly side was that the Baltic states were fast to implement the murderous anti-Semitic policies that would become the 'Final Solution of the Jewish Problem'.

THE TACTICAL AREA OF OPERATIONS for Army Group North resembled the areas in East Prussia in which its units had been assembled. It was flat with occasional uplands, sandy moors, lakes, swamps and thick woodland. Only the coastal region was fertile agricultural land. To the northeast the terrain became more wooded and desolate. The roads were poor and even the good ones were narrow and in such poor repair that in rain they deteriorated rapidly.

The rivers flowing from east to west into the Baltic were major obstacles. The Nemunas (Niemen in German) was about 64km (40 miles) from the German start line, while about 322km (200 miles) away from the border the Daugava (Dvina) was a more formidable obstacle. General Erich von Manstein, however, commanding the LVI Corps, knew that a major river obstacle faced his forces closer to the border: 'On the very first day it had to thrust 50 miles (80km) into enemy territory in order to capture the crossing over the Dubysa at

Left: Decked with a Swastika, a captured KV-1B is driven to the rear by its delighted German crew. The tank has been modified, with an extra 25 to 35 mm (1–1.33in) armour bolted to the turret and a hull machine gun has been added.

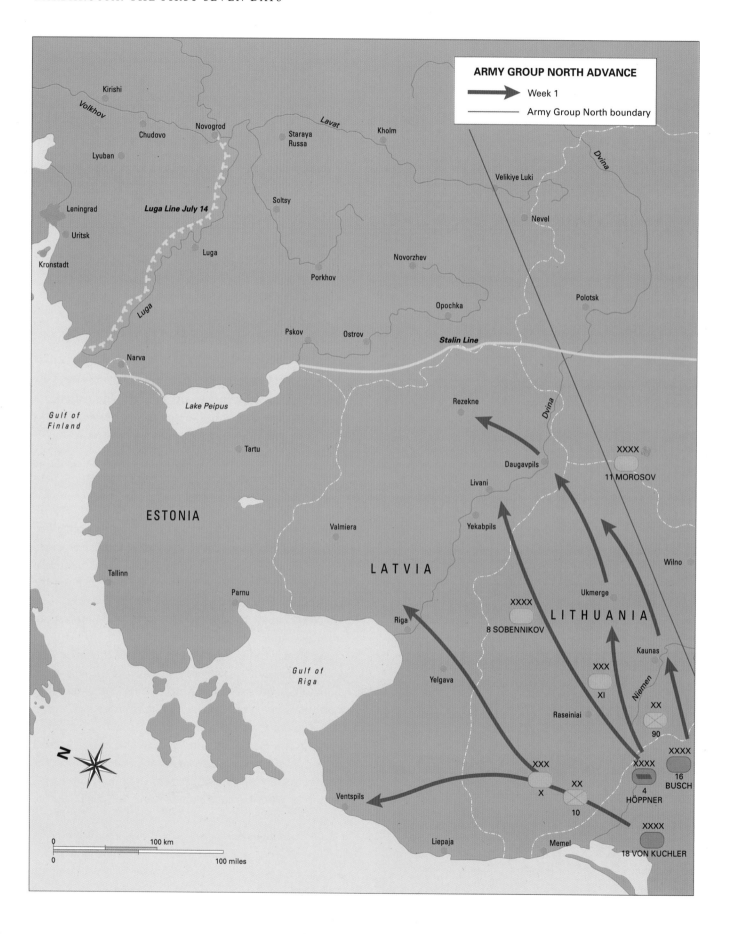

> Surprise and then forward, forward, forward.
>
> *Slogan adopted by Army Group North*

Ariogala. I knew the Dubysa sector from World War I. What we should find there was a deep, ravined valley whose slopes no tank could negotiate. In the First War our railway engineers had laboured there for months on end to span the gap with a masterly construction of timber. If the enemy now succeeded in blowing up the big viaduct at Ariogala, the corps would be hopelessly stuck and the enemy would have time on the steep bank of the river to organize a defence that would be extremely difficult to penetrate.'

Since the Baltic states of Latvia, Lithuania and Estonia had been occupied only recently by the Soviet Eighth and Eleventh Armies under General F.I. Kuznetzov, there had been less time to prepare defences. Units were still moving from their depots and positions in the USSR, however, so they were deployed in depth. There was, for example, a large reserve of tanks east of Pskov on the old border.

Leutnant Heinz-Georg Lemm with the 12th Infantry Division recalled that, 'We received only poor information on the enemy and terrain in the area of attack. We had been able to recognize that the Russians had high wooden guard towers; we had been able to observe the relief of the sentries and their supply procedure, and furthermore could see vivid entrenching activities about 800–1000 metres behind the border. From aerial photographs some firing positions of Russian artillery field positions were known. The division expected a troop strength of about one to two Soviet

Left: The axis of attack for Army Group North took it across some formidable river barriers as well as through areas of marshland and thick woods. The roads were poor, though logisticians were confident that the railways would still be European gauge.

regiments in front of its sector, which would presumably fight a delaying action in their field positions and developed bases. The maps we received were poorly printed and provided hardly any information on altitudes, road conditions and forest vegetation.'

WAR AT SEA

The land war in the Army Group North area may have begun on 22 June, but the war at sea had started ten days earlier. On the night of 12 June the *Kriegsmarine* minelayers KMS

Below: A grin from a crewman of a PzKpfw III as he glances back at infantry plodding through the mud of a Lithuanian forest. Both soldiers and tank crews knew they were joint members of an all-arms team that offered mutual protection.

Above: The commander of a PzKpfw 35(t) raises his hatch to observe a burning chateau. Some of the grand houses in these areas of the Baltic had been the homes of Prussian aristocrats during the time of the Kaiser before World War I.

Tannenberg, Brummer and *Hansestadt Danzig* laid the Apolda minefield around Fan-Fjord and the northern tip of Dagö (now Hiiumaa) as well as the Corbetha field between Kallabada-Grund and Pakerort (Pakri). During these operations, a Soviet reconnaissance aircraft had opened fire on the *Brummer* north of Dagö and so fired the first shots of the Barbarossa campaign. In the late afternoon of 18 June the KMS *Preussen, Grille, Skagerrak* and *Versailles* put out from the Baltic port of Pillau (now Baltiysk) carrying 3300 mines and laid the Wartburg minefield between Öland and the Lithuanian–Latvian border.

At Hanko (Hangö), a Finnish port and naval base that dominated the approaches to the Gulf of Finland and had been ceded to the USSR on a 30-year lease following the Winter War of 1939–40, its commander Major General Kabanov followed the personal 'recommendations' of Admiral V.F. Tributs, commanding the Baltic Fleet. He ordered the evacuation on a fast steamer of 6000 women and children who were dependants of Hanko's naval and military personnel.

The seas were rapidly becoming much more dangerous. The ex-Latvian steamer *Gaisma* was intercepted by four E-Boats off Gotland at 03:20. They began by shelling her and then launched torpedoes until, under the impact, the ship broke in half. As the burning wreck slid under the waves at 04:15 the signals officer sent his last message: 'Torpedoed, *Gaisma* sinking. Good-bye'.

THE ATTACK BEGINS

Leutnant Ekkehard Maurer, serving with the 32nd Infantry Division, recalled: 'On the morning of 22 June 1941 my battalion commander and myself (I was his adjutant at the time) were in our foxholes, very close to the barbed wire. Just before the artillery barrage began, he whispered over to me something like, "Don't ever forget 22 June 1941, at 3:15 in the morning", then he paused for a moment and said, "Well, I don't think I have to tell you not to forget it anyway! At this very moment, the worst decline – the worst disaster – of German history in many centuries, is going to happen.'"

Following the hour-long bombardment that hit frontier positions and fortifications Army Group North moved from its start lines. Though the strength of the opposition varied, in some places it was bitter. When, in the first minutes of Barbarossa, the 7th Company of the 501st Infantry Regiment hit a Soviet position north of Klaipeda, a platoon commander, *Leutnant* Weinrowski, was killed by machine gun fire from a bunker disguised as a farm cart and so became the first German to die in the East. The regiment pushed hard, despite taking casualties among its junior leaders, towards its immediate objective, a bridge over the river Mituva.

The situation reports were optimistic and by 06:00 units of the Sixteenth Army were between three and 12km (8 miles) inside Soviet territory, although the 121st Infantry Division was fighting in the village of Kybartai. *Panzergruppe* 4 had advanced 12km (eight miles) and, though the 291st Infantry Division in the Eighteenth Army was entangled in house to house fighting in Kretinga, the 61st had captured the bridge near Gargzdai.

STUBBORN RESISTANCE

A *Luftwaffe* reconnaissance sortie identified Soviet fortifications along the Daugava between Daugavpils (Dünaburg) and Jākabpils (Jakobstadt). Aircraft located Soviet convoys south of the river Daugava, to the southwest of Siauliai (Schaulen) and south of Riga. In the ground attack operations that followed 40 trucks were destroyed near Siauliai. The Soviet 48th Rifle Division, which was still deploying and lacked supporting artillery and air cover, was hammered from the air and, attacked by *Panzerdivision* 3, broke, beginning a disorganized retreat.

Within a day the men of Army Group North were discovering, as were their comrades in the two other army groups, that the Soviet soldier could be a stubborn, almost suicidal fighter. While reinforcements for the 2nd Battalion, Infantry Regiment 422, part of the 126th Infantry Division, were moving up, a Soviet machine gun crew, who had remained hidden in cornfields and allowed the first wave to pass their position, opened fire and inflicted heavy casualties. It needed a company fighting for three hours to destroy them.

In the right of Army Group North the II *Armeekorps* pushed back the Soviet 5th and 33rd Rifle Divisions, part of the XVI Rifle Corps. The immediate German objective was

---

NAVAL ADVERSARIES

At the beginning of the Barbarossa campaign, the opposing German and Soviet navies in the Baltic were as follows:

Marinekommando Nord
Admiral Claasen HQ Kiel

- Battleships: KMS *Schlesien* and *Schleswig-Holstein* (did not participate in any attacks)
- Submarines: 22nd *U-Bootflotilla*, *Korvettenkapitän* Ambrosius commanding (U-140, U-142, U-144, U-145, and U-149)
- Minesweeper group: *Grille*, *Preussen*, *Skagerrak* and *Versailles*
- Minesweeper group Nord: 5th, 15th, 17th, 18th and 31st Sweeper Flotillas
- *Sperrbrecher* group: 6th, 8th and 138th Flotillas
- Submarine chasers: 11th Submarine chaser flotilla, 11th and 12th *Räumbooteflotilla*
- Naval Group 'D': Minesweeper group 'Cobra'
- 1st Torpedo-boat flotilla (S26, S39, S40, S101, S102 and S103)
- 5th Torpedo-boat flotilla (S27, S28, S29, S45 and S47)
- Half of the 5th Minesweeper flotilla (R56, R57, R58, R60, R61 and R62)
- Depot ships *Carl Peters* and *Tsingtao*
- 3rd Finnish coastal patrol flotilla (V304–308 and V310–314), *Ilmarinen*, *Väinämöinen*, *Hämeenmaa*, *Karjala*, *Turunmaa* and *Uusimaa*, plus 3 submarines

Soviet Baltic Fleet
Admiral V.F. Tributs

3rd Battle Group
- Battleships: *Marat* and *Oktyabraskaya Revolustiya*
- Destroyers (flotilla leaders): *Leningrad* and *Minsk*
- Destroyers: *Artyom*, *Engels*, *Jakov Sverdlov*, *Kalinin*, *Karl Marx* and *Volodarsky*

Light Battle Group
- Cruisers: *Kirov* and *Maksim Gorkiy*
- 1st Destroyer Division: *Gnevnoy*, *Grodnoy*, *Grozhjashtshy*, *Smetlivoy* and *Steregushtshy*
- 2nd Destroyer Division: *Storozhevoy*, *Stoiky*, *Silnoy* and *Sereditoy*

All former Estonian, Latvian and Lithuanian merchant and navy ships were now in Soviet service.

the Lithuanian city of Kaunas (known to the Russians as Kovno). About 18km (11 miles) from the city Soviet resistance hardened and the advance slowed down. Inside the city, elements of the population rose against their Soviet occupiers and occupied the radio station. At 19:30 on 23 June a representative of the 'Lithuanian Army Command' broadcast a plea to the German High Command to direct air attacks against the city and the Soviet forces who were withdrawing.

THE POGROMS BEGIN

At noon the following day, as the Soviet withdrawal continued, a fighting patrol from the 123rd Reconnaissance Battalion under *Leutnant* Florret pushed into the city and linked up with the 'Lithuanian Army' and took over the radio

station. By 17:15 the advanced guard of the II *Armeekorps* under *Oberst* Holm reached the city and was quickly followed by Infantry Regiments 89 and 405, accompanied by the 121st Reconnaissance Battalion. By 26 June the 501st *Propaganda Kompanie* had taken over the Kovno radio station and made the first broadcast in German.

In 1939 approximately 40,000 Jews lived in Kaunas, constituting nearly one quarter of the city's total population. Before the German attack several thousand had escaped before the city was occupied and made for the interior of the USSR, some of them losing their lives as they fled. Even before the German entry into the city, however, bands of Lithuanians went on a rampage against the Jews, especially those living in the Slobodka suburb.

The murder of Jews continued when the Germans occupied the city and took charge of the killings. It is reported that SS troops released criminals and the insane and sent them to join in the killings, beating Jews to death with iron bars. Thousands of Jews were moved from the city to other locations, such as the Seventh Fort (one of a chain of forts constructed around the city in the nineteenth century). Here, before they were shot, they were brutally mistreated by the Lithuanian guards. It is estimated that 10,000 Jews were murdered in June and July of 1941.

The defence of Kaunas was the responsibility of Lt General V.I. Morozov, commanding the Eleventh Army. He had been unable to contact Colonel-General Kuznetsov at the North-Western Front HQ and so, under pressure, had pulled his forces back from Kaunas to Jonava where he knew the 'relatively fresh' 23rd Rifle Division under Major-General V.F. Pavlov was concentrating. He then attempted to recapture the city in attacks that cost Pavlov his life. Eventually Morozov contacted Kuznetsov on the telephone, but the latter refused to listen to his situation report and finally denounced his subordinate as 'a German spy'.

Left: Tension marks the faces of young German soldiers of Army Group North in the opening hours of June 22 as fire crackles through the woods following the bombardment at 03.15. Many officers had strong reservations about the unprovoked attack on Russia.

Left: The severe appearance of Ritter von Leeb masked a man who was critical of the Nazis and a devout Catholic. Professionally his fault was that he failed to understand the dynamics of armoured warfare and the need for aggression and speed.

houses of the villages were poor and run down.' On a grimmer note, *Einsatzgruppe* A, operating behind Army Group North, reported: 'To our surprise it was not easy at first to set in motion an extensive pogrom against Jews … During the first pogrom in the night from 25 to 26th June, the Lithuanian Partisans (with German encouragement) did away with more than 1500 Jews, set fire to several synagogues, or destroying them by other means, and burned down a Jewish dwelling district consisting of about 60 houses. During the following nights about 2300 Jews were made homeless in a similar way. These self-cleansing actions went smoothly because the Army authorities who had been informed showed understanding for this procedure.'

Brutality was not one sided, however, and General von Manstein noted that early in the campaign a Soviet counter-attack overran a forward position near the Daugava. An attack by *Panzerdivision* 2 recovered the position, where they 'found the bodies of three officers and thirty men who had lain wounded in a dressing-station captured by the enemy the previous day. Their mutilations were indescribable.'

'BATTLE OF THE FLOWERS'

On 23 June the 290th Infantry Division reported the greeting they received from the people of the Baltic states who saw them as liberators: 'The Lithuanians greeted us with shouts of "*Swieks gyos*" and offered us flowers. In front of the houses they loaded tables with milk, coffee, eggs, bread, and butter and cakes for snacking. And the *Landser* had learned to say thank you in their native tongue: "*Swieks gyos, Marijana!*"' To the *Landser* this seemed almost like a *Blumenkrieg* ('battle of the flowers'), the traditional summer parades, and memorably the victory parade held in Berlin in 1940 following the defeat of France, in which the girls of the BdM had covered the streets with flowers and tucked posies into the soldiers' tunics.

The 58th Infantry Division, however, moving up as part of the second echelon, were not impressed by the country: 'As we crossed the border, it was as if we had entered another world. The roads were poor, the forests on either side of the road were unattended and overrun with shrubbery, the

WILHELM RITTER VON LEEB

Von Leeb was born in Landsberg am Lech, Bavaria, on 5 September 1876. A career soldier, he was sacked during the 1930s following a scandal in the German army known as the Blomberg-Fritsch crisis. With the outbreak of war he was recalled to the army at the age of 63. He commanded Army Group C on the Western Front and was promoted *Generalfeldmarschall* on 19 July 1940. Although he protested to Hitler that the German army was ill-equipped for a campaign in Russia, he served loyally and effectively, commanding Army Group North from June 1941 to January 1942. He was eventually sacked by Hitler when he urged withdrawal to shorten the lines around Leningrad. Wilhelm Ritter von Leeb was a devout Catholic, cautious and conservative in his outlook, calm and detached in his manner and critical of the Nazis. Like many of the senior German generals he did not understand the characteristics and capabilities of armour. He died at Hohenschwangau, Bavaria, on 29 April 1956.

*Above: Waves and Nazi salutes greet a motorcycle crew as it roars
through a Baltic village. A young woman darts forward to throw flowers
into the sidecar – this is almost a* Blumenkrieg. *Images like this were
superb propaganda in newspapers and magazines in Germany.*

The minefields laid by the *Kriegsmarine* claimed their first
victims early in the war. On 23 June the destroyer *Gnevniy*
was heavily damaged and later sank. The cruiser *Maxim
Gorky* was badly damaged and limped into the naval base at
Kronstadt. *U-144*, commanded by *Kapitänleutnant* von
Mittelstedt, torpedoed and sank the Red Navy submarine
M-78 west of Windau.

BATTLE FOR LIEPĀJA

By 24 June the reconnaissance patrols of the 505th Infantry
Regiment, part of the East Prussian 291st Infantry Division,
were 50km (31 miles) away from the Latvian port of Liepaja
(Libau to the Germans). Here Soviet resistance became

stronger and the regimental commander, Colonel Lohmeyer,
waited for the division to close up before he attacked. The
following night at 01:30 the 291st Infantry Division,
supported by sailors of a naval assault detachment under
Kapitänleutnant von Diest, launched a surprise attack on
Liepāja. They charged across the narrow neck of land towards
the fortifications but were thrown back. A second attack was
launched by the Naval Artillery Detachment 530 under
Kapitänleutnant Schenke. The assault on the naval base was
beaten off by elements of the Soviet 67th Rifle Division and
sailors fighting as naval infantry. Their commanding officer
had signalled at 05:00: 'Bombs falling on military installations
and on the region of the aerodrome; no serious damage'.

A Soviet breakout attempt directed towards the north and
northeast encountered little resistance from the German 2nd
and 3rd Battalions of Infantry Regiment 504 but was halted
by fire from the 291st Division's artillery. Two days later the
garrison attempted another breakout and, although suffering

heavy casualties, small groups were able to reach the Lithuanian interior. Most of the 67th Rifle Division were halted by the Germans and forced back into the port. Here Infantry Regiment 505, supported by a naval assault battalion commanded by *Kapitänleutnant* von Diest and the Special Naval Command under *Kapitänleutnant* Bigler penetrated the fortified harbour from the south. The divisional history reports: 'The house and street battle was very bitterly fought. Enemy machine-gun fire spat from camouflaged embrasures. The resistance could only be broken by heavy infantry guns firing over open sights and fire from heavy field howitzers and mortars.'

The port was finally occupied by 28 June and Naval Command 'C' under *Konteradmiral* Claasen moved in to establish and man the coastal defences. The 1st Naval Communications Battalion under *Korvettenkapitän* Glaeser also began operations. The *Kriegsmarine* command then set about salvaging the warships that the Baltic Red Banner Fleet had scuttled, eventually raising the damaged destroyer *Lenin*, as well the submarines *S-1*, *M-76*, *M-83*, *Ronis* and *Spidola*.

COUNTER-ATTACK AT RASEINIAI

Inland, Reinhardt's XLI Corps had pushed back the Soviet 125th Rifle Division. As they approached the village of Raseiniai (Rossieny) on 23 June they were hit by a heavy

counter-attack by a force of 300 tanks from three divisions of the III Mechanized Corps commanded by Major-General Kurkin. Supported by cavalry and artillery, they attacked frontally in waves, impetuously and without skill. Among the tanks was an unknown vehicle that German tank crews and anti-tank gunners were to discover was a formidable enemy – the Kliment Voroshilov I (KV-I). Raseiniai was the first tank battle of the war in the East. It confirmed that some Soviet weapons and equipment, though crudely made by Western standards, were a match for their German counterparts, even if in action the German soldiers' tactical experience and radio communications gave them an edge.

The initial weight of the Soviet attack had hit the lead elements of *Panzerdivision* 6, commanded by *Generalmajor* Landgraf. As reports came in Reinhardt ordered *Panzerdivision* 1 to attack the Soviet flank. There are conflicting dates for the first contact with the KV-I. On 25 June at around 08:20 the *Panzerdivision* 1 war diary recalls the first encounter with Soviet KV-I and KV-II tanks near the State Farm Gut Saukotas, an infertile area of moorland and

Below: Soviet troops on the march. The man in the centre is armed with the Pulemet Degtyareva Pekhotnii *(DP) light machine gun, a simple gas operated weapon with only six moving parts and a 47-round drum magazine. It fired at 520 to 580 rounds a minute.*

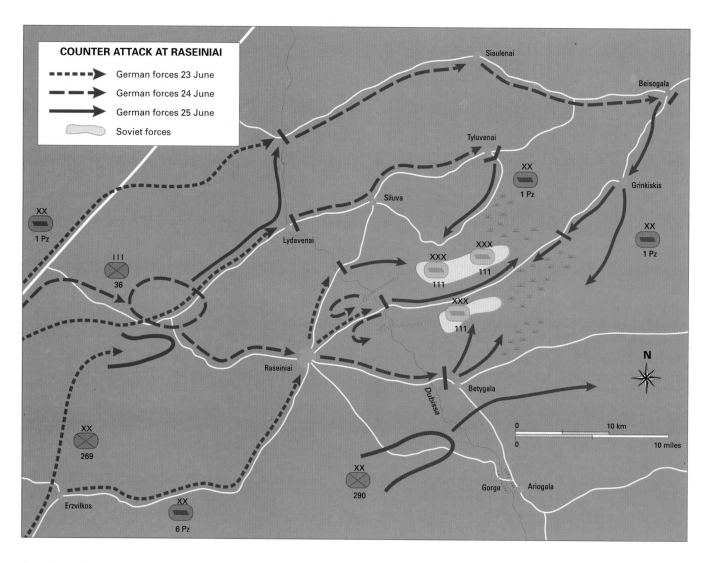

COUNTER ATTACK AT RASEINIAI

- ▶ German forces 23 June
- ▶ German forces 24 June
- ▶ German forces 25 June
- Soviet forces

marshes with poor road communications. In a report the 2nd Battalion, Panzer Regiment 1, Panzer Division 1 stated, 'The 6th and 7th companies of Panzer Regiment 1 opened fire at about 800 metres [870yds] but the fire remained ineffective!

> We were walking across a meadow and came under artillery fire… Standing next to me was my commanding officer and you had to play the hero. You couldn't just lie down, which would have been easier. And then over there lay a German soldier. His hand was raised in the air, which made his wedding ring shine in the sun, and his head – a little reddish and puffed up – had a mouth with lips full of flies. That was the first dead man I had ever seen in my life.
>
> *Leutnant Hubert Becker*
> *Heeresgruppe Nord*

We moved closer and closer to the enemy, who for his part continued to approach us unconcerned. Very soon we were facing each other at from 50 to 100 metres [55–110yds]. A fantastic exchange of fire took place, without any visible German success! The Russian tanks continued to advance undisturbed. All armour-piercing shells simply bounced off their plating… Panzer Regiment 1 therefore about-faced and rumbled back along with those KV-I and KV-IIs, roughly said, rolling in line with them! At last we were able to outmanoeuvre them and knock out many. In the course of this astonishing operation we finally succeeded in immobilizing some with special purpose shells [*Rotkappchen*] at a range of 30 to 60 [32–64yds] metres.'

A description of this action is also recorded on 24 June at 15:00. *Leutnant* Ritgen with the 6th Division noted: 'These hitherto unknown Soviet tanks created a crisis in *Kampfgruppe* "Seckendorff", since apparently no weapon of the division was able to penetrate their armour. All rounds simply bounced off

Left: The Soviet counter attack at Raseiniai was a shock to Panzerdivision 1 since it was the first encounter with the heavily armoured KV-1. Only the superior tactics and radio communications of German tank crews allowed them to defeat the counter-attack.

the Soviet tanks, and 8.8cm [3.45in] Flak guns were not yet available. In the face of the assault, some riflemen panicked. The super-heavy Soviet KV tanks advanced against our tanks, which concentrated their fire on them without visible effect. The command tank of the company was rammed and turned over by a KV and the commander was injured.'

TANK BUSTING

German soldiers from Pioneer Battalion 37 used hazardous tactics to defeat the KV-Is. Using improvised demolition charges they closed with the huge tanks and pitched the charges at tracks or turrets. It was a technique pioneered by Spanish and Finnish troops and would be used by the Germans throughout the war in the East. Successful soldiers would be awarded tank destruction badges. The crews of 8.8cm (3.45in) Flak guns of 1st Battalion Flak Regiment 3 were also critical in the German victory at Saukotas, the flat trajectory and high velocity of their guns proving well capable of knocking out heavy armour. Reinhardt reacted quickly and confidently with a counter-attack in which the Soviet force was pushed back into marshy ground, losing 180 tanks and over 100 guns. He followed up by moving across the marshy ground on a broad front towards Krustpils and nearby Lievenhof on the Daugava. After the fighting was over Major Graf von Kielmansegg spoke with the commander of

Below: The KV-1 was armed with a 76.2mm (3in) L/41 ZiS-5 gun and four 7.62mm (0.3in) DT machine guns. Its armour was between 30–75mm (1.18 – 2.95in). The V-2K V-12 diesel engine gave a road speed of 35km/h (21.75mph) and range of 150km (93.2 miles).

KLIMENT VOROSHILOV I

Taking the cumbersome dual turreted T-100, Z. Kotin, the chief engineer of the Kirov-Zavod factory, designed a more compact tank that was originally known as the Kotin-Stalin but later designated Kliment Voroshilov (KV) after the then Commissar for Defence. The KV-I was upgraded during its operational life, the most important changes being the KV-IA's longer L/41.5 76.2mm (3in) gun and the cast turret of the KV-IB and C. It was unstable and very vulnerable.

In June 1941 the Soviet Army had 508 KV-Is in the field. The KV-II used the same chassis but was armed with a huge 152mm (6in) howitzer and was intended for a direct support role. At Saukotas the HQ of the 1st Panzer Division received a fearful radio report, 'KV-I and KV-II tanks have overrun the 2nd Battalion of Armoured Rifle Regiment 1. Neither the infantry's anti-tank guns nor those of our own *Panzer Jäger* platoons, nor the tank cannons of the medium and heavy German tanks are able to pierce the plating of the heavy Russian tanks! What can be done to stop those heavy Russian tanks?' To the south one KV-II astonished the Germans of Army Group Centre when it survived 11 hits from PzKpfw IV 7.5cm guns.

the 6th Division, 'Herr General this is a totally different war from what we have experienced with Poland or France'. As he later reported, it had been 'a hard battle with hard soldiers. Early panic was mastered finally only by the attitude and discipline of the officers. At the division level we saw, for the first time in the war, the danger of a serious defeat. This was one of the heaviest strains I experienced during the war.'

Men of the *Waffen-SS* Division *Totenkopf* also encountered fierce resistance as they moved towards Deguciai to cross the Daugava at Daugavpils on 29 June.

After extricating his vehicle columns from an enormous traffic bottleneck near the Kedainiai crossroads early on 27 June, *SS-Gruppenführer* Theodor Eicke led the division through central Lithuania. However, the Russians had recovered from the shock of the initial assault and were reacting violently. The *Aufklärungs-Abteilung*

Above: A KV-1 burns in its wooded hide. Wide tracks gave the Kliment Voroshilov greater mobility across snow and soft ground, which allowed it to operate in conditions on the Eastern Front that immobilised the German PzKpfw III and IV tanks.

(reconnaisance battalion) was forced to halt and repel a series of armoured counter-attacks – they knocked out three and drove off the survivors. Still the Soviet infantry continued to make suicidal charges and only after three human-wave assaults had been defeated did the survivors withdraw into the woods. The men of the *Waffen-SS* were shaken by the fanaticism of their opponents, but decided that these units of stragglers were 'bandits' who had been organized and fanaticized by commissars and hard-line Red Army officers. This rationalization allowed Max Simon, the commanding officer of Infantry Regiment 1 in the division, to issue orders that stragglers were to be shot even if they had surrendered.

Left: Smoke rises from a light tank knocked out by fire from a hastily deployed 3.7cm (1.41in) Pak 35/36. The German anti-tank gun was obsolete by 1941 and was known by soldiers as 'the Army's door knocker' because of its poor performance against most tanks.

With an understandable desire for vengeance following its losses in the Winter War of 1939–40, Finland declared war on the Soviet Union on 26 June. A day earlier Soviet forces were reported to have attacked Finnish positions and launched air attacks against Helsinki. Baron Mannerheim described the new conflict as a 'holy war'. Finnish troops began to push towards Murmansk on 28 June.

Four days earlier a recruiting drive had started in Occupied Europe to attract volunteers to fight for the Germans in the Soviet Union. Men from France, Belgium, the Netherlands and Scandinavia, along with men from Franco's Spain, were encouraged to join the fight against Soviet Communism.

BA-10

Built on the reinforced chassis of the GAZ-AAA commercial truck, the BA-10 first appeared in 1932. It was used in the invasion of Poland in 1939 and large numbers were captured by the advancing Germans, who used them for anti-partisan operations. As a covering screen they were effective in 1941 and earned the nickname *Panzerferde* ('armoured horses') because of the cavalry style tactics adopted by their crews. Surviving vehicles were stripped down by Soviet engineers and used as armoured personnel carriers.

SURPRISE AT DAUGAVPILS

On 26 June the German Brandenburger Special Forces Unit went into action. The 8th Company from the secretive *Lehr* Battalion 800 'Brandenburg', disguised as wounded Soviet soldiers and commanded by *Leutnant* Wolfram Knaak, captured the two strategically important bridges over the Daugava at Daugavpils, both 300m (984ft) long, carrying the Kaunas–Leningrad highway and, 1.5km (1 mile) upstream, the railway. The weapons, uniforms and helmets had been acquired from the Finns, who had captured them in 1940. Using two captured Soviet trucks the Brandenburg company, which included Lithuanian as well as German soldiers, approached the objective through the disrupted Soviet lines. When they passed Soviet positions the drivers joked with outposts, 'The Germans are a long way back!' At Varpas, a village 3km south of the river they split to attack the two bridges. The Soviet demolition guard had positioned GAZ BA-10 armoured cars to cover the approaches but when the fire fight developed on the bridges the armoured car crews were unable to differentiate between friendly and enemy forces. In the confusion *Feldwebel* Kruckeberg was able to climb into the structure of the road bridge and cut suspected demolition cables.

CROSSINGS SECURED

At 08:00, about an hour after the attack, General von Manstein received the signal, 'Surprise of Daugavpils town and bridges successful. Road bridge intact. Railway bridge slightly damaged by demolition charges, but passable.' Writing after the campaign, he commented, 'Before the offensive started I had been asked how long we thought we should take to reach Dvinsk, assuming that it was possible to do so. My answer had been that if it could not be done inside four days, we could hardly count on capturing the crossings intact. And now, exactly four days and five hours after zero hour, we had actually completed, as the crow flies, a non-stop dash through 200 miles of enemy territory. We had brought it off only because the name of Dvinsk had been foremost in the mind of every officer and man, and because we had been ready to face heavy risks to reach our appointed goal.'

On the rail bridge Knaak and five men were killed when a tank shell hit their truck. As tanks of Panzer Regiment 10, from the 8th Panzer Division, closed on the bridge their crews had the same problem as Soviet soldiers in differentiating friend from foe, but they made the crossing and secured the far bank with the Brandenburgers. For the rest of the day Soviet armour, infantry and aircraft made fruitless attacks in an attempt to destroy the bridges. By the end of the day 20 Soviet light tanks had been knocked out along with 20 field guns and 17 anti-tank guns. It had been a hard fight, with Soviet infantry attacking tanks with grenades and attempting to penetrate to the bridges to reignite the fuses. The Soviet demolition guard commander was captured and confessed under interrogation 'I had no order to blow up the bridge. Without such an order I could not take the responsibility. But there was no one about whom I could ask.'

It is reported that at the end of the day, one of the surviving Brandenburgers, dusty, bloodstained and so exhausted that he was barely able to speak, and still dressed in his Soviet uniform, was filmed by a passing PK cameraman. He was a perfect example of the Soviet 'sub-humans' that German forces were now fighting.

FURTHER OBJECTIVES

Hitler was delighted by the news of the capture of the Daugavpils bridge and on 27 June began to interfere in low level operations. This would be disastrous for the *Ost Heer* (Army of the East), restricting initiative and later forcing German soldiers to hold indefensible positions. Through

---

Certain officers of these staffs ... continued to regard the telephone as the basic means of communication. In the event of the land lines being cut, they were faced with a lack of signals with subordinate units, although the radio links still worked. In such cases, in suggesting the use of radio to transmit vital information, this so often brought the reply: 'What sort of signals is that, radio?'

T.P. Kargopolov
Lt General (Signals), North Western Front

Above: The crew of an 8cm (3.1in) sGrW 34 mortar take cover and block their ears against the muzzle blast as a brown 3.5kg (7.72lb) HE bomb is loaded. The mortar had a maximum range of 2400m (2,265 yds) and effective range of 400–1,200m (437–1,312 yds).

General Keitel he instructed Halder to alter the axis of advance of the XLI Panzer Corps and put all armoured formations across the Daugava behind von Manstein. The order also included detailed instructions about another crossing that was to be seized for use by infantry formations.

Under Directive 21, von Leeb was instructed by Hitler to destroy the enemy in the Baltic area and secure the occupation of Leningrad. The directive issued via the OKH was not specific about the relative priorities of the two tasks and this would produce dissent and later recrimination. On 27 June Höppner flew up in his *Storch* liaison aircraft to the bridgehead near Daugavpils to confer with von Manstein. Manstein later commented that he was surprised that Höppner appeared not to have been informed about the new orders. Four days later von Leeb arrived at the tactical HQ of

BRANDENBURGERS

Formed in October 1939 at Brandenburg with the cover name *Baulehr-Kompanie zbV 800* (Special Duties Construction Company 800), the Brandenburger special forces unit quickly expanded to a battalion. It was directly subordinate to Admiral Wilhelm Canaris, head of the *Abwehr*, the counter-intelligence department of the OKW. One Brandenburger veteran, Eduard Steinberger from the South Tyrol, explained that they recruited many non-Reich Germans, such as Czech speakers from the Sudeten area of Czechoslovakia, and in May 1941 the *Abwehr* established the *Nachtigall* (Nightingale) and Roland military battalions made up of Ukrainians. These men, who had been drafted into the Polish Army in 1939, were later recruited from PoW camps after the fall of Poland.

In the fighting around the Baltic, Latvians or Estonians would drive captured Soviet trucks and so could converse with enemy soldiers at checkpoints. The Nightingale Battalion enjoyed the dubious reputation of being not only being rabidly anti-Communist but also of having settled a number of private scores against Poles, Jews and Russians. Brandenburgers were delivered to their targets in the Soviet Union by a variety of means. While some crossed porous front lines in captured Soviet Army vehicles, others were parachuted. Perhaps the most unusual were those who were smuggled into the USSR hidden under loads of sand or gravel in goods trucks crossing over the rail bridge at Brest-Litovsk.

In 1940 in the Netherlands Brandenburgers disguised as Dutch soldiers escorted German 'deserters' onto the bridges before doffing their disguises and attacking. The ruse was only successful at Gennep but this opened the road to Hertogenbosch for *Panzerdivision* 9. In North Africa the *Afrika Kompanie*, a detachment commanded by *Oberleutenant* von Koenen, made deep penetration raids behind British lines, with some of their number disguised as Arabs. If a divisional commander was assigned a Brandenburger company he always deployed them with forward units where they would be the first to make contact with the enemy.

Panzergruppe 4 at Utena to give Höppner an outline of the plans. The two generals clashed almost at once – Höppner was an outspoken cavalry officer and an outstanding Panzer leader, Leeb an elderly and conservative officer with reservations about the wisdom of Barbarossa. Leeb was soon in a 'lose-lose' situation. Höppner was at times rash, but he had an excellent feel for the battle and the daily list of worries transmitted by Hitler via the OKH in East Prussia.

On 28 June the Brandenburgers attempted another coup by capturing a bridge across the Daugava at Jekabpils. The city had been captured bythe 1st Panzer Division, commanded by *General-Leutnant* Kirchner. Russian demolition guards, however, were alert and destroyed the bridge. The 2/113 Infantry Regiment under Major von Kittel brought assault boats to the river and made an assault crossing under fire. In nine and a half hours the engineers of the 37th Engineer Battalion and 26th Bridge Construction Battalion quickly built a 20-ton bridge across the 166m (545ft) wide river.

STALIN LINE BROKEN

A day later the Finns launched an assault on the Karelian peninsula, which had been seized from them by the Soviet Union at the end of the Winter War. The plan envisaged a link up with Army Group North, which was pushing northeast through the Baltic states. Riga, the capital of Latvia, was captured on 1 July and a day later the Germans broke through the Stalin Line defences on the Latvian border.

The fight for Riga, held by the Soviet Eighth Army, had been tough with Regimental Group Lasch under *Oberst* O. Lasch suffering heavy casualties. The attack had begun at 03:10 with three assault guns of the 3/185 Assault Gun Battalion, commanded by *Oberst* Geissler, the Flak guns, a 3.7cm (1.45in) Pak, and part of the 10th Company, Infantry Regiment 43 with supporting engineers racing across the 600m (1969ft) railway bridge. They crossed safely only to see it disappear in a roar of exploding demolition charges. The small force set up a perimeter on the far bank and bore the brunt of subsequent attacks by the 10th, 11th and 90th NKVD Divisions supported by an armoured train. The small German force lost nine officers and 82 men in the street fighting.

During the night of 1 July elements of the 5th Battalion, 61st Infantry Division were ferried across the Daugava by the 667th Engineer Regiment commanded by *Oberst* Ullersperger. When dawn broke and the German forces began to probe into the city they discovered that the Soviet forces had withdrawn. Before departing, however, they had torched three landmarks in the Latvian capital, the guild house of the Brotherhood of Blackheads, the Arthaus and St

Peter's church. As the men of Army Group North moved through the city, the Latvians greeted them as liberators.

Four years later Lasch, the hero of Riga, now a General, would be the last defender of the Baltic port of Königsberg (now Kaliningrad), which was surrounded by the 3rd Belorussian Front under Marshal Ivan Bagramyan. Despite suffering heavy air and artillery bombardments and concerted attacks, *Festung Königsberg* held out until 9 April 1945 behind a belt of improvised defences. Lasch could see no point in continued resistance that was causing huge civilian losses. His humane decision provoked Hitler, who ordered that his family should be arrested and the general condemned to death *in absentia*.

By 28 June, Army Group North had captured 400 armoured vehicles, 200 guns, several hundred aircraft and a number of warships, but only 6000 prisoners – many Soviet soldiers had fought to the death.

ATTACK FROM THE COLD NORTH

In the far north, within the Arctic Circle, the Soviet 52nd Rifle Division was deployed in the Murmansk area, with the 205th Regiment covering the port and naval base of Murmansk. During the short Arctic night of 22 June, it was put on alert

and the commander of Fourteenth Army 52nd Rifle Division was ordered to block any attempts by German or Finnish forces to penetrate into the Kola peninsula. These moves had been made on orders from Lt General V.A. Frolov, commander of the Fourteenth Army, the Leningrad Military District, who had taken the decision 'at his own risk' after the Defence Commissariat had refused him permission to deploy his forces. It was a bold and very risky move, given the fate that Soviet officers could suffer for insubordination or failure.

In fact German ground forces were not committed against the Soviet Union until one week after the war had begun, although bombers of *Luftflotte* V under *Generaloberst* Hans-Jurgen Stumpff, operating from Finnish and Norwegian airfields, attacked Soviet airfields in the Kola peninsula on 22 June. That day the German army and *Waffen-SS* troops had moved from Norwegian Kirkenes into Finnish Petsamo (now Pechenga), and German army engineers in civilian clothes had reconnoitred the approaches to the Petsamo

Below: Soviet soldiers move through a village supported by a GAZ BA-32 6 x 4 armoured car. The armoured car was based on the commercial 1.5 tonne (1.47 ton) GAZ-AAA truck chassis which was also used for the Katyusha multiple rocket launchers.

8.8CM FLAK 18/36/37

Known by the British in North Africa as the 'Eighty Eight', the 8.8cm (3.46in) Flak 18/36/37 was similar to many other medium anti-aircraft guns developed between the wars. The difference was that the Germans brought it into the front line and used it as an anti-tank gun. With a muzzle velocity of 795m/sec (2608ft/sec) when firing armour piercing ammunition it could penetrate the armour of all existing tanks. Firing HE it had a muzzle velocity of 820m/sec (2690ft/sec). Shells weighed 9.4kg (20.7lb). The maximum vertical range was 9900m (10,830yds) and horizontal 14,813m (16,200yds). The practical rate of fire was 15 rounds a minute but an experienced crew could fire faster. In action the 8.8cm Flak weighed 4985kg (4.6 tons). Designed in 1931 by a team from Krupps working secretly in Sweden at the firm of Bofors, it was put into production after Hitler repudiated the Versailles Treaty. The gun would be modified and improved during the war and fitted in tanks like the Tiger 1.

river. On the eve of Barbarossa the entire German 163rd Infantry Division was allowed to pass through neutral Sweden, halting at the fortress-town of Boden, 'the Gibraltar of Sweden', on its way to Karelia.

On 29 June the *Gebirgskorps* '*Norwegen*' under *Generalleutnant* Eduard Dietl launched Operation *Platinfuchs* (Silver Fox) against Murmansk. The corps consisted of the 2nd and 3rd Mountain Divisions, commanded respectively by *Generalmajor* Schlemmer and *Generalmajor* Kreysing, and the separate Finnish 'Ivalo' Border Guard Battalion. An armoured battalion equipped with PzKpfw I and II and French Hotchkiss tanks, which had been captured at Narvik in 1940, was briefly employed in support. Dietl had attempted to explain to Hitler how difficult the fighting would be in the north. 'My *Führer*, the landscape up there in the tundra outside Murmansk is just as it was after the Creation. There's not a tree, not a shrub, not a human settlement. No roads and no paths. Nothing but rock and scree. There are countless torrents, lakes and fast flowing rivers with rapids and waterfalls. In summer there's swamp – and in winter there's ice, snow, and it's 40 to 50 degrees below.' Map analysis using Russian maps was more encouraging: the border might be trackless, but not far behind was a network of roads and tracks that would allow an advance on the key base of Murmansk.

Right: Finnish soldiers move through rough, wooded terrain in southern Finland. Veterans of the Winter War of 1939–40, they were keen to recover the territory lost to the Soviet Union in that heroic but one-sided conflict, but would not press further into the USSR.

The first obstacle for the German forces was the Titovka river with a Red Army and NKVD Border Guard camp at its mouth. German planners were concerned about the ability of Soviet troops in the *Rybachiy* or Fisherman's Peninsula to counter-attack. *Gebirgsjäger* Regiment 136 from the 2nd Division was tasked with blocking the isthmus and attacking Stary Titovka. They completed their mission, finding the camp unoccupied. To the south the regiment hit a line of bunkers that were defended with determination. The Siberian and Mongolian soldiers in the bunkers 'fought until they were shot dead, beaten dead, or burnt to death. Only a hundred prisoners were taken.' A fortuitous Arctic fog descended and this allowed the mountain troops to infiltrate past them. The bunkers were subsequently neutralized by artillery fire and Stukas.

ROUGH TERRAIN

By 30 June the lead units of the 2nd Division were on the Litsa river. The 3rd Division had laboriously struggled past Lake Chapr, searching for the Soviet road that German intelligence had reported was over the border. It was believed that roads linked the town of Motovskiy to the border and Litsa to the mouth of the Titovka. When the mountain troops reached the area they found nothing; only after the *Luftwaffe* had flown reconnaissance missions did it emerge that there were no roads. It transpired that the lines on Soviet maps showed telegraph lines and the routes used by the Lapps and not, as OKH planners had presumed, tracks and roads. The fighting slowed down as the men from RAD groups K363 and K376 moved up to build roads in the tundra wasteland. It was going to be a long, dark and cold war.

The 'smooth period' lay between two parts. The first was the battles fought directly on the frontier – these were very, very hard. Next came a blocking action on the so-called 'Stalin Line', which was where Russian reinforcements were fed in. But to speak of 'overrunning', even though Goebbels may have asserted this, was an overstatement from the start.

Major Graf von Kielmansegg
6th Panzer Division

CHAPTER SIX

ARMY GROUP CENTRE

Army Group Centre was the most powerful of the three army groups. Its *Panzergruppen* 2 and 3 would cut off the Bialystok salient and then push deep into Belorussia, taking the strategically important cities of Minsk and Smolensk and capturing huge numbers of enemy soldiers cut off in pockets. Army Group Centre's final and most important objective, Moscow, lay further to the east. To the optimistic German soldiers it seemed an attainable goal that could be reached before the onset of winter.

WHEN THE ORDERS FOR THE ATTACK on Russia were passed down to lower formations in Army Group Centre, Eberhard Wagemann, a platoon commander with 13th Company, Regiment 67 of the 3rd Infantry Division, visited a fellow officer Ekkehard Maurer. As he recalled, Maurer was a courageous officer, respected by the officers and men in the regiment, and it gave him pause when Maurer said, quietly, 'This is the end of Germany'.

Opposite the German forces the commander of the Soviet Third Army, General V.I. Kuynestov, reported that his patrols had seen German troops clearing the barbed wire on their side of the border northeast of Augustów, near one of the border crossings. The thick woods made concealed movement easy and German reconnaissance patrols and agents had penetrated the area to identify defences, routes and the class of bridges. In the attractive city of Brest-Litovsk Colonel L.G. Starinov recalled that, 'On the warm evening of

Left: A German patrol armed with MP38/40 submachine guns and a Kar 98k rifle hesitantly approaches a peasant cottage. For men nurtured in the comfort of houses in Western Europe the primitive living conditions of rural workers in Russia came as a shock.

21 June 1941, the staff officers of the Fourth Army, which was covering the approaches to Brest, were following a typical Saturday routine.' Georgij Karbuk, living in Brest, remembered that he met with friends in the park in the evening: 'Many people were in the park. In fact it was the only place where you could get together. Orchestras and brass bands were playing, people danced, and we were happy. It was lovely and pleasant.'

In the Minsk Officers' Club the popular comedy *The Wedding at Malinovka* was playing to a full house that included Colonel General Pavlov, his chief-of-staff

Below: Wielding wire cutters, a soldier breaches a barbed wire obstacle. He is prone because all obstacles were normally covered by small arms fire since they were designed to delay or halt an attacking enemy long enough for the defenders to inflict casualties.

> In many of the former Polish areas, the German soldiers were greeted as liberators. However, even in old Russia, they come with flowers and friendly greetings.
>
> *General Geyer*
> *Commander, IX Armeekorps, 22 June 1941*

Klimovskikh and district deputy commander Lt General Boldin. Their enjoyment was briefly interrupted by Colonel Blokhin, the senior Intelligence Officer for the Western Special Military District, who reported that 'the frontier was in a state of alarm'. German troops were at full combat readiness and firing had been reported in some sectors. Pavlov passed the information to Boldin with the comment that it was 'some kind of rumour'.

From the far bank General Guderian watched and noted, 'We had observation of the courtyard of Brest-Litovsk citadel and could see them drilling by platoons to the music of a military band. The strongpoints along the bank of the Bug were unoccupied.'

Another German officer who had sombre memories of the last moments before Barbarossa exploded was *Oberleutnant* Erich Mende of the 8th Silesian Infantry Division. He was standing with his commanding officer, a man twice his age who had fought the Russians in 1917 on the Narwa front. It was now after 23:00 and the attack had not been cancelled. As they watched the hands on their watches creeping towards 03:15 he said, 'We will only conquer our deaths, like Napoleon, within the wide Russian expanse. Mende, remember this hour, this is the end of old Germany. *Finis Germania!*'

The initial attack by Army Group Centre would fall on the left flank of Lt General V.I. Morozov's Eleventh Soviet Army in the North West Front and the whole of the Soviet West Front in Byelorussia

Right: The attack by Army Group Centre in easterly and south-easterly directions trapped many units of the Western Special Military District under General Pavlov. Pavlov's failure to halt the attacks meant that he was doomed to be a scapegoat for Stalin.

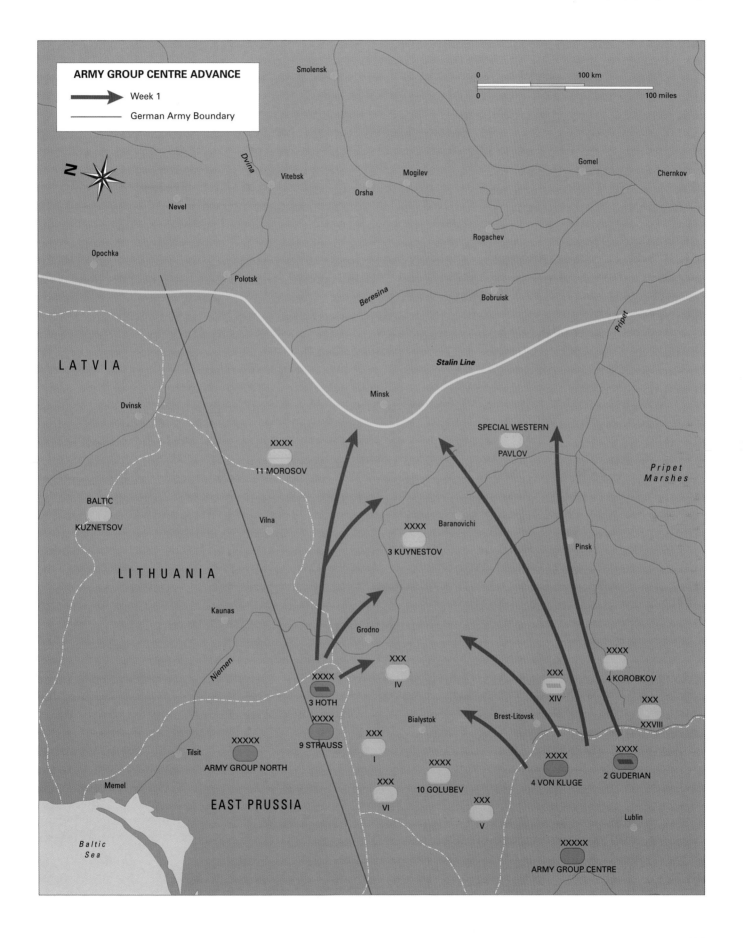

commanded by General D.G. Pavlov. This front had the Third, Tenth and Fourth Armies deployed against the frontier with its own mechanized corps under command. Further mechanized and cavalry corps were held in the front reserve.

The Germans would make two thrusts, one along the axis east of Brest and the northern from Suwalki. The aim was to fight major battles of encirclement in Byelorussia, but even as the pioneers were crossing the river obstacles and the tank crews were examining the terrain before them, their commanders were still unsure of how the battle should be fought. On the third day of the war Generals Hoth and Guderian remained undecided whether to close the jaws of their *Panzergruppen* on Minsk or on the further city of Smolensk.

THE ATTACK BEGINS

The first attack in Army Group Centre was actually launched by an assault pioneer detachment from the 3rd Company, 39 Engineer Battalion commanded by *Leutnant* Moellhoff.

Convinced that the sound of approaching aircraft would alert the Soviet border troops, he led his platoon over a bridge across the Bug at Koden, south of Brest, at 03:00. He captured four Russian guards, removed demolition charges and secured the bridge before the opening artillery barrage. Ten minutes later the report of the capture of the bridge was passed rapidly by field telephone to *Oberstleutnant* Bayerlein, Chief of Operations, at the tented command post of the XXIV Panzer Corps.

On the Soviet side of the border the impact of the artillery barrage was awesome. The Fourth Army War Diary recorded, 'like thunder from a clear sky, throughout the depth of the frontier zone, unexpectedly, the roar of a barrage. The surprise Fascist artillery-fire burst on those

Below: A German gunner prepares to fire a 21cm (8.26in) Mrs 18. He is holding the lanyard under tension and has his right hand ready to give it a jerk when he is ordered to fire. The howitzer fired a huge 113kg (250lb) shell to 18,700m (11.5 miles).

TAUCHPANZER PZKPFW III AND IV

In preparation for Operation Sealion (the planned German invasion of Britain in 1940) armoured vehicles were modified for amphibious and even submerged operation down to a depth of 15m (49ft). Between September and October 1940 three units were formed from Panzer Regiment 2, named *Panzerabteilungen* A, B and C. Their PzKpfw III and IV tanks were made submersible and trials conducted at the coastal training area of Putlos in Holstein.

All existing openings in the vehicles were sealed and the air intake for the engine eliminated. The turret ring was sealed with a rubber ring, and rubber covers were fitted over the main armament, gun mounts and commander's cupola. All had detonator cord embedded with the covers, so that when the tank surfaced they could be blown off and the tank would be ready for action.

While the tank was driving under water, fresh air was supplied through a wire mesh reinforced, 20cm (7.8in) diameter, 18m (59ft) flexible hose that stayed on the surface attached to a buoy. For submerged communications a radio antenna was also attached to the buoy. The exhaust silencers were equipped with high pressure valves to keep water out, but the engine was cooled by seawater during submerged operations. Seepage could be extracted from the tank via a bilge pump.

Navigation under water was by a directional gyro, but coordinates for underwater travel were generally provided via radio link from the transport ship from which the tanks were offloaded. *General der Panzerkorps* Reinhardt, who commanded the trials in 1940, ordered that the tanks should be painted in camouflage that resembled seawater.

points where the Rifle and Engineer units building fortifications were spending the night, on sections located on the Brest training ground and on the frontier guards' posts. The most intensive artillery fire was directed against the military cantonments of Brest and especially on the Brest fortress. The latter was literally covered all over with uninterrupted artillery and mortar fire.'

When the fighting began Wagemann encountered for the first time the tenacity of some Soviet soldiers: 'The garrison in the newly built bunkers of Sklody defended them down to the last man. During the advance march we were confronted with the horrific effects of modern weapons of war, as we passed alongside mile-long columns of Russian tanks, which had been destroyed by our Stukas.'

Among the soldiers with General Walther Model's 3rd Panzer Division, 28-year-old Martin Hirsche recalled that, after crossing the river Bug, they waited for orders and that 'various rumours started going round, quite absurd now, looking back on them. Rumours like, there would be no war in the east as such, instead the British would go in with us to encircle the Russians and liberate the world from Communism … On the advance to Brest-Litovsk I got my first taste of the horror to come. There was a huge field of corpses and wounded Russian soldiers. These had, I think, been hit by the advance bombing by the *Luftwaffe*. One Russian soldier was bleeding heavily and I tried to bind his wounds, when suddenly a soldier from another unit, whom I didn't know, came over to me. "What are you doing here?",

he asked. I told him I was bandaging a soldier. He said it was not my job to look after these "sub-humans".' For Hirsche, who had grown up in an actively democratic and republican family, a wounded enemy soldier was no longer an enemy and it was his duty to help him.

Eighty amphibious tanks from 1st Battalion *Panzerdivision* 18, commanded by Manfred, Graf Strachwitz, were employed in Operation Barbarossa to cross the river Bug underwater; the first of these, commanded by *Unterfeldwebel* Wierschin, entered the water at 04:45. From his HQ at Hrodna (Grodno) General Kuznetsov, commanding the Soviet Third Army, reported: 'Germans crossing the border, Grodno being bombarded. Telephone contact with the border interrupted, two radio stations have fallen …'

CROSSING THE BUG

Guderian crossed the Bug near Kolodno at 06:50 without waiting for the vehicles from his HQ, which came over later. These consisted of two SdKfz 251 radio vehicles, cross-country vehicles and motorcycle despatch riders, and it was with this force that he captured the bridge over the river Ljasnaja (Lesna) ahead of the advancing tanks. A small group of Russians guarding the bridge ran off pursued, against orders, by two officers from the HQ. The fleeing Russians turned, opened fire and the two officers were killed.

By 09:00 the first assault bridge had been built over the Bug by German engineers in the Fourth Army area. However the river Bug was not the only obstacle, since sand and

marshes in the area also slowed down men and vehicles. Across the whole front the dust and grit would wear out engines in the ensuing months as it clogged or abraded the working parts.

On the first day of Barbarossa the men of the 3rd Panzer Division under General Model were so slowed down by the poor going in marshland near Stradecz (Stradez) that by the afternoon they had advanced only 20 of the assigned 80km (50 miles). At 15:00 the commander of the XXIV Motorized Corps, General Baron Geyr von Schweppenburg, ordered a halt and then diverted the 3rd Panzer Division to the north, where they were able to advance more quickly at the special *Panzerstrasse* 1 high-priority rating.

A FLUID FRONTLINE

Enemy defences slowed down the advance in other sectors. The 7th Panzer Division's Panzer Regiment 25, under its highly decorated commander *Oberst* Rothenburg, holder of the *Pour le Mérite* from World War I and the *Ritterkreuz* (Knight's Cross) in World War II, lost half its vehicles in front of Alytus (Olita). The Panzer Regiment had advanced so rapidly that units had become mixed up and some tanks had fallen out with mechanical problems and others had overtaken them.

At the upper Nemunas, two battalions of the regiment raced for the same objectives, two bridges across the river. After about 20 tanks of the 3rd Battalion had crossed the northern bridge the next tank was hit by a camouflaged Russian tank. A German officer watched as the Soviet tank then withdrew under fire from about 30 German tanks whose 37mm (1.45in) guns made no impact. The Germans had encountered their first T-34.

Left: Water streams off a PzKpfw III Ausf E after it has forded a Russian river. Timber has been positioned by engineers to reinforce the right bank so that the tracks of the tanks do not churn it into a slippery mess.

Stray rounds exploding from a burning tank severely wounded Rothenburg soon after the contact at Alytus. He required immediate evacuation, but the regiment had advanced so fast that it was not in direct contact with the division. The commanding officer of the 7th Panzer Division offered his Fieseler Fi 156 *Störch* liaison aircraft, which was capable of landing on unprepared strips for an airborne evacuation. Rothenburg was aware how vulnerable the aircraft would be and declined it, as he did an SdKfz 231 armoured car. Travelling back in a convoy of two 4 x 4 *Kubelwagens*, the group was intercepted by Soviet soldiers at large in the fluid front line. All were shot and their bodies were not recovered until a fighting patrol was sent out the following day. The incident was not untypical of the fighting on the Eastern Front – it was recorded at the time only because of the celebrity of the man who died.

At about the same time *Hauptmann* Dr Alfred Durrwanger, commanding an *Infanterie-Geschütz Kompanie* in the 28th Infantry Division, survived his encounter with a Soviet soldier when, as a pillion passenger on a motorcycle on a narrow wooded track, he and the rider had an unexpected encounter: '[A] Red Army soldier … five steps before us, aiming his (SMG) at us. He was, I remember well, a young man, well dressed, with a keen face, a pink collar-patch, and with only a cap. In our confusion the cyclist and I remembered only one Russian word: *Stoi* (stop)! The Russian soldier stopped abruptly without doing anything. The cyclist discontinued and we both put our left foot on the ground. One second later the cyclist let go of the handlebars – unexpectedly for me – and the cycle fell on the ground, dragging me to the ground as well. Unaware of this, my soldier fled behind some trees. Now the Russian soldier only had to aim, first at the flying cyclist, then calmly at me lying

Below: In the hazy light of the morning of 22 June 1941 soldiers cross a bridge over the River Bug into Soviet-controlled Poland. In most cases the NKVD border guards were overwhelmed, but in some positions they fought with determination from their bunkers and barracks.

under the cycle. I tried eagerly to reach the trigger of my [MP40], but it seemed to me an entire eternity before I got to it. My subsequent shots went into the blue sky and nothing happened! The Russian soldier, perhaps frightened by the shots, quickly disappeared and my cyclist came back.'

LOGISTICAL PROBLEMS

Guderian knew that, once across the Bug, there were only two good axes of advance on the Brest to Babrujsk (Bobruysk) road and the road to Minsk. He and his staff knew that they would have to handle 27,000 vehicles from his *Panzergruppe* as well as the 60,000 logistics, HQ and communications troops that would be following behind. Guderian introduced three priority ratings for armoured traffic or *Panzerstrasse*.

For any vehicles classified as No 1 the roads must be cleared. Any vehicle with a No 2 priority had to yield precedence. Only when all No 1 and No 2 vehicles had passed along the roads could No 3 traffic begin to use them.

When word reached Berlin that a convoy of vehicles from a communications unit from the Herman Goering Regiment

Above: A motorcycle despatch rider puzzles over a map with two NCOs as Russian urchins watch the scene. The vast areas and poor roads made navigation extremely difficult for men who were only familiar with the well signposted roads of western Europe.

had been assigned a No 3 priority, the *Reichsmarshall* was enraged. He demanded that the unit commander report to Guderian for an immediate upgrade to No 1. The convoy of nearly 2000 *Luftwaffe* vehicles halted the 19th Panzer Division for hours.

'Can telegraph posts shoot?' asked the general of the unfortunate *Luftwaffe* officer.

'Of course not, *Herr Generaloberst*.'

'And that is why you'll keep No 3 priority.'

The *Luftwaffe* officer, unable to report failure and face the wrath of Herman Goering, is reported to have shot himself.

This was not the only mistake, however, for the Ninth Army staff, forgetting the traffic priorities, began to order infantry divisions forward, urging them to form mobile detachments by centralizing their limited number of trucks. This was a crude attempt to give the infantry greater

> As the infantry moved forward, the morning darkness was filled with the sounds of shouting, the crack of rifle shots, the short bursts of machine guns, and the shattering crashes of hand-grenades. The rifle fire sounded like the clatter of metal-wheeled carts moving fast over cobblestone streets. Our infantry overran the barbed wire the Russians had erected on each side of their no-man's land and stormed the guard towers and bunkers the Russians had built immediately beyond the death-strip.
>
> *Oberleutnant Siegfried Knappe*
> *87th Infantry Division*

mobility, since a complete marching division took up 35km (22 miles) of road and could take 24 hours to pass through a location. The partially mobile infantry now further slowed down the tanks.

ON TO VILNIUS

Other Soviet tanks from the 5th Tank Division were in hull down and reverse slope positions covering the southern bridge across the upper Nemunas near Alytus. East of this bridge German tanks were ambushed and six were knocked out by anti-tank guns. The Russians then counter-attacked with tanks and infantry but lost 70 tanks. When German troops saw flames rising from the villages to the rear of the Soviet positions they knew that the battle at Alytus had gone in their favour and Soviet troops were withdrawing. They were replenished during the short summer night and moved from the southern bridgehead to seize the heights dominating Vilnius.

In a dramatic move the 7th *Panzeraufklarungs* (Armoured Reconnaissance Battalion), moving ahead of the main force, seized an undamaged bridge 10km (6¹/₂ miles) west of Vilnius, allowing Panzer Regiment 25 to bypass the town and, moving by night, take up positions to the east. At 05:00 on 24 June the motorcycle battalion of the 7th Panzer Division succeeded in occupying the Vilnius

Right: General Hermann Hoth commanding Panzergruppe 3 *wears the M1938 side cap with gold wire trim. It is more practical headwear than a peaked cap, particularly when travelling in vehicles. His britches have the distinctive red stripes of a staff officer.*

Right: Traffic control was at times difficult during the early days of the invasion. Here a column of staff vehicles, many modified civilian saloons, and motorcycle despatch riders move along a road that is not only in good condition, but also uncongested.

airfield and pushed into the town. Here the population had decorated their homes with Lithuanian flags and greeted the motorcycle troops as liberators.

If the fast moving pace of operations was clear to German staff officers as they marked blue arrows on their maps, the opposite was not the case with Soviet forces. On 24 June at his HQ near Bialystok, Lt General V.I. Boldin, commanding the Tenth Army, received a flying fact-finding visit from Marshal G.I. Kulik. Like Marshal Budenny, Kulik was an old Civil War crony of Stalin's and both men were woefully ill-equipped to command large formations in a fast moving war. Boldin was startled to see Kulik dashing in wearing leather flying kit. The beleaguered commander explained his situation – low on fuel and ammunition, without communications with many of his sub-units and in danger of being encircled. Kulik could offer no advice, orders or help except the banal and obvious 'Get on with it'. He left at noon and as his aircraft climbed into the sky I.S. Nikitin, then a corps Commander, muttered 'Strange visit'.

NEAR MISS

At 11:30 on 24 June, Guderian arrived at the HQ of the 17th Panzer Division on the outskirts of Slonim. Here he found not only the divisional commander General von Arnim, but also the corps commander General Lemelsen. It was an excellent opportunity for an operations update, and as the senior officers were conferring 'there was a sudden outburst of lively rifle and machine-gun fire in our rear; our view of the road from Bialystok was blocked by a burning lorry, so we were in ignorance of what was going on until two Russian tanks appeared from out of the smoke … The Russian tanks noticed the group of officers, of which I was one, and we were immediately subjected to a rain of shells, which, fired at such extreme close range, both deafened and blinded us for a few moments. Being old soldiers we had immediately thrown ourselves to the ground.' Two officers were wounded, one fatally, but the Soviet tank crews, who drove on into Slonim where they were knocked out, would never

Above: A Feldgendarmerie NCO stands rigidly to attention as the staff car of Generalfeldmarshall *Fedor von Bock stops to allow his ADC to dismount. The military policeman would probably have been on traffic control duties at a crossroad or junction directing convoys.*

know what a high value target they had engaged. Guderian survived another close brush with death that day when, returning to his HQ, his staff car encountered trucks with Soviet infantry aboard near Slonim. 'I ordered my driver, who was next to me, to go full-speed ahead and we drove straight through the Russians; they were so surprised by this unexpected encounter that they did not even have time to fire their guns.'

Guderian had encountered men of the 121st Rifle Division who, with the 55th, had been ordered forward respectively from Babrujsk and Slutsk by General Korobkov, commander of the Fourth Army. He was responding to reports that German units had penetrated to Slonim and were threatening Baranavichy. Colonel Konov, commanding the 121st, attacked a German column on the Ruzhana–Slonim road in which General Guderian was travelling.

On 25 June the soldiers of Rifle Regiment 6 reached the Stalin Line defences between Poland and the Soviet Union at Molodeczno (now Maladzechna). They attacked off the line

FEDOR VON BOCK

Born in Küstrin (now Kostrzyn), Brandenburg, on 3 December 1880, Fedor von Bock was the son of a famous general. He attended the Potsdam Military Academy and joined the Kaiser's Foot Guards in 1898, serving on the General Staff in World War I. In 1917 while commanding an infantry battalion he won the top gallantry decoration the *Pour le Mérite*. In 1938 he was promoted to full general and commanded the forces that entered Austria in the *Anschluss*. At the outbreak of World War II, aged 59, he commanded Army Group North in the invasion of Poland. In the West in 1940 he led Army Group B through the Netherlands and Belgium into western France up to the Somme. He was promoted *Generalfeldmarschall* on 19 July 1940. He commanded Army Group Centre in Russia, but was dismissed by Hitler when the attack on Moscow broke down. He was recalled to command Army Group South from 16 January to 15 July 1942. A difficult officer with both superiors and subordinates, he was relieved of his duties after clashing with Hitler and was killed in an air raid on 4 May 1945.

of march at 06:00 but met with very strong resistance that lasted for a day before they broke through. Similar resistance faced Rifle Regiment 7 and Panzer Regiment 25, which had reached the area south of Radaskovicy, where the Red Air Force added to the discomfort of the German forces by damaging the bridge there in repeated attacks.

RIVER CROSSINGS

On 24 June *Panzerbattalion* 1, part of the 3rd Panzer Division, reached the Sczcara river defensive line. The Soviet defenders had set fire to the timber bridge across the river and a strip of marshland 800m (half a mile) wide. As the reconnaissance troops approached the crossing, heavy artillery fire crashed down around them. As sunset approached the battalion commander came forward and quickly organized an assault group drawn from the 2nd Tank Company platoon with infantry in inflatable assault boats under command, parts of the 4th Tank Company and a light tank platoon. At 20:00 in the light summer evening, the

assault group carefully approached the still burning bridge. The company commander dismounted, grabbed a few riflemen and raced across the bridge as his tanks gave supporting fire. They had punched through the Sczcara line. Images of troops paddling the pneumatic assault boats as bridges blazed in the background would be captured by the PK still and cine photographers.

A blazing bridge at the Pritsch river, a branch of the Pripet, faced the 3rd Panzer Division on 28 June. Over the previous four days the division had advanced 150km (93 miles), always in contact with Soviet forces. As it pushed through local defences many Russian soldiers went to ground and logistic vehicles following behind were ambushed by small parties of hidden enemy. As Guderian

Below: Two tank experts confer. Generals Hoth and Guderian discuss the next phase of operations. They favoured a far bolder approach than Hitler and the more conventional senior officers in das Heer and would have pushed faster and deeper into Soviet territory.

Above: A 76.2mm (3in) Infantry Gun Model 1927 (76–27) commanded by D. Solodnov waits in ambush. The little gun was very successful, weighing only 780kg (1720lbs) in action. It fired a 6.21kg (13lbs) shell to a maximum range of 8,555m (9,300yds).

had already discovered HQ and logistics troops were forced to dismount and fight as infantry in these local actions.

At the Pritsch three German tanks made a dash for the blazing bridge and reached the far bank before it collapsed behind them. On the near bank the brigade commander and some of his staff dismounted and went forward to reconnoitre. German tanks that remained in the rear saw these figures by the bridge and, presuming they were Russian, opened fire. The brigade commander was wounded and lost an arm. It was a tragic but far from unique example of what today would be called 'friendly fire'. After a long detour a crossing point was found over the Pritsch. It was marshy ground across which all the wheeled vehicles would have to be towed by those with tracks. At dawn two light tank platoons and a mechanized company, which had become an

ad hoc advanced guard, reached the outskirts of Babrujsk on the Berezina (Biarezina) river. They roared into the town passing buildings ablaze from artillery fire and raised the Swastika on the castle at 05:00. The town was not defended strongly, but having destroyed the bridge Soviet forces held the east bank in strength. As a thunderstorm rumbled and flashed across the steppe the Soviets launched local counter-attacks. Model, the hard-driving Panzer general, arrived later in the day and ordered 2nd Battalion, Rifle Regiment 394, to cross the river and secure a bridgehead. As an artillery barrage

Yesterday I knocked off a Russian tank, as I had done two days earlier! If I get in another attack, I'll receive my first combat badge. War is half as bad as it sounds and one thing is plain as day: the Russians are fleeing everywhere and we follow them. All of us believe in early victory!

Karl Fuchs
PzKpfw 38 (t) gunner, 7th Panzer Division

LANDSER

The German infantry soldiers (*Landser*) wore serge uniforms and calf-high leather jackboots with studded leather soles, which were known to the soldiers as 'dice shakers'. They carried a 7.92mm (0.3in) Kar98k bolt action rifle, weighing 3.9kg (8.6lb), and 60 rounds in leather pouches. NCOs had the 9mm (0.35in) MP40 submachine-gun with six magazines and officers a P08 Luger or P38 pistol. Tucked into their leather load-carrying belts were *Stielgranate* 24 (stick grenades), which weighed 0.56kg (1.31lb) each. On the belt was a bayonet, entrenching tool, M1938 respirator in its metal cylinder, M1931 water bottle and M1931 bread bag.

His large pack would contain his personal belongings, together with a greatcoat and camouflaged tent quarter strapped on the outside, along with the two-piece cooking pot. If he was lucky this pack might be carried in the horse-drawn unit transport. The total weight would be about 30kg (66lb), but on top of this the soldier would also carry spare ammunition for the MG34 machine gun or light mortar. It is

little surprise then that German soldiers often used captured Soviet troops as ammunition carriers.

The marching soldiers were exhausted at the end of each day. *Leutnant* Heinrich Haape, the Medical Officer for Infantry Regiment 18, recalled the fatigue: 'The hour and a half's sleep had done no more harm than good. It had not been easy to awaken the dog-tired men. Our bones were cold, muscles stiff and painful and our feet were swollen. We pulled off our field boots only with great difficulty.'

Curzio Malaparte recalled the end of a day's march: 'In the evening, when we halted in the villages for the night – we were by then in the heart of the ancient Cossack land of the Dnieper – and fires were lighted to dry the soaked clothes on our backs, the soldiers cursed softly between their teeth and greeted one another scornfully saying '*Ein Liter* (one litre).' They did not say '*Heil Hitler*!' and they laughed as they stretched toward the fire their swollen feet, covered with little white blisters.'

---

crashed into the Russian defences the German infantry launched rubber assault boats and, despite heavy resistance, achieved a lodgement that they held for a day. Engineers assembled a bridge and soon, as the bridgehead expanded, the Russians withdrew. The first week had been a hard fight, but the Division was deep into western Russia.

THE POISON PAWN

To the north of the invasion's start line at Koden the 'poison pawn' of Brest-Litovsk was still holding out, delaying troops and producing horrific casualty figures. It was essential that the fort be neutralized quickly because it covered road and rail bridges that were to be *Rollbahnen*, the vital axes for the German armoured formations that would be pushing eastwards.

At the close of the war with Poland in 1939, the USSR and Nazi Germany had settled on the river Bug as the new national border. Eastern Poland had been absorbed into the Soviet Union and western Poland into Greater Germany, while the rump became the General Government ruled by Hans Frank. Most of the fortress at Brest-

Litovsk lay on the east bank of the Bug and therefore became Soviet, while the outer forts on the west bank were under German control.

This gave the 45th Infantry Division an advantage since it had already penetrated the defences. In the weeks leading up to 22 June the nine German battalions from Regiment 130 and 135 had practised attacks across rivers and waterways – training that had initially been fun. The men of the 2nd and 3rd Battalion Regiment 135 were to take the North and Western Island and the central area with the barracks.

In preparation for the attack the intelligence staff had

Below: The Soviet T-35 heavy tank had a 76.2mm (3in) gun in its main turret with two auxiliary turrets with 37mm (1.5in) guns similar to the BT-2 and two with machine guns similar to those on the T-37 light tank. It had a crew of 10.

Left: German riflemen and a 5cm (2in) leGrW 36 light mortar crew engage Soviet positions from the perimeter wire at the fortress at Brest-Litovsk. The little mortar fired a 0.9kg (2lb) bomb to a maximum range of 520m (1700ft) but even at 15–25 rounds a minute would have had little effect against the thick masonry of the fort.

defects in the artillery, anti-aircraft and logistics units in and around Brest, some of which had been rectified over the next 19 days. On Sunday morning the garrison was not at full strength – it was, after all, the weekend. Out of a possible 8000 men some 3500 were inside the fortifications. Many of these, however, were sleeping in tents and would be killed or wounded in the opening barrages.

About three hours after the first German barrages crashed into the fortress and town of Brest, Major General A.A. Korobkov, commanding the Soviet Fourth Army, sent a situation report from his HQ at Kobrin to the Western Special Military District at Minsk: 'I report: at 04:15 on 22 June 1941 the enemy began to fire on the fortress at Brest and the region of the town of Brest. At the same time enemy aviation began to bomb the airfields at Brest, Kobrin and Pruzhany. By 06:00 artillery shelling intensified in the region of Brest. The town is burning.' Soon afterwards at 06:30 the Fourth Army HQ was blasted by waves of Stukas and the surviving staff moved 5km (3 miles) away to Bukhovich.

These bald facts conceal the violent reality of what was happening. Georgij Karbuk recalled the jolt from peace to war: 'We had a foreboding that war would soon break out. We had certainly seen the Germans behind the Bug, but in spite of this we did not want to believe it. Then when we saw the first wounded and dead lying on the pavement and all the blood – we had to believe now there would be a war.'

Among the German soldiers awaiting the assault, Gerd Habedanck, serving with the 45th Infantry Division, watched from the safety of the battalion HQ bunker. He heard a single artillery piece fire and then, 'We had barely heard it when the earth shook, boomed and rolled. Strong draughts of air blew into our faces … I risked a quick look outside the casement. The sky over us was lit up bright red. An infernal whistling, droning and crackle of explosions filled the air. Young willows

built a model of the objective based on aerial photographs and captured plans taken in 1939. Two battalions from Regiment 130 would attack the South Island and attempt to capture Brest town further south. The importance of seizing the bridges dominated by the fort had been impressed on the infantry. Without them, the Panzers would not be able to begin their drive into Russia. Supporting the battalions breaking into the fort, troops drawn from a further 18 infantry battalions would advance covering the flanks.

AMPHIBIOUS ATTACK

At the same time that German infantry were honing their assault river crossing skills, the Soviet Fourth Army had staged a practice alarm on 3 June. This revealed various were bent over as if in a storm … It is not yet quite light and thick clouds of smoke darken the sky.'

On the receiving end of this massive barrage, Katschowa Lesewna, a nursing sister in the surgical hospital, one of the 36 buildings on the South Island, recalled, 'Immediately with the initial bombardment the buildings forming the surgical clinic went up in flames as did the others. We thought the Fascists would spare the hospital, there was a large red cross painted on the roof.' As the wooden buildings began to burn fiercely the first casualties were brought i

Rudolf Gschöpf, the chaplain with the 45th Division who had earlier watched the last trains between Nazi Germany and the USSR, recalled how, 'as 03:15 hours struck, a hurricane broke loose and roared over our heads, to a degree never experienced before or indeed later in the war. This all embracing gigantic barrage literally shook the earth. Great fountains of thick black smoke sprang up like mushrooms from the ground. As no counter fire was evident at that moment, we thought everything in the citadel must already have been razed to the ground.'

THE ASSAULT

After the bombardment lifted, Habedanck moved down the riverbank as the soldiers manhandled the wooden assault boats into the river. 'Boat after boat slid into the water. There were excited cries, splashing and the howling of assault boat engines. Not a shot from the other bank as blood red flames dance in the water. We jump on shore and press forwards.'

The barrage that covered the assault was timed to creep forward 100 metres (110yds) every four minutes. It was a

Right: Men of the Waffen-SS *Division* Das Reich *cross a water obstacle in a* Sturmboot – *assault boat. They have the distinctive spring pattern green and brown camouflaged smocks and helmet covers – the smocks were reversible with autumn camouflage on the inside.*

technique that had been refined in World War I and designed to give the attacking infantry protection while they consolidated their position and prepared for the next bound of the assault. *Gefreiter* Hans Teuschler had watched the men of Infantry Regiment 135 in the first wave begin the attack on the northern axis in their rubber assault boats at 03:19. The memory of the supporting barrage remained with him forever, 'The sky was filled with bursting shells of every calibre. It was an awful roaring, exploding, crackling and howling as if hell was actually about to come on earth.'

After being under siege for a week, the Fascists penetrated the fortress. They took out all the wounded, children, women and soldiers, and shot them all before our eyes. We sisters, wearing our distinctive white hats and smocks marked with red crosses, tried to intervene, thinking they might take notice. But the Fascists shot 28 wounded in my ward alone, and when they didn't immediately die, they tossed in hand grenades among them.

Medical Sister Katschowa Lesewna
Surgical Hospital, South Island, Brest

The four-span railway bridge to the north of the fortress was captured in a classic coup as *Leutnant* Zumpe led his 3rd Company from Regiment 135. Once they secured the bridge they located a demolition charge that was quickly disconnected and dumped in the Bug. Within 15 minutes of the start of Barbarossa, armoured cars were crossing the bridge into Soviet-controlled Poland.

CRACKING THE NUT

Close to the railway bridge a mixed amphibious assault group composed of pioneers from Regiment 130 and 81st Pioneer Battalion in nine assault boats had launched into the river. Under the command of *Leutnant* Kremer, their mission was to seize the bridges onto the Citadel and the road bridge allocated to *Panzergruppe* II as its *Rollbahn* or *Panzerstrasse*. As the boats took to the river they were hit by a terrifying barrage. The secret *Nebelregiment* 4 (ZbV Nr4) had opened fire with multi-barrelled rocket launchers and dropped their barrage short, killing 20 men and wrecking four boats. With superb leadership the young officer rallied the shaken group and they moved along the river to land close to the bridges.

One group reached the Citadel island and would remain trapped there for two days. The amphibious assault was supported by a land attack by 'Stosstrupp Lohr', also from Regiment 130. The men under *Leutnant* Lohr gave covering fire for the surviving boats as they made their way to the road bridge. This was taken at 03:55 and the elated Kremer pulled a folded Swastika from his tunic and raced for a flag-pole close to the bridge. As he hauled up this symbol of victory and success, he was killed by a Soviet sniper.

Left: The crew of a Flammenwerfer 35 engage a Soviet bunker. The flamethrower had a range of 25–30m (80–100ft) and a duration of fire of ten seconds. The operator carried a heavy load of 11.8 litres of fuel that weighed 35.8 kg.

Towards midday the battalions of the 135th and 130th had forced their way deep into the fortress in some places. However, the eastern fort of the Northern Island, as well as the officers' club and the barracks block of the Citadel island, were still in Soviet hands. By now both attacks and defenders were closely interlocked and consequently the German artillery could not provide effective support.

In the afternoon Infantry Regiment 133, the corps' reserve, was committed and StuG III assault guns moved up to give direct fire support with their stubby 7.5cm (2.95in) guns. By the evening 21 officers and 290 NCOs and men had been killed. The dead included *Hauptmann* Praxa and *Hauptmann* Krauss, the commander of the 1st Battalion Artillery Regiment 99 and the HQ staffs. It was realized that

AUFTRAGSTAKTIK

One of the strengths of German operational procedures in the Soviet Union was the *Auftragstaktik* system, which had been developed from experience in World War I. Here commanders realized that once troops had been committed to attack, had crossed no-man's-land and were in the enemy trenches it was almost impossible to pass new orders or 'run' the battle. It was better to give a framework set of orders without detailed instructions and let the subordinate commanders operate within these parameters. It is ironic therefore that, while the German army had developed this superbly flexible operational philosophy, Hitler, who should have given overall strategic aims, would meddle at operational and tactical level and negate the benefits of *Auftragstaktik*. General Herman Hoth pinpointed the problem when he censured the OKH for undertaking a war without written plans on the basic strategy, all moves being made as a consequence of day-to-day conversations between Hitler and his staff. The philosophy behind *Auftragstaktik* has now become a standard planning procedure within NATO.

A veteran of the Eastern Front, *Hauptmann* Dr Alfred Durrwanger of the 28th Infantry Division, explained it at a symposium in 1987: 'The order to fulfil a certain military mission is only given within broad parameters and all further details regarding its fulfilment are left to the subordinate. The principle can be applied to all forces. It is the result of long experience and especially of a belief that better know-how in warfare decides the issue of who will prevail in battle.'

Above: Following its recapture in 1944, a Soviet aircraft flies over the central core of the fortress of Brest-Litovsk. In the background, left of centre, is the garrison church that was one of the centres of the defence.

the fortress would need to be bombarded again and so the infantry were pulled back, except for a small group from the 3rd Battalion huddled close to the fortress church. Although sound in principle this allowed the Soviets to reoccupy positions they had lost.

Two German propaganda vehicles with loudspeakers were moved up to the North Island and, after a murderous 15 minute bombardment beginning at 17:00, offered the survivors a 90-minute amnesty. With the gravity feed water reservoir in the Terespol tower destroyed, many of the civilians and soldiers were beginning to suffer and 1900 emerged shakily from the ruins.

Nikitina Archinova, the wife of a Soviet officer, recalled, 'We women were taken with the older children from out of the casemates and thrown outside. The Germans sorted us

out and handled us as if we were soldiers, but we had no weapons, and led us off into captivity.' Her five-year-old son would suffer permanent deafness from the bombardment. Although her family would suffer grievously in the war, she and her children survived owing to the kindness of the German soldier who was escorting them to detention. Out of sight of other soldiers, he told them to get away and go home.

At noon on the third day, an assault group from the 1st Battalion Infantry, Regiment 133, broke through to the men trapped by the church. They had been in radio contact and had survived German artillery and Soviet small arms fire. The 45th Infantry Division announced 'the citadel has been taken and isolated infantry is being mopped up'. The optimism was premature.

SITTING IT OUT

On the fourth day *Leutnant* Schneiderbauer of the 45th Division's 5cm (2in) anti-tank platoon was ordered to bring his guns forward to give direct fire. As they moved across the

MESSAGES FROM THE DEAD

Inside the citadel and other buildings at Brest Soviet soldiers scratched messages in the plaster and brickwork. They suggest that, though resistance may have ended on 29 June, men survived in the tunnels and cellars and there were reports of sniping in the vicinity of the fort as late as July.

We are three men from Moscow – Ivanov, Stepanchikov and Shuntyayev. July 1941

I am alone now. Stepanchikov and Shuntyayev have been killed. The Germans are inside the church. I have one hand grenade left. They shall not get me alive.

Things are difficult, but we are not losing courage. We die confidently. July 1941

I will die but I will not surrender. Farewell, native country. 20.7.41

South Island, he noted that, 'Buildings were for the most part destroyed and brick rubble, and dead Russians and horses covered the roads. The oppressive stench of burning and corpses was all-pervasive'. He watched German assault pioneers employ pole charges against Soviet-held positions as the anti-tank guns gave supporting fire. The Soviets, however, 'sat it out in secure cellars and, despite the heavy artillery strikes, would take up the fire again after the demolitions had exploded.'

The officers' club on the Citadel had held out and subjected the German troops on North Island to enfilading fire. The 81st Assault Pioneer Battalion was tasked with reducing the position, climbing onto the roofs and lowering charges in front of windows and embrasures. The divisional report stated 'one heard the screams and moans of Russians wounded in the explosions, but they carried on firing'.

On 26 June the pioneers closed up to a building identified

Below: Seconds after a demolition charge has exploded and the defenders are still stunned, an infantry assault group with grenades, rifles and submachine guns storms through the smoke and dust into a fortified Soviet position. Speed and aggression were critical for a successful outcome in this type of fighting.

On 24 June I left my headquarters at 08:25 and drove towards Slonim. The 17th Panzer Division had meanwhile arrived at this town. Between Rozana and Slonim I ran into Russian infantry, which was laying down fire on the main road. A battery of the 17th Panzer Division and dismounted motorcyclists were returning the enemy fire without any particular success. I joined in this action and by firing the machine-gun in my armoured command vehicle succeeded in dislodging the enemy from his position; I was then able to drive on.

General Heinz Guderian
Panzergruppe II

as the Communist Officer School on the North Island and placed a huge charge against the metre-thick walls. Following the shattering explosion they took 450 stunned prisoners. All that now remained on North Island was the position known to the Germans as the *Ostfort*. The defenders were so determined that the staff of the 45th Division reverted to the most ancient tactics of siege warfare. 'The only option left was to oblige the Russians to give up through hunger and especially thirst. All other means were to be employed to

Below: The crew of a 3.7cm (1.3in) Pak 35/36 anti-tank gun depress the gun to -8° to engage a Soviet bunker at close range. One man can be seen bracing the split trail to give the gun greater stability on the concrete surface.

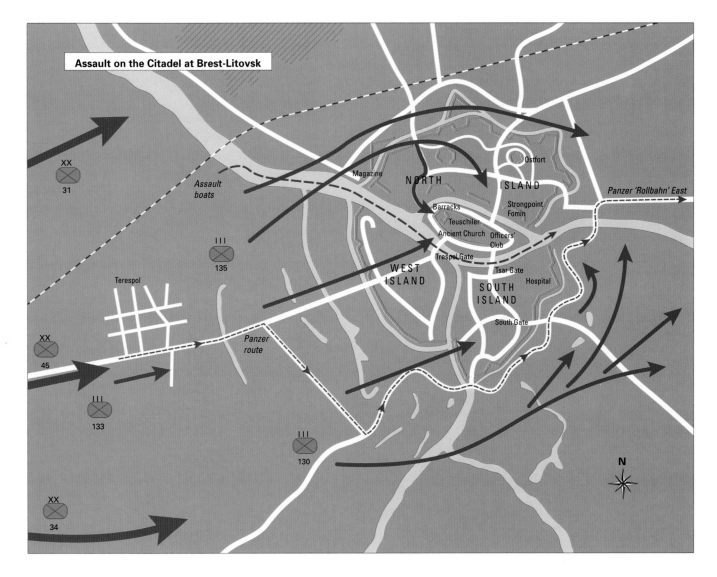

Assault on the Citadel at Brest-Litovsk

XX
31

XX
45

XX
34

III
135

III
133

III
130

Terespol

Assault
boats

Panzer
route

Magazine

NORTH
ISLAND

Ostfort

Strongpoint
Fomin

Barracks

Teuschiler

Ancient Church

Officers'
Club

Trespol Gate

Tsar Gate

Hospital

WEST
ISLAND

SOUTH
ISLAND

South Gate

Panzer 'Rollbahn' East

N

accelerate this process of wearing him down, such as constant harassing fire with heavy mortars, preventing movement in trenches or houses, using direct tank fire, employing loudspeaker appeals to surrender or by firing surrender leaflets.'

Inside the fort, Georgij Karbuk recalled, 'The Germans set up huge searchlights on their bank and illuminated our side, turning night into day. Every bush was lit up, and if any of us attempted to go down to the river, even to fetch a tin can full of water, he was immediately taken out. Many of us ended up lying there.'

THE OSTFORT IS TAKEN

Six days into the siege a Soviet deserter from the *Ostfort* told his captors that the defence was built around 20 officers and 370 men of the 393rd Anti-aircraft Battalion of the Soviet 42nd Rifle Division. They had a quad 7.62mm (0.3in) AA

Above: The attack on the fortress of Brest-Litovsk had been carefully planned. After 18 months occupation, the German forces had had plenty of opportunity to study the position at close range. What they had not considered was that the garrison would put up a determined fight even though cut off.

machine gun, 10 light machine guns, 1000 hand grenades and plenty of ammunition and food. Although water was short they had enterprisingly sunk boreholes. The two men who were the core of the resistance were a major and a commissar. The *Ostfort* was attacked by pioneer teams with flamethrowers. The men moved forward carefully with the 21kg (46lb) Model 41 flamethrowers strapped to their backs. These terrifying weapons were capable of producing ten bursts with temperature of 4000ºC and a flame 30m (98ft) long. Flamethrowers could incinerate their victims, or in enclosed spaces consume all the available oxygen and suffocate them. Georgij Karbuk recalled what it was like to be on the receiving end: 'The Germans deployed flamethrowers. They simply poked the nozzles into cellar windows and held them there. They avoided actually penetrating the cellars themselves. They held them there and burned everything. Even the bricks melted. Others threw grenades into the cellars where families were hiding.'

The *Ostfort* tower was still in Soviet hands by the end of the sixth day. Even though an 8.8cm (3.45in) Flak gun as well as

captured Soviet tanks and other armoured vehicles from Panzer Platoon 28 were engaging any obvious apertures, sniper and machine gun fire was still hitting German soldiers.

DEFIANT SURRENDER

It was 28 June and *Generalmajor* Schlieper, commanding the 45th Division and reluctant to expend any more of his soldiers' lives, called in the *Luftwaffe* based at the neighbouring Malaszewieze airfield to hit the position with heavy calibre bombs. The mission was delayed by low cloud until 08:00 the next day, when a bomber dropped a single SC-500 500kg (1100lb) bomb, but despite the huge explosion the garrison did not surrender. The following day the bomber returned to deliver a similar payload – with similar results. It was followed by an attack with an SC-1800. This huge 1800kg (3960lb) bomb produced a massive explosion and its detonation marked the effective end of resistance in the *Ostfort*. Some 389 men emerged to surrender.

The demeanour of the Soviet soldiers was caught by PK still and cine cameramen. Though their hands were raised in surrender, they held their heads high and looked defiantly into the lens and at their captors. They had fought long and hard. The bodies of 2000 Russian soldiers were found in and around Brest and it is estimated that as many as 3500 may have died, but they exacted a heavy toll. The 45th Division had lost 462 men in the campaign in France in 1940, but in about a week at Brest 482 men had been killed and 30 officers and 1000 soldiers wounded.

For Stalin the fact that Brest-Litovsk

Left: Thirsty, exhausted and probably deafened by the massive bombardment that has fallen on the fortress, a Soviet defender looks defiantly at the German photographer as he emerges from the citadel to surrender. A small number of men fought on into late July, sniping at German convoys.

Above: A Werhmacht light gun crew take up position as they prepare to assault a village in Belorussia in June 1941. They are all wearing heavy-duty harness straps over their shoulders to asist in manhandling the gun.

was a defeat and that some survivors surrendered meant that it was not a fit subject for celebration or respect. In the USSR it was not until 1956 – three years after Stalin's death – that the historian Sergey Smirnov tracked down 400 survivors. The central citadel had been held by a force commanded by Commissar Fomin, Captain Zubachev, First Lieutenant Semenenko and Second Lieutenant Vinogradov. The soldiers holding out in the *Ostfort* were commanded by Major Petr Mikhaylovich Gavrilov of the 44th Rifle Regiment. A group led by Fomin, Zubachev and Vinogradov attempted to break out on 25 June, but the three officers were captured. Gavrilov, however, survived the war.

Smirnov summarized their fates: 'Commissar Fomin, before the break-out, put on the uniform of a private soldier who had been killed; but he was identified in the PoW camp by another soldier, denounced and shot. Zubachev died in

MOLOTOV COCKTAIL

Named in the West after the Soviet Foreign Minister Vyacheslav Molotov, this weapon is now more widely known as a petrol bomb. It consisted of a thin walled 1 litre (1½ pints) or 0.75 litre (1¼ pints) bottle containing about half a litre of petrol with a rag stuffed into the open neck. The petrol could be thickened with one part oil or a piece of raw rubber. Immediately before throwing the bottle was tipped up so that the rag was soaked with petrol and it was then lit. When the bottle hit the target and shattered flaming petrol would splash over an area about 2 to 3 metres (6–9ft) square, burning for up to five minutes. The aim was to pitch the bottle so that it landed on the rear deck of a tank and the burning petrol entered the engine space. Soviet soldiers would sometimes follow up an attack with bottles filled with petrol to stoke the fire started by the Molotov Cocktail. It could look spectacular when it burst, but the lethality varied.

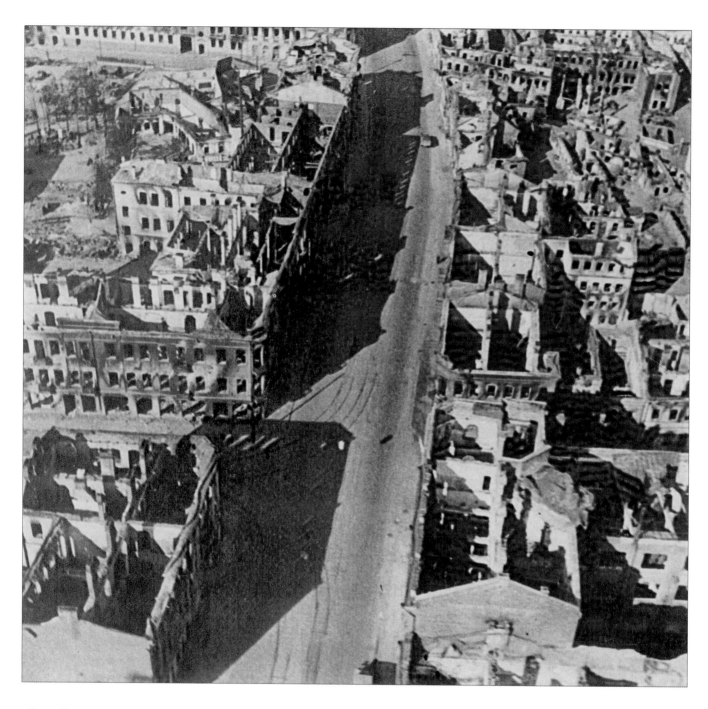

Above: The gutted apartment blocks in central Minsk following its capture. For the populations of cities with little access to smallholdings or gardens, starvation was a very real prospect. German policy in occupied Russia exacerbated the problem.

captivity. Major Gavrilov survived his captivity although, seriously wounded, he had resisted capture by throwing a hand grenade and killing a German soldier.' The determination of Soviet soldiers was also evident at Sokal, a town in the western Ukraine, where Yaroslav Branko witnessed a desperate one-sided fight that typified the spirit of Russian resistance: 'A tank made straight for the ruins of what had been a border command post where, in the basement, women and children had taken cover. At that moment a man in flaming clothes dashed towards the armoured monster. Tearing off the burning coat he threw it on the grille on the engine hatch and then flung himself like a blazing torch under the tank. An explosion followed. The fascists turned back … This occurred on the first day of the war, 22nd June, at about 9 am.'

The frontier post and wooden bridge at Sokal was the responsibility of a border detachment commanded by Captain Bershadskii. His wife and 11-year-old son were among the civilians in the basement and were soon to die in the fighting. At 19:00 on 25 June the Soviet II Rifle Corps staff reported an enemy tank column moving unhindered 50km (31 miles) northwest of Minsk. During the night the 100th Rifle Division without its supporting artillery was ordered to take up a blocking position. By a strange twist of fate the division found that it was digging in on its old pre-war training area. Without anti-tank weapons the divisional commander raided the local *Belarus* glass bottle plant and took its stock to make 'Molotov Cocktails'.

CLOSING THE TRAP

The battle for Minsk was joined on 26 June. In the morning General Pavlov had evacuated his HQ to Mahilou (Mogilev). Even though he was out of touch with many higher formations, orders for attacks were still being issued. Within the city Colonel Sandalov of the Fourth Army searched on foot for the District commander. He found only a shattered city with 'a flood of vehicles in the streets' making for the bridges across the Svisloch river or the other eastern exits.

During the night of 26/27 June, General Nehring, commanding the 18th Panzer Division, was searching in his SdKzf 251 staff car for the ancient château of the Polish Radziwill family at Niasviz (Nieswiez in Polish), which was now the HQ of Guderian's *Panzergruppe* II. As he approached the PzKpfw III that was guarding the gates it was obvious that the crew of the German tank were dozing. Nehring halted his vehicle 40m (130ft) from the tank and shone his torch at the Panzer.

Suddenly out of the darkness came the noise of tracks and two Soviet light T-26s appeared, driving towards the officer's staff car. 'Break away half right!', Nehring shouted to his driver. As the

PZKPFW III AUSF C

Built initially by Daimler-Benz in the late 1930s, the PzKpfw III was not available in large numbers at the time of the invasion of Poland. Some 17 Ausf C and 30 Ausf D were deployed as well as some Ausf E. The Ausf C had a brief operational career before being scrapped after the campaign in Poland. Later marks of the tank were armed with a more powerful 5cm (2in) L/42 gun, which made the tank a formidable opponent in North Africa. However, like the PzKpfw IV, it was no match for the T-34 and German engineers were forced to develop new designs like the Tiger and Panther.

staff car took evasive action the PzKpfw III crew woke up and went into action with commendable alacrity – three rounds were sufficient to reduce the Russian tanks to blazing wrecks. Inside the château HQ, which had previously been used by a Soviet HQ, German staff had been busy installing map boards and communications links. In the attic they were amused to discover a framed photograph of a hunting party taken in 1912. In the centre was the guest of honour – Kaiser Wilhelm II of Germany. With the HQ set up in the château and the area secure, the population of Niasviz approached General Guderian for permission to hold a Thanksgiving Service for their liberation.

The push eastwards was now beginning to accelerate. As it did so many of the tactical principles that would have been observed during earlier campaigns were jettisoned by the Panzer columns. The men were fighting a 24-hour war and this carried risks as well as advantages. The tanks and vehicles of the 7th Panzer Division were now speeding along on the surfaced road that ran from Minsk to Moscow, but they were not alone. The PK correspondent Bernd Overhues reported a shouted warning about Soviet tanks ahead: 'What had happened? A number of small Soviet AFVs had joined the middle of the German column. It seems they had driven along together for a short stretch and then suddenly

Left: The PzKpfw III Ausf H had an improved suspension and track – it was wider by 40mm (1.7in). The tanks coming off the production line were fitted with an extra 30mm (1.2in) of armour to the front faces of both hull and superstructure.

opened fire from a quadruple MG mounted on a lorry, shooting all barrels straight into the German vehicles. The sharp voice of a German officer icily restored order. The Soviet tank and lorry were shot into flames and put out of action.' Captain Ivan Krylov, commanding a company covering the approaches to Minsk, was assured that the attacks by Army Group Centre would be held, 'provided our troops fight to the end. The men have been ordered not to die before taking at least one German with them.'

Below: A Sturmgeschütz III grinds past a burning building. The assault gun – normally abbreviated to StuG III – was cheaper to build than a PzKpfw III, though it used the same chassis. It was designed to give close artillery support for the infantry.

'THE SIGNPOSTS OF OUR MARCH'

For *Oberleutnant* Siegfried Knappe the advance into Russia with his artillery battery was like a scene from Napoleon's invasion in 1812: 'Burning villages, the bodies of dead Russian soldiers, the carcasses of dead horses, burned out tanks and abandoned equipment were the signposts of our march. The infantry had to move on foot, but we rode either on horseback or on the equipment being pulled by our horses. Occasionally, when there was resistance up ahead,

Right: An exhausted infantry platoon collapsed by a roadside. The long marches down poor roads in the heat of summer taxed even the toughest German infantry even though they were not carrying their full pack but normally an assault order, with weapons and ammunition.

Ninth Army would send trucks back to rush the infantry forward more quickly.'

By midday on 26 June Hoth's *Panzergruppe* 3 was only 29km (18 miles) north of Minsk. At the same time Guderian, who was still thrusting eastwards, was ordered by Army Group Centre to turn the bulk of his forces to close the pocket at Minsk. He was told that XXIV *Panzerkorps* on his right flank could continue to push towards Babrujsk on the Berezina and thence onwards to Rogachev (Ragacov) on the

If you are wounded sham death, and when the Germans approach kill one of them. Kill them with your rifle, with the bayonet, with your knife, tear their throats out with your teeth. Don't die without leaving a dead German behind you.

Soviet West Special Military District Orders

Dnieper. Both Hoth and Guderian were reluctant to obey the order since they could see a greater victory if they linked up further east near Smolensk.

At Rastenburg there was tension and disagreement between Hitler, the OKH and Army Group Centre. In the original orders from the OKH issued on 31 January Minsk had been designated as the point where the Panzer pincers should snap shut. Von Bock favoured a deeper thrust and tried to get the orders altered. Now with the Blitzkrieg enjoying obvious success Hitler became fearful that the *Panzergruppen* would overreach themselves and the large numbers of Soviet troops trapped in the pocket between Bialystok and Nowogrodek (Navagrudak) would break out eastwards.

On 25 June he sent his personal aide *Oberst* R. Schmundt to Army Group Centre HQ – Hitler wanted the pocket to be closed to the west of Minsk at Navagrudak. Von Bock, an officer with courage and a strategic rather than tactical vision, resisted these instructions with all the eloquence and professional expertise at his command.

Halder confided to his diary that he hoped the forces on the ground would

Left: A female medical orderly of the Red Army tends the leg wound of a German Obergefreiter – senior corporal – *in July 1941. To the surprise of the Germans, Soviet women were employed in a huge range of front line roles including tank crews and snipers.*

Above: A German infantryman pauses near the burning outbuildings of a collective farm. The scorched earth policy of the Soviet forces was cruel to the civilian population, but to Moscow any civilians who refused to be evacuated eastwards and remained in occupied territory were suspect.

do the correct thing and cross the Dnieper at Mogilev and Rogachev. The acerbic von Bock, who backed Guderian and Hoth, had become infuriated with von Brauchitsch, who was passing on Hitler's orders, while at the same time hoping that Army Group Centre would adopt a tactically sound course. Hoth and Guderian were convinced that they should secure the Vitebsk–Orsha–Smolensk triangle and land bridge and prevent the Soviets from forming a defence line on the Dniepr.

On 23 June, following a telephone conversation with von Brauchitsch, von Bock insisted that all his orders should be in writing.

MOPPING UP THE POCKETS

The pincers closed on the Bialystok pocket around 29 June and by 3 July the enemy in the area had surrendered. By 8 July the prisoner count stood at 290,000 including several corps and divisional commanders, 2500 captured or knocked out tanks and 1500 guns. The Germans estimated that 22 rifle divisions and the equivalent of seven tank divisions and

> The impression that the battles left on me will be with me forever. Believe me, dearest, when you see me again, you will face quite a different person, a person who has learned the harsh command: 'I will survive!' You can't afford to be soft in war, otherwise you will die.
>
> *Karl Fuchs*
> *PzKpfw 38 (t) gunner, 7th Panzer Division*

six mechanized brigades had been destroyed. The Red Army troops encircled came from the Third and Tenth Armies, some elements of the flanking Fourth and Eleventh Armies and the larger part of the Thirteenth Army.

It was a crushing German victory and General Pavlov paid for this defeat with his life. His forces were well equipped and numerically as strong as their opponents; although the Soviet tanks and armour may have been qualitatively inferior they actually outnumbered the forces of Army Group Centre. Soviet historians have, however, been harsh with their comments about Pavlov. He was the only Front commander to be executed in the war, yet two months later Marshal S.M. Budenny was responsible for a greater defeat at Kiev on 19 September. On Stalin's orders Budenny would be flown out of the pocket in which the five armies under his command were trapped – but then Budenny was one of

PRISONERS OF WAR

During the war in the East the Soviet army would lose around 6 million as prisoners, of whom only one in ten would survive to return home. Tragically, in the spirit of Marxist orthodoxy, the Soviet Union did not sign the 1929 Geneva Convention and in 1941 Stalin had promulgated Order No 274, which stated that all prisoners were traitors to their country. When his eldest son Yakov, an artillery captain, was captured in Byelorussia and featured on the cover of *Signal*, Stalin disowned him and had his wife imprisoned under a statute that provided for the punishment of the relatives of PoWs.

In a briefing to Italian war correspondent Curizio Malaparte, a staff officer serving with a Panzer unit attached to Army Group South talked about the enemy: 'He spoke as a soldier, objectively, without exaggeration, without using any argument not of a strictly technical order. "We take few prisoners", he says, "because they always fight to the last man. They never surrender. Their material can't be compared with ours, but they know how to use it."'

Early in the fighting, however, artillery *Oberleutnant* Siegfried Knappe was astonished by the numbers of prisoners that were taken: 'We had started taking prisoners from the first day of the invasion. The infantry brought them in by the thousands, by the tens of thousands and even by the hundreds of thousands.'

For ordinary Soviet soldiers who surrendered, the distances and climate did not favour their survival. In the first winter of the war, German soldiers took the felt boots, hats and coats of captured or dead Soviet soldiers. In sub-zero temperatures this doomed the Soviet PoWs. In the summer the long columns of prisoners were marched across the dry steppe and many died from dehydration. Some men who surrendered were simply shot as a matter of course. If they survived and reached Poland and Germany a grim fate awaited them. Some were used as slave labour in munitions factories, mines and in constructing defences. Working for long hours on starvation rations, many died. Others were used and expended in medical experiments in extermination camps and in the first trials of Zyklon B poison gas.

Faced by the prospect of death by starvation, and in many cases motivated by anti-Communist conviction, many Soviet PoWs assisted the Germans. The most dramatic form of this collaboration was the Vlasov Army, led by the former Red Army General Andrey Vlasov. Some 800,000 former Soviet PoWs worked as individual *Hilfswillige* or *Hiwis* (auxiliary troops) in the German Army. Several thousand Cossack troops in German service in the Fifteenth Cossack Cavalry Corps fought in anti-partisan operations in France and Yugoslavia and eventually surrendered in northern Italy to the 2nd British Armoured Division.

German prisoners on the Eastern Front would not perish in extermination camps: they would, however, work on starvation rations on reconstruction projects in the Soviet Union long after the war had ended. Many of those who returned to Germany arrived home in the mid-1950s. The *Waffen-SS* practice of tattooing a soldier's blood group under his left armpit, while it made excellent sense for combat first aid, also meant that members of the *Waffen-SS* could not disguise themselves as soldiers in the *Wehrmacht* if they were captured. On the Eastern Front few soldiers of the *Waffen-SS* survived capture. A captured Soviet Fifth Army document recorded: 'It has frequently occurred that Red Army soldiers and commanders embittered by the cruelties of the fascist thieves … do not take any German soldiers and officers prisoner but shoot them on the spot.'

There were reports that starving and desperate German and Soviet prisoners, herded into exposed barbed wire enclosures, resorted to cannibalism in order to survive. Portions of flesh were cut from buttocks and thighs of dead prisoners and cooked – producing, it was said, a meat similar in flavour to pork.

Above: A Waffen-SS Rottenführer (NCO) guards a column of Soviet prisoners. Some have blanket rolls in which they have stowed any personal items they have managed to retain and some even have water bottles – crucial for survival in the summer heat and dust.

Stalin's old comrades from the Civil War. A sinecure command was created for him and he lived to die of old age in 1973, whereas his successor in the Kiev pocket, Colonel General Kirponos, along with his chief of staff Lt General Tupikov, would die attempting to fight their way out of encirclement. With their deaths and the collapse of resistance 665,000 prisoners, 3718 guns and 884 armoured fighting vehicles were taken at Kiev.

The large Minsk pocket had been closed a week into the Barbarossa campaign, and there were also three smaller ones, including the fort at Brest. The tanks of *Panzergruppen* 2 and 3 then pushed eastwards and, like steel jaws, closed around the Smolensk pocket on 16/17 July. Here, caught in four small pockets and one large one, they took 310,000 prisoners. These victories, however, presented unforeseen problems. Unlike the Polish troops in 1939 or the French in 1940, many of these

pockets continued to fight and this in turn meant that strong cordons had to be in place to prevent these enemy troops moving east to link up again with their own forces.

At the Minsk pocket, two *Panzergruppen* and 23 infantry divisions were required to contain and destroy the Soviet forces. This was half of the fighting power of Army Group Centre. At Smolensk a similar operation tied up two *Panzergruppen*, composed of 10 Panzer divisions, and six motorized divisions along with 14 infantry divisions, some 60 per cent of the fighting power of Army Group Centre. Each victory delayed the advance on the real objective, Moscow.

141

CHAPTER SEVEN

ARMY GROUP SOUTH

The Soviet troops facing Army Group South were commanded by General Kirponos, who is one the unsung heroes of Barbarossa. His men fought an effective defence until command was passed to Stalin's old comrade Semion Budenny, a former cavalry NCO whose moustache 'was bigger than his brain'. When Budenny was surrounded at Kiev, he was flown out of the pocket. Kirponos took command and died fighting his way out of the encirclement.

IN THE SOUTH, WHERE SOVIET FORCES were strongest, the German advance was much less rapid, as had been planned. Red Army Colonel General M.P. Kirponos had managed to establish a defence in depth, rather than line his armies along the frontier. He had four armies in two groups sited in depth with well-sited and camouflaged bunkers and artillery positions. Nature also assisted him with his defences since the rivers Prut, Dniester, Southern Bug and Dniepr run south east into the Black Sea, while there was broken marshland to the south of the Pripet Marshes.

Stalin had always considered that if an attack was launched on the USSR it would be aimed at the Ukraine with its wheat and coal reserves and related industries. The area was better defended than the north or centre with a total of 45 rifle, 20 tank, 10 mechanized and six cavalry divisions. Zhukov states that Kirponos was in his battle HQ at Tarnopol (now Ternopol) by midnight on 21 June and

Left: Smoke rises from a distant battle as PzKpfw III and II tanks group near an SdKfz 250 half track. The picture gives an idea of the huge scale of tank battles in the East which were fought over distances that many urban Germans found intimidating.

Above: Cossacks of Lieutenant General Kirichenko's XVII Cavalry Corps ride in loose formation across the steppe near Lvov. Cavalry were ideal troops for patrolling and reconnaissance in the vast spaces of the Ukraine and Belorussia.

reported to Moscow that a deserter had brought news of the impending attack. Army Group South and *Luftflotte* 4 consisted of three million men, 600,000 vehicles, 750,000 horses, 3580 tanks, 7184 guns and 1830 aircraft. The front they covered totalled 1350km (840 miles), of which the Carpathian Mountains accounted for 250km (155 miles) in which no German soldiers were positioned. Although Soviet forces would inflict quite heavy casualties on the Germans, their own losses were infinitely greater. Kirponos would then squander his tank formations by rushing them into the battle before they could deploy effectively. As with Army Group North and Centre, there was a mixture of nervous anticipation, fear and confidence among the German forces waiting for the order to attack. 'The war with Russia will last only four weeks', *Hauptmann* von Rosenbach-Lepinski told the motorcycle crews of his reconnaissance company.

THE BUILD-UP

On Saturday 21 June, the day before the German attack was launched, Nikolai Kirillovich Popel, the Chief Political Officer of the VIII Mechanized Corps of the Kiev Special Military District, attended a show at the unit's Red Army Garrison House. Throughout the entertainment he was distracted and kept wondering what was happening on the opposite bank of the San river. 'No it wasn't a premonition', he recalled. 'How many times afterwards did I hear of that night "my heart told me" or "my mind felt it"? Neither my heart nor my mind told me anything. It was just that I – like many of the senior officers in the frontier formations – knew more facts than I could explain.'

Near the Polish-Ukrainian city of Lvov (now L'viv), the capital of Galicia, Colonel Nikolai Yeryomin, a staff officer with the Soviet 41st Rifle Division was awoken at 02:00 on 22 June with a report that the frontier guards had telephoned the headquarters. He hurried to the HQ thinking that this was the first time that the frontier guards had contacted him at night. On a crackling line he heard a worried voice, 'Comrade Colonel, this is the commander of the Lyubycha–Krulevkaya

KARL RUDOLF GERD VON RUNDSTEDT

One of the most experienced officers in the German Army, Gerd von Rundstedt was born in Aschersleben on 12 December 1875. He served as a General Staff officer in Wor War I, fighting in France and Turkey. He rose rapidly in the *Reichswehr*, but was retired as a *Generaloberst* after criticizing the action against Czechoslovakia in 1938. He wa reinstated in time to command Army Group South in the Polish campaign of 1939, followed by Army Group A in France and the Low Countries in 1940. He was promoted to *Generalfeldmarschall* after the fall of France.

In the USSR in 1941 he commanded Army Group South as it pushed into the Ukraine. Hitler sacked him on 12 December 1941 for a tactical withdrawal near Rostov, but

he returned on 1 March 1942 as Commander-in-Chief of Army Group West in France. Here he was responsible for preparations against the expected Allied invasion. He was again dismissed on 2 July 1944 following the failure to stop the D-Day landings, only to be brought out of retirement to command the Ardennes offensive of December 1944. He knew about the July bomb plot but did not participate, and after its failure he presided over the Court of Honour that dismissed the conspirators from the Army.

After the war von Rundstedt served a sentence for transmitting the Commando Order of 18 October 1942. He was released on 5 May 1949 owing to serious illness and died at Hanover on 24 February 1953.

sector speaking. All along the state boundary the posts of my sector are reporting unusual behaviour by the Germans. Troops and armour movement can be heard on their side. Our listening posts have discovered that infantry has been massing since dusk. We've never had such a situation and I decided to report it to you. Will there be any instructions?'

In a letter home to his mother in Germany, 28-year-old Ulrich Modersohn wrote confidently of the Soviet forces, 'It was never possible for him to muster any worthwhile resistance. Our artillery and Stuka fire must have been pure hell for him. By midday assault bridges were across the Bug and ready. Now our troops are rolling over into Russia. This afternoon I saw how the earth shook and the sky hummed … Everything is following the set plan.'

In the moments before the artillery barrages came crashing down the XLVIII Motorized Corps commander reported, 'Sokal is not blacked out. The Russians are manning their posts, which are fully illuminated. Apparently they suspect nothing.'

CROSSING THE BUG

On the left flank the Sixth Army commanded by *Feldmarshall* von Reichenau crossed the Southern Bug and, despite heavy fighting, the 56th and 62nd Infantry Divisions had penetrated 14 km (8^{1}/$_{2}$ miles). As darkness fell two forward battalions were counter-attacked so violently that they were cut off.

The divisions of the Seventeeth Army under General von Stülpnagel had to fight bunker by bunker through the positions covering Lvov and Przemysl. The first echelons of the Soviet Fifth and Sixth Armies had managed more or less

Below: Generalfeldmarshall *Gerd von Rundstedt was an officer who was not afraid to speak his mind or give orders to withdraw if the tactical situation merited this manoeuvre. This enraged Hitler who sacked him and then reinstated him twice during the war.*

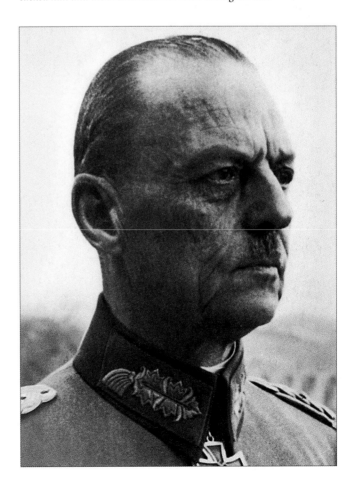

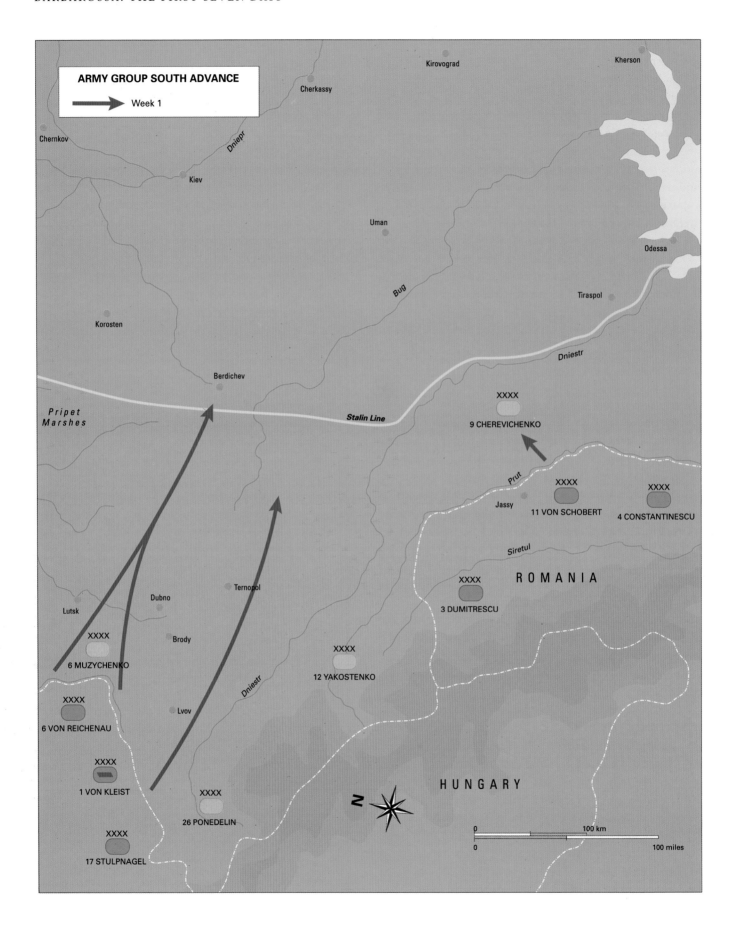

successfully to man their bunkers. The reduction of the southern front between the Pripet Marshes and the Carpathian Mountains took much longer than expected.

Feldmarshall von Reichenau's Sixth Army crossed the Styr river but found itself continually harassed by Soviet forces cut off in the wooded swampland on its left flank. Reichenau was so enraged by the constant setbacks that he ordered prisoners to be executed as partisans, whether or not they still wore uniform. Red Army units also shot their German captives, especially *Luftwaffe* pilots who had baled out. There were few opportunities for sending them to the rear to prisoner-of-war camps, and they did not want them to be saved by the enemy advance.

Left: The attack by Army Group South was split by Hungary – German and Rumanian troops attacked in June 1941 and were later joined by Hungarian forces. A slight delay in the attack meant that Soviet forces were alert and resistance was tougher.

Wir besiegen unsere Toten – We conquer our own dead.

Generaloberst Ritter von Schobert
Eleventh Army, Army Group South

'SLOW BUT SURE PROGRESS'

General Hube, commanding the 16th Panzer Division, reported his operations during the first few days of Barbarossa as 'slow but sure progress', but this was not what the OKW wanted to hear. The plans called for deep penetration and entrapment of the Soviet forces in Galicia and Western Ukraine. By the morning of 23 June, Army

Below: As small arms fire cracks overhead two Pioniere *use the directional outboard motor to steer a* Sturmboot *loaded with infantry across a river. The man on the left has the metal case for spare MG 34 machine gun barrels slung on his shoulder.*

Group South had penetrated the Soviet lines. *Panzergruppe* Kleist finally broke through east of Lvov, creating a 48km (30 mile) gap on the boundary between Potapov's Fifth and Muzychenko's Sixth Soviet Armies. With its vehicles marked distinctively with the letter 'K', the group began a *blitzkrieg* offensive in the direction of the town of Rovno.

Captain Curzio Malaparte, an Italian *Alpini* liaison officer and observer with Army Group South, watched by the banks of the River Prut as a German armoured column moved past. 'The exhausts of the Panzers belch out tongues of smoke. The air is filled with a pungent, bluish vapour that mingles with the damp green of the grass and with the golden reflection of the corn. Beneath the screaming arch of Stukas the mobile columns of tanks resemble thin lines drawn with a pencil on the vast green slate of the Moldavian plain.' They were followed by infantry transported on lorries, and to the poet in Malaparte the men on the wooden benches 'were so white with dust, they looked as if they were made of marble … [they] … had the appearance of statues'.

To block this advance Kirponos planned to use all the armour drawn from the Mechanized Corps attached to the two armies as well as the Twenty-Sixth Army in one heavy counter blow. His first problem, however, was to assemble the scattered armoured forces, which included the IV Mechanized Corps under the command of General Vlasov. Although he was to fight a successful defensive action near Moscow, Vlasov would become one of the most controversial figures of World War II.

The forces committed to action by Kirponos included vulnerable light tanks but also the formidable KV-I and KV-II. Although German tank and anti-tank gun crews were shocked at how ineffective their weapons were against these massive tanks, they had little trouble with the cumbersome T-28 medium tank. This multi-turreted monster was a throwback to an outdated theory of armoured warfare. Developed in 1932 as a 'breakthrough tank', its armament consisted of a central turret with a 76.2mm (L/16.5) gun and two auxiliary machine gun turrets, similar to that fitted on the T-37 amphibious tank, located forward of the vehicle on either side. It looked like a land-based battleship. Versions of the T-28C with improved armour had performed reasonably well in Finland in 1940, but pitted against PzKpfw IIIs and IVs in 1941 it was hopelessly outclassed.

Right: As Soviet prisoners make their way hesitantly across a stream to the left, infantry aboard a PzKpfw III watch a farm burning on the sky-line. The tank has the usual litter of spare road wheels, tracks, bucket and improvised stowage bin.

COUNTER-ATTACK AT RADZIECHOW

The counter-attack planned by the Military Soviet of the South-Western Front, a three man group composed of the Commander Kirponos, Chief-of-Staff Purkayev and Commissar Nikita Khrushchev, was perhaps too ambitious. Two mechanized corps were to operate with their own infantry formations, the Fifth and Sixth Armies. The remaining four (the Eighth, Fifteenth, Ninth and Nineteenth) would cover the crisis points at Lutsk, Rovno, Dubno and Brody, and eliminate the German penetration with a concentric blow.

The main weight of the counter-attack would be borne by the VIII and XV Mechanized Corps. General Potapov's Fifth Army would have the IX and XIX Mechanized Corps under command working in concert with the VIII and XV. Potapov would attack on the axis of the Lutsk–Brody railway line. The IX, which was concentrated in the woods north of Rovno, would attack from Klevany and the XIX would attack from the Rovno area towards Dubno. The VIII and XV together would be designated the 'Front Mobile Group'; the VIII

under General Ryabyshev would advance on Berestecko from Brody and the XV from Toporiv to Radziechow (now Radechiv). H-Hour was 09:00 on 26 June.

General Karpezo's XV Mechanized, which had taken heavy punishment since 23 June, was now committed to crossing very difficult terrain composed of five rivers with intervening marshland. On the morning of the attack he had only one division ready. To the right the VIII Mechanized had travelled from Uman and was formed up near Brody; the 12th Tank Division (part of the VIII Mechanized) had only 60 tanks and the 34th Tank Division only 150. To reinforce the XV General Vlasov was ordered to transfer the 8th Tank Division from his IV Mechanized Corps. Another division is reported to have been lost in a swamp when its commissar overruled the commanding officer.

A CONFUSED ACTION

The four-day tank battle was a confused action. General Karpezo's available division hit the XLVIII *Panzerkorps* southern flank at Radziechow. During the night of June

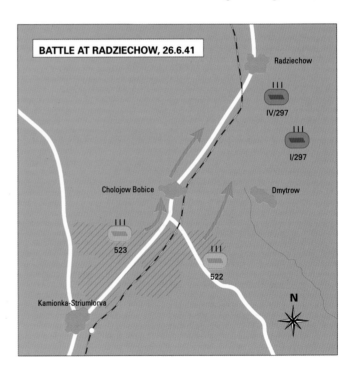

Left and above: The Soviet armoured counter-attack at Radziechow that had been ordered by General Kirponos was uncoordinated and consequently did not hit Army Group South with the planned full weight. It was what Soviet tacticians would call an 'encounter battle' with mobile forces arriving on the battlefield at the same time. It was a surprise to the Germans who fell back on their good communications and superior tactical training to defeat the Soviet attack.

26/27 Kirponos ordered the VIII Mechanized to fight its way to Verba and Dubno, with the XV attacking towards Berestecko. Just like his tank formation, Karpezo had been battered by the *Luftwaffe* and handed over to his deputy Colonel Yermolayev when his HQ was put out of action. Ryabyshev, with his units still scattered, decided to form a 'Mobile Group' from the 34th Tank Division, a tank regiment and a motorcycle regiment under the command of Brigadier Commissar N.K. Popiel. This force recaptured the city of Dubno – in reality the 11th *Panzer Division* had passed through the town and its supporting infantry had not moved up to consolidate the capture, so it was in a vacuum.

A critical factor in the fighting was the role of the *Luftwaffe*, which intercepted the Soviet armoured columns before they reached the combat zone. Popiel's Mobile Group was later encircled, but on 2 July he decided to break out eastwards and eventually reached Soviet lines in August.

Riding with the 11th Panzer Division into its encounter battle at Radziechow was Arthur Grimm, a photojournalist with the German international pictorial propaganda and style magazine *Signal*. He captured the action about 05:20 as SdKfz 251 half tracks bucketed across the steppe and the tanks opened fire on their distant targets. He ended his report, 'The Soviets left the battlefield after a duel lasting eleven hours. More than 40 Soviet tanks were destroyed. The pursuit continues. Only five of our tanks were disabled.'

Curzio Malaparte watched German soldiers examining a knocked out KV-I.

Right: A German Oberfeldwebel *takes a close look at a battle-damaged Soviet tank. Collecting technical intelligence from enemy equipment could be very valuable but also a gruesome task since the remains of the crew were often still inside the wrecked vehicle or aircraft.*

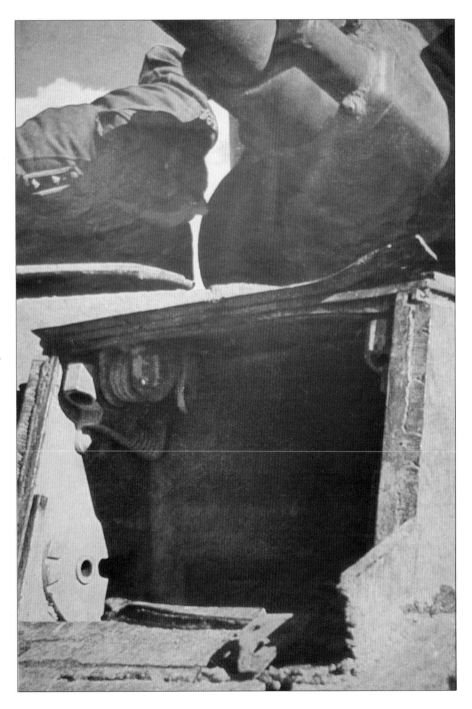

'They looked like experts conducting an on-the-spot enquiry into the cause of an accident. What interests them most of all is the quality of the enemy's matériel and the manner in which that matériel is employed in the field … They shake their heads and murmur *"Ja, ja, aber"* … The whole secret of the German success is implicit in that *"aber"*, in that "but".'

Post-war analysis by Soviet historians pointed to poor or non-existent communications between tanks and higher formations as the reason for the failure of the battle. Many

Soviet tanks lacked radios and coloured flags were used for signalling. Troop or squadron commander's tanks had radios and these were often obvious since the antenna was a complex frame around the turret – in a tank battle they became the first target.

On 29 June Kirponos issued a special directive on eliminating operational shortcomings, covering such areas as security of flanks, proper organization of intelligence, use of radio and infantry–artillery coordination. They were sound instructions issued emphatically, but this could not compensate for acute shortage of equipment or simply lack of spares. The XV Mechanized had only two radio units instead of eight, the XXII Mechanized had lost 119 tanks in the first eight days, but 58 had been blown up by their crews for lack of spares needed for minor repairs.

The 11th Panzer Division had by now pushed as far as

Ostroh and was threatening the huge Soviet logistics base at Shepetivka. General M.F. Lukin, the commander of the Sixteenth Army was waiting at the base for his troops, who would then move to join the men of the Western Front (formerly the Kiev Special Military District). With the civilian telephone system out of use, Lukin was connected to Kirponos's HQ via the railway telephone system and spoke to Kirponos's deputy Lt General Yakovlev, who told him to hold

LT-GENERAL ANDREY VLASOV

Born at Lomkino near Nizhni Novgorod on 1 September 1890, Vlasov joined the Red Army in 1919. When Germany invaded the USSR he had reached the rank of general and commanded the IV Mechanized Corps. During the defence of Kiev in September 1941 he was Commander-in-Chief of the Thirty-Seventh Army and played a successful part in the defence of Moscow in December 1941. In March 1942, while commanding the Second Shock Army on the Volkhov front, his forces were surrounded and he was finally captured on 11 July. Disenchanted with Stalin's leadership he put himself at the disposal of the *Smolensker Komitee*, a group of anti-Stalin Soviet senior officers and politicians, and wrote leaflets that were dropped behind Soviet lines urging Soviet soldiers to desert. He sought to set up a military formation to fight the Soviet forces. The Germans used him for propaganda, but only at the end of the war was he given command of the Vlasov Army, a force of two divisions dressed in German uniforms with distinctive arm shield insignia and mostly armed with captured weapons of Soviet origin. Captured by the British at the end of the war, Vlasov was handed over to the Soviet Union, tried for treason in Moscow and executed on 2 August 1946.

Shepetivka 'or the Front will have no ammunition'.

What followed was one of those nightmares of bureaucracy. When the supply dump staff refused to issue ammunition without the correct requisitioning forms Lukin moved in. Some 250 trucks standing idle 'at the disposition of the district military commissariat' were put to use moving the ammunition while civilians were loaded onto trains. Lukin then formed 'Group Lukin', composed of elements of the 213th and 109th Rifle Divisions and the XIX Mechanized Corps. Communication was via the railway telephone system. It was a temporary grouping in which leadership was by example – all the company, two-thirds of the battalion and five regimental commanders were killed in action. 'Group Lukin' fought until it was eventually relieved by the VII Rifle Corps.

Left: Like the victors of a cavalry charge the crews of PzKpfw III dismount to examine a battery of 57mm (2.15in) Model 1941 anti-tank guns with which they have fought an intense action. The Germans were impressed by the gun and used captured examples.

LVOV LIBERATED

On 30 June Lvov was captured by the Germans, who discovered that the NKVD had slaughtered 4000 political prisoners and Ukrainian intellectuals in Brygidsky prison, which they then set on fire, and in the former Samastinov military prison, to prevent their release. This savagery was no doubt partly triggered by the atmosphere of suspicion, chaos, drunkenness and looting in the city. Lvov had been subjected not only to air attacks but also to sabotage by groups of Ukrainian nationalists organized by the Germans.

> Although the tanks could see no infantry in the open, the Soviet infantry remained hidden in the cornfields. German infantry trying to winkle them out were also invisible. And then the awful work began, hand-to-hand fighting took place in the weak light of dawn. The fields were infested with enemy riflemen. Every metre of ground was fought over. The Soviet soldiers did not give up. Even hand grenades did not bring them out of their hiding places.
>
> *Arthur Grimm*
> *PK correspondent, 11th Panzer Division*

Above: Panzergrenadiere *emerge through the double door at the back of their SdKfz 251 half track. An MG34 machine gun is mounted at the back of the vehicle for local defence and for anti-aircraft protection. The* Panzergrenadiere *and tanks made a potent team.*

The mood of violent fear had been fuelled just before the tanks reached the city by jibes from the non-Russian population, 'The Germans are coming to get you'. Within the Ukraine Admiral Canaris and the *Abwehr* had established diversionist groups formed from a Ukrainian nationalist organization known to the Germans as *Bergbauernhilfe* and to the Ukrainians as the Organization of Ukrainian Nationalists or OUN (B). They cut rail and telephone communications, blew up fuel and ammunition dumps and attempted local uprisings, although these were suppressed with considerable brutality by the Red Army and NKVD.

Once they secured the city, German broadcasts urged people to come to the prisons to identify the bodies. Maria Seniva, whose husband had been arrested by the NKVD, walked into a courtyard filled with bodies. 'I stopped to look at one of the dead bodies, it was covered by a blanket. I lifted the blanket and there he was, I'd found him, but his face was all black. He had no eyes, nothing there, and no nose.'

German soldiers who saw, and smelled, the corpses in the prison at Lvov were horrified by the brutality and an SD report on morale produced in the second week of July noted that Lvov had 'produced a deep impression of disgust. It was often asked what fate must our own soldiers expect if they become prisoners, and what are we doing on our own side with the Bolsheviks "who are no longer human?"' Nazi propaganda teams were quick to capitalize on the murders, posting photographs of the victims with the caption 'Jewish killings'.

ANTI-JEWISH MEASURES

The NKVD murders were not the first or the last tragedy that the culturally diverse city of Lvov would suffer. Founded in the thirteenth century in Eastern Galicia, the city (as Lemberg) was under Austrian rule from 1772 to 1918; Poland, from independence in 1918 until annexation to Soviet Russia in late September 1939; Germany, from June 1941; and the Soviet Union again, following the defeat of Germany in 1945.

Before World War II Lvov had the third largest Jewish community in Poland. The city was known as both a cultural and industrial centre, with a lively Jewish cultural scene.

In how many fields and woods and ditches were German soldiers dying, waiting for help that would not come – or that would be too late when it did arrive? Surely, I thought, the army could have made better arrangements to deal with the hellish mix of confusion, terror and despair that was left behind by the relentless forward march of our storm troops.

The organization of the fighting troops and paraphernalia of war seemed to have been worked out with amazing precision, but there appeared to have been a criminal disregard of the necessities behind front line troops. Surely it would even have been better to advance more slowly if it would have given us time to find and treat our wounded and bury our dead.

Leutnant Heinrich Happe
Medical Officer, Infanterie Regiment 18

Below: A Soviet vehicle burns following an encounter with a German Pak 35/36 anti-tank gun. These small anti-tank guns could be quickly deployed to counter a Soviet tank threat, but were ineffective against the better armoured KV-1 and T-34.

Above: With their clothes marked with a yellow star a family of rural Ukrainian Jews make their way to an uncertain fate probably in 1942. Many Jews who had been told they would be rehoused were killed by the Einsatzgruppen *at sites outside towns and villages.*

Following the German invasion of Poland on 1 September 1939, and the annexation of Lvov into Soviet territory three weeks later, approximately 1000,000 Jews from Nazi-occupied Poland found refuge in Lvov. The following year the Soviet authorities exiled many of these Polish Jews to distant regions of the Soviet Union.

Following its capture in June 1941, extremely harsh anti-Jewish measures were implemented immediately. Over the summer, during what later became known as the 'Petliura Days', there was a series of massacres of the Lvov Jews, designated *Aktion Petlura* and carried out by both Germans and Ukrainians. The pogroms had been named symbolically

Left: A Soviet patrol commander armed with a PPD 1940 submachine gun observes an enemy position. Behind him are soldiers armed with SVT-40 automatic rifles – the Germans were impressed by Soviet small arms which were robust and reliable in mud and snow.

after the former Ukrainian prime minister who, 15 years earlier, had been assassinated in Paris by a Jew.

Ukrainian disenchantment with Moscow and Stalin's Soviet Union dated back to the 1930s when Soviet collectivization of all private farms took away the peasant farmers' land and livestock; the German administrators of the occupied Ukraine were to maintain the collective farms but called them 'cooperative farms'. In 1933 Ukraine suffered a man-made famine organized by Lazar Kaganovich, who followed Stalin's orders to the letter. About 7 million Ukrainians died of starvation in this famine.

Later in the 1930s thousands of Ukrainians whose patriotism was suspected by the NKVD were arrested. These included members of the intelligentsia, writers, artists and even musicians: this repression of writers, poets and playwrights was later called the *Rozstrilaniy vidrodzhennia* ('Executed Renaissance') period of Ukrainian literature. Both the Ukrainian churches, Orthodox and Catholic, were banned and only the Russian Orthodox Church was allowed to function in the region, although they were allowed to practice under German rule. The Soviet terror of the 1930s convinced many Ukrainians that there was nothing worse than Communist Russian slavery and consequently the Army Group South were viewed as liberators. Following the capture of Lvov an independent Ukrainian state was proclaimed in the city by Yaroslav Stetsko and the new wing of the OUN (B) led by Stepan Bandera. It was very short-lived, however, since on 12 July the Ukrainians in the Stetsko government were arrested and Bandera, Stetsko and others were taken as prisoners to Sachsenhausen concentration camp in Germany.

Hungary, under its pro-German, authoritarian leader Admiral Miklós Horthy, declared war on the Soviet Union on 27 June and Hungarian troops were placed under von Rundstedt's command on 3 July. These troops were designated a Mobile Force, under General Ferenc Szombathelyi, but they were only partially motorized,

> The incessant gruelling marches and the continuous fighting over several days had taxed the tank crews to the utmost. Since the beginning of the war the officers and men had not had a single hour's rest and they seldom had a hot meal. Our physical strength was leaving us. We desperately needed rest.
>
> *Stephan Matysh*
> *Soviet 32nd Tank Division*

comprising two motorized brigades, a cavalry brigade and ten Alpine battalions, six of which were mounted on bicycles. The tiny Italian puppet state of Albania also declared war on the USSR on 28 June.

Below: German officers examine a KV-2 that was abandoned when it sank into a marsh. The KV-2 was armed with a powerful 152mm (6in) howitzer, but the big turret made the tank unstable and production stopped after the German invasion in June 1941.

Right: A Soviet prisoner smiles hopefully up at the German photographer as he passes in a truck. Few would survive their four years as prisoners and those that did and were liberated by the Red Army would be treated as collaborators by Moscow.

STAVKA

The Soviet Union actually went to war in 1941 without a commander-in-chief, since the post had been abolished in the reforms of the 1920s. The highest military post was the Peoples' Commissar for Defence, held by Kliment Voroshilov. Reorganization of the Army in the 1930s had actually made the army less efficient, with a cumbersome bureaucracy that included the Defence Commissariat, the post of Defence Commissar and the *Voennyi Soviet* (Military Soviet). In 1938 the Army acquired the *Glavnyi Voennyi Soviet RKKA* (Main Military Soviet) and the Navy had an equivalent body. There was also a *Komitet Oborony* (Defence Committee), although its role was vague and did not include any command functions.

On Monday 23 June a decree signed by Stalin and the *Sovnarkom* produced the *Stavka Glavnovo Komandovaniya* (High Command Headquarters), an organization that would soon be known simply as *Stavka*. This was both an institution and a location. As an institution it included Marshals of the Soviet Union, the Chief of the General Staff, the heads of the Navy and Air Force, and, as the war progressed, the heads of the armed services. *Stavka* was also a command centre in the Kremlin with its own war room and sophisticated communications links.

During the first two months of the war Stalin engineered himself into the position of commander-in-chief and so it was *Stavka* and Stalin that set the strategic objectives of the war. Some were unattainable in the opening chaos, but by early 1943 it was well in control of the 'big picture' on the Eastern Front. Admiral Kuznetsov, the Soviet Navy Commander-in-Chief, recalled that Stalin had worked his way to the top 'little by little', but by 8 August he was *Verkhovnyi Glavnokommanduyushchii* (Supreme Commander of the Soviet Armed Forces).

That day the 13th Panzer Division reached the Rovno area, but lacked sufficient infantry support to push further since the infantry divisions had swung south to contain a critical situation developing around Dubno. By reinforcing their positions near Lutsk and withdrawing elements of the IX and XXII Mechanized Corps from the Dubno area, the Soviet command were able to build a fairly firm defensive line running north and southeast of Lutsk to just north of Rovno. The Soviet Fifth Army reinforced this line and it became a threat to Army Group South. This led to the decision to deploy Army Group Centre's main axis of attack southwards out of the Smolensk area and against Kiev.

DELAY IN ROMANIA

To the far south on the Romanian–Soviet border, where the Eleventh Army under *Generaloberst* Ritter von Schobert was in position, nothing was happening at dawn on 22 June. There was some patrol activity across the River Prut, which was hazardous since the banks offered little cover, and the Red Air Force launched some bombing raids. Infantry Regiment 30, part of the 198th Infantry Division, carried out a reconnaissance in force on 22 June and occupied the village of Sculeni on the far bank of the Prut.

Curzio Malaparte was in a forward command post with *Generaloberst* Ritter von Schobert as he observed his armoured units go into action near the Dnieper: 'General von Schobert was smiling. The shadow of death was already hovering over him – an extremely light shadow like a spiderweb: and no doubt he felt that shadow weighing on his brow … he would die a few days later landing in his small plane, a *Storch*, on the airport of newly-occupied Kiev: that the wheels of his *Storch*, gliding over the grass of the landing field, would touch off a mine, and he would disappear among a cluster of red flowers in a sudden explosion, and only his blue handkerchief with his white embroidered initials would drop intact on the grass of the airport … On the Dnister he said to me, "*Wir besiegen unsere Toten* – We conquer our own dead". He meant that the last, the final laurels of the German victories would spell the death of the German people, that the German nation and all its victories will win death as the only reward.'

Owing to operational delays by forces further to the north it was not until the beginning of July that major operations were undertaken. The Eleventh Army was tasked with entering the USSR as part of the border battles of encirclement and its delay was intended to fit into a larger timetable. Army Group South had had a hard fight, but by 16 July *Feldmarschall* von Rundstedt, now supported by Romanians, Hungarians and the German Eleventh Army, had surrounded vast numbers of Soviet troops in a huge pocket at Uman, between Kiev and Odessa. It was not finally reduced until 8 August, yielding 100,000 prisoners, but as with Army Group Centre the price for this victory would be further delay in a timetable that was constrained by the onset of winter. The advance into the Ukraine across the open, rolling steppe filled with sunflowers, soya beans and unharvested corn now seemed unstoppable.

However, victory came with a price, and by the close of the year the bill in human lives destroyed or wrecked would be terrifying. Kirponos reckoned that the mauling his forces had given to *Panzergruppe* 1 had prevented a potentially vital breakthrough behind and into his centre and left. Perhaps the greatest tribute to Kirponos came from General Halder, who commented ruefully that he had done a 'good job'. The Soviet forces had not collapsed under the impact of the *Blitzkrieg* and, though they had suffered heavy losses, they had inflicted them as well. Kirponos's forces were now pulled out of the salient formed around Lvov.

In Moscow a Soviet Defence Committee, including Stalin, Molotov, Voroshilov, Malenkov and Beria, was formed on 29

Below: Soviet soldiers find time to share a joke as they prepare for the expected German advance in a bunker on the Stalin Line in the southern Ukraine. The Stalin Line slowed but did not halt the advance by Army Group South.

June that would prosecute the war with a terrible ruthlessness. The next day the newly-constituted *Stavka* authorized the South Western Front and the right wing of the Southern Front to pull back to what was effectively the old Soviet–Polish frontier. This reduced the frontage covered by Kirponos by 322km (200 miles) and had the added benefit that he was falling back on the defences of the Stalin Line. It is a bitter irony that much of this good work would be undone by Marshal Budenny in the next few weeks and that, after he had marched to defeat at Kiev, on Stalin's orders he handed the impending disaster back to Kirponos.

THE END OF THE BEGINNING

As summer began to fade into autumn and the lightning war slowed down, German soldiers marching towards endless horizons, and their commanders planning new battles of encirclement with dwindling armoured formations, knew that the war would not be over in 1941. Travelling alongside them, Curzio Malaparte noticed 'the white stain of fear growing in the dull eyes of German officers and soldiers. When Germans become afraid, when that mysterious

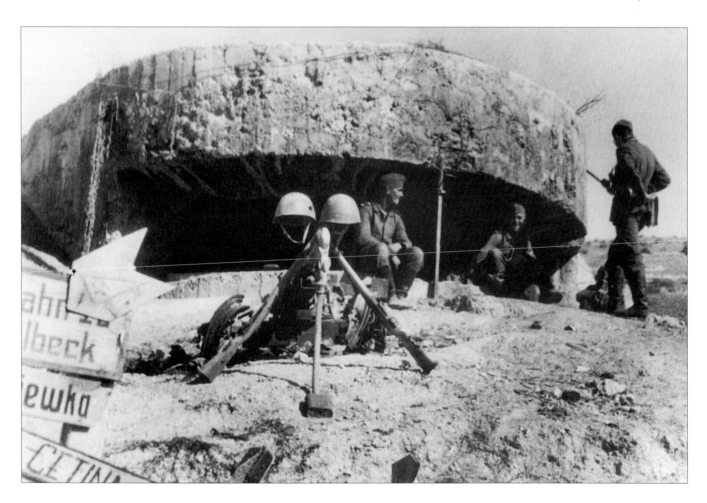

German fear begins to creep into their bones, they always arouse a special horror and pity. Their appearance is miserable, their cruelty sad, their courage silent and hopeless. That is when Germans became wicked … They began killing prisoners whose feet were blistered and who could no longer walk. They began setting fire to the villages that were unable to hand over a fixed number of loads of wheat and flour, a certain number of loads of corn and barley and of heads of horses and cattle to the requisitioning platoons. When only a few Jews remained, they began hanging the peasants. They strung them up by their necks or by their feet to the branches of trees in the little villages … side by side with the rain-washed corpses of the Jews that had been dangling for days.'

Left: Landsern *give German Army horses an envious glance as they drink from a trough filled with water that has been raised from a village well. The dust that covers the infantry made many men look like statues made from white marble.*

Below: As fire destroys her wood and thatch farmhouse a Russian peasant weeps. Some buildings caught fire during artillery bombardments or were hit by tracer, but others were destroyed by Soviet forces as part of the ruthless 'Scorched Earth' policy to deny the enemy cover.

ITALIAN OBSERVER

Curzio Malaparte, who was born Erich Suckert in Prato, near Florence, in 1898 to a German father and Italian mother, was no stranger to war by World War II. At the age of 16 he had enlisted in Peppino Garibaldi's volunteer legion and served in France until May 1915. In 1918 he was exposed to mustard gas on the French front, which caused his death from lung cancer in 1957.

Before World War II Malaparte joined the Italian Fascist Party. Even though his reports for the newspaper *Corriere della Sera* sometimes angered the Fascist and Nazi authorities, he was granted exclusive rights to follow the advancing German troops in the Soviet Union and report back in daily articles. His collected correspondence from France in 1940–1 was published as *Il sole è cieco* (1947) and from the Eastern Front in 1941–2 as *Il Volga nasce in Europa* (1943). He was fascinated by literature and politics and, as a respected author and editor, enjoyed considerable access in World War II. Towards the end of the war he served as the Italian Army Contingent liaison officer with the Allied Command.

CHAPTER EIGHT

DEATH IN THE SNOW

The *Blitzkrieg* ran out of energy as Army Group Centre were virtually within sight of Moscow. At the same time the winter set in and the cold was so intense that it killed men and animals and caused weapons and machines to malfunction as lubricants thickened and Buna rubber took on the consistency of wood. At this point the Red Army launched a decisive counter-attack, and forced the invaders back from the capital.

ONE MONTH INTO THE CAMPAIGN, the *Führer*, who had been increasingly interfering in operational matters, issued Directive No 33 at his pretentiously-named *Wolfsschanze* (Wolf's Lair) HQ in Rastenburg, East Prussia. This stated that the priorities were now to be Leningrad and the Ukraine. If the OKW staff questioned this change, Hitler silenced them by saying that they did not understand economics and that the coal, wheat and factories of the Don Basin and Ukraine were the target to the south. To achieve this Army Group Centre had to hand over its tanks to the two Groups to north and south.

The *Luftwaffe*, however, was ordered to launch air attacks on Moscow. The first mission by *Luftflotte* II, commanded by *Generalfeldmarschall* Albert Kesselring, was on 22 July, when 127 aircraft hit the Soviet capital. During the rest of the year there were 75 attacks, of which 59 were by formations of fewer than 60 aircraft.

Left: A Soviet 7.62mm (0.3in) DP light machine gun crew take aim at a distant target. The crew of an automatic weapon would normally never take up an exposed position in a window where the muzzle flash would be obvious to the enemy.

> It is hardly too much to say that the campaign against Russia has been won in fourteen days.
>
> General Franz Halder
> diary 3 July 1941

Stalin broadcast to the Soviet Union on 3 July and ordered the imposition of a 'scorched earth' policy. This ruthless tactic, which had been used in the Russo–Japanese war, made no concessions to the civilian population. It was a militarily sound command, but one that added cruelly to the suffering of the civilians in the Ukraine and Belorussia. Stalin spelled it out: 'In the case of a forced retreat of Red Army units, all rolling stock must be evacuated; the enemy must not be left a single engine, not a single railway carriage, not a single pound of grain nor gallon of fuel … In occupied regions conditions must be made unbearable for the enemy and his accomplices. They must be hounded and annihilated at every step and all their measures frustrated.'

SMOLENSK SURRENDERS

The Smolensk pocket surrendered on 5 August and 310,000 Soviet prisoners marched into captivity. Yet just a month after this victory Hitler changed his mind again. Moscow would now be the priority. Army Groups North and South were ordered to hand over or return the armoured forces that had been loaned to them or were under their command. In the

Below: Autumn 1941 – German infantry relaxing in the sunshine wait on the start line as Stukas and artillery bombard a Soviet position. With no threat from the air or from artillery the soldiers have not dug in or camouflaged themselves and are bunched together.

Right: Month by month, Army Groups North, Centre and South pushed eastwards during Barbarossa. However, as they moved deeper into the USSR their logistic chain became extended and the frontage wider: supplies of fuel, food and ammunition to the front line became erratic.

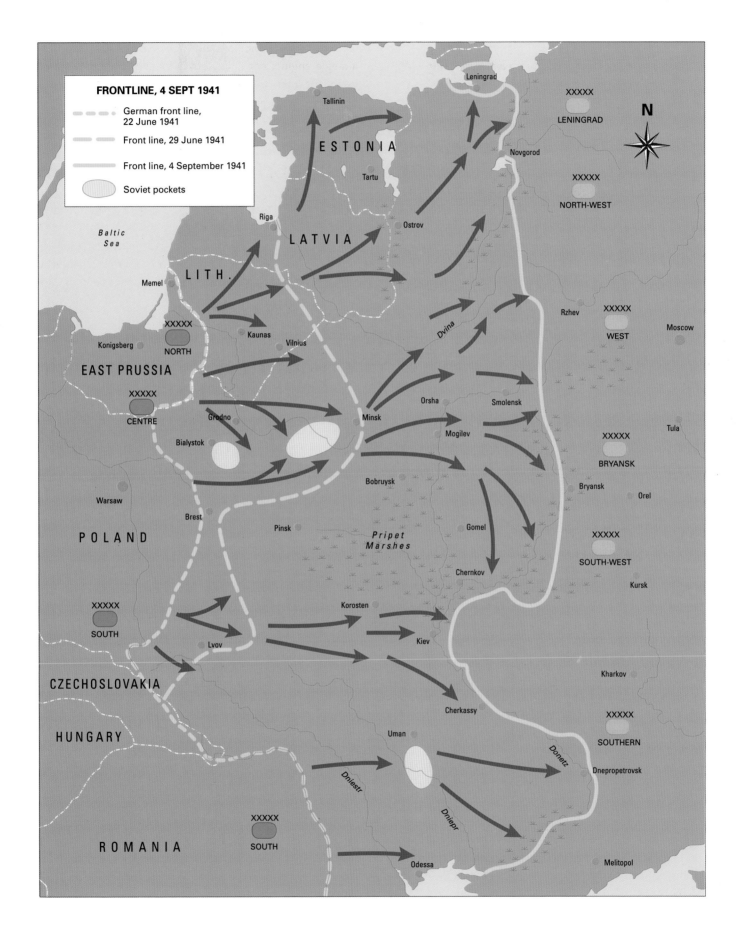

FRONTLINE, 4 SEPT 1941

- - - - German front line, 22 June 1941

━ ━ ━ Front line, 29 June 1941

━━━ Front line, 4 September 1941

⬭ Soviet pockets

Baltic Sea

Leningrad

XXXXX
LENINGRAD

N

Tallinin

E S T O N I A

Novgorod

XXXXX
NORTH-WEST

Tartu

Riga

L A T V I A

Ostrov

Memel

L I T H .

Rzhev

XXXXX
WEST

Moscow

Konigsberg

XXXXX
NORTH

Kaunas

Vilnius

Dvina

EAST PRUSSIA

XXXXX
CENTRE

Grodno

Minsk

Orsha

Smolensk

Tula

Bialystok

Mogilev

XXXXX
BRYANSK

Warsaw

Bobruysk

Bryansk

Orel

Brest

Pinsk

Pripet Marshes

Gomel

P O L A N D

XXXXX
SOUTH-WEST

Chernkov

Kursk

XXXXX
SOUTH

Korosten

Lvov

Kiev

Kharkov

CZECHOSLOVAKIA

Cherkassy

XXXXX
SOUTHERN

H U N G A R Y

Uman

Donetz

Dnepropetrovsk

Dniestr

XXXXX
SOUTH

Dniepr

R O M A N I A

Odessa

Melitopol

167

Above: Mozjayskoye Shosse *boulevard in Moscow prepared for street fighting in October 1941. The population was mobilised to construct defences both around and in the city. A narrow access through the hedgehogs has been left for vehicles on the left of the barricade.*

south this was easier to order than implement, since Army Group South had surrounded the huge pocket at Kiev and was in the process of reducing it. It was a major victory but would delay the drive on Moscow and so give the Soviet Army and civilians enough time to build defences around the capital city. The construction of these fortifications was largely undertaken by women and youngsters, because all able-bodied men had now been called up.

In November they built 1428 artillery and machine gun positions, dug 160km (100 miles) of anti-tank ditches and laid 112km (70 miles) of triple coil barbed wire obstacles as part of the city's outer defences.

Hitler never fully grasped the scale of operations in Russia. The victories in Poland and the West had been because roads were good and the distances short. The Germans had attacked from well-stocked and accessible depots and the action was so fast that Hitler had little chance to interfere. Had he made Moscow the priority target from the outset the two *Panzergruppen* that straddled the Moscow highway, the only metalled road outside of the cities, could

have used it to push through to the city. If Moscow had been captured, it might have been fought for like Stalingrad a year later, but its loss would have been a savage blow to Soviet morale. It would also have severed the north–south rail communications in the USSR.

MUD AND SNOW

The first autumn rains began to fall on 27 September. As German planners had predicted, the dusty roads turned into sloughs and movement halted. Yet three days later Operation *Taifun* (Typhoon) was launched with Moscow as its objective. The II *Panzerarmee* and *Panzergruppen* 3 and 4 were faced by three Soviet Fronts: the West Front under General Ivan Konev, composed of seven armies; the Bryansk Front under General Andrey Eremenko, with three armies;

and in the rear Marshal Semyon Budenny, Stalin's old comrade from the Civil War, commanded the Reserve Front of five armies. It was a formidable force but a greater threat was 'General Winter', the severe Russian winter, which was beginning to show itself after the autumn rains. The poor roads caused the German supply system to break down, and the delivery of food, fuel and ammunition became erratic.

At Bryansk the II *Panzerarmee* under Guderian quickly cut off and surrounded Soviet forces in a pocket, while to the north the Ninth Army under General Strauss and the Fourth Army under *Generalfeldmarschall* von Kluge cut off another group at the railway town of Vyazma. Bryansk and the bridge over the Desna had been taken in a swift coup on 6 October by the men of General von Arnim's 17th Panzer Division.

The city was full of troops, heavy artillery and NKVD units and in store for a planned defence were 100,000 Molotov cocktails. Its capture put one of the most important railway junctions in European Russia in German hands. The German forces were closing in on Moscow and still inflicting

Below: Women and elderly men are conscripted to dig an anti-tank trench near Kiev. An anti-tank trench was normally 'V' shaped and designed to trap a tank nose down in the ditch. Both sides used civilians for these types of construction tasks.

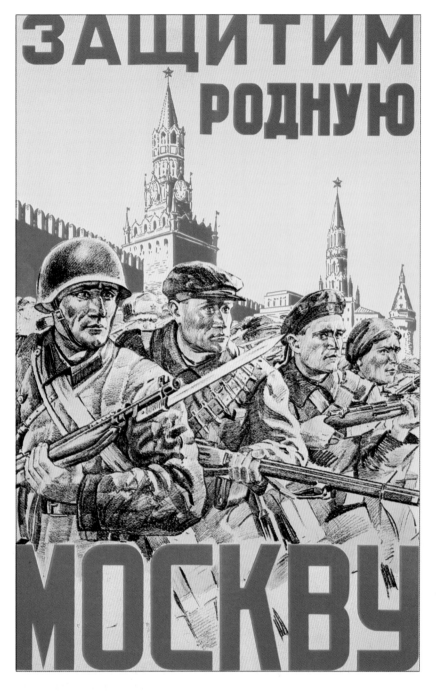

Left: A Soviet patriotic poster mobilizes the population of Moscow for the capital's defence. In the background are the towers of the Kremlin, while in the foreground a soldier, militiaman, sailor and woman defend the population and level their rifles at the enemy.

men had been able to break out eastwards, some 50,000 prisoners began the grim march westwards.

Like a military dilettante, Hitler changed his mind again – Moscow was not to be attacked directly, it was now to be outflanked. Fear gripped the city in mid-October; although Stalin remained in the capital, most of the foreign embassies and the government ministries were evacuated to Kuybyshev behind the river Volga. The British and American defence attachés were convinced that the capital would fall. Martial law was declared in the city and even the jails were scoured for likely reinforcements. An office in the Kremlin with a window visible to Muscovites in Red Square was reported to be Stalin's and at night the light was left on to convince the citizens that Stalin was working.

Significantly, early in the war the Soviets had already dismantled its major armaments factories and moved them by rail hundreds of kilometres to the east beyond the Ural Mountains. Although this had caused much disruption, it now placed them out of range of the *Luftwaffe*. At Chelyabinsk the production lines of the huge Tankograd tank factory were producing the formidable T-34. Tanks were also being built at Gorki (now Nizhny Novgorod) and Kirov – the USSR was already beginning to win the production battle.

staggering defeats on the Soviet Army. In Berlin on 3 October Hitler boasted, 'Russia has already been broken and will never rise again'.

ZHUKOV APPOINTED

On 10 October General Zhukov took over command of the West Front and with it the defence of Moscow. The Front consisted of eight armies on a 280km (174 mile) line centred on Mozhaisk, 100km (62 miles) west of Moscow. Four days later the Bryansk pocket surrendered and, although many

You get excited as you look for a target. The engine starts and the ground bumps up and down as you charge forward. You sight the gun and the driver shouts 'Fire!' When you hit a German tank in battle and blow it up, instead of firing at another tank you open the hatch. You look out and make sure you got it!

Lt Alexander Fadin
T-34 commander

T-34/76

The T34/76 had been developed from the pre-war BT series of fast tanks that used American-designed Christie suspension. Early T-34s had a two man all-welded turret that was cramped and lacked a radio and vision devices for the commander. The short-barrelled 76.2mm (3in) gun was soon replaced by one with a longer barrel and better anti-armour performance. It required a larger turret and this was fitted with a cupola for the commander. The range of the T-34 could be extended by topping up from two or four spare fuel drums secured to the rear decking. In June 1941 the Soviet Army had deployed 967 T-34s. They were the first of tens of thousands of what proved to be the most effective tank of World War II.

MOSCOW REACHED

On 18 October men of the German Ninth Army reached Mozhaisk and penetrated the outer defence line of Moscow. Next day the Vyazma pocket collapsed, yielding some 670,000 prisoners, 1000 tanks and 4000 guns. The Second *Panzerarmee*, however, failed to capture Oryol on 30 October because it was almost out of fuel and the mud had reduced the mobility of those tanks that still had full tanks. There was a pause as reinforcements and supplies were moved up for the attack on Moscow.

By 7 November snow and frost had frozen the soft mud, so that vehicles could move more freely and the decision was taken to attack again, although by now there were an estimated 80 Soviet divisions in position in front of Moscow. In just over two weeks of hard fighting the Germans pushed to positions 60km (37 miles) northwest of Moscow. In the south troops reached Kashira on the river Oka, 120km (74 miles) from the capital. In his order of the day to *Panzergruppe* 4 on 17 November, General Erich Höppner wrote: 'Arouse your troops into a state of awareness. Revive their spirit. Show them the objective that will mean for

Right: The T-34/76 tank was armed with a 76mm (3in) gun and two 7.62mm machine guns. Its 500hp V-2-34 12 cylinder diesel engine developed 500hp and gave a road speed of 54km/h (33.5mph) and cross country range of 300km (186.3miles).

them the glorious conclusion of a hard campaign and the prospect of well-earned rest. Lead them with vigour and confidence in victory! May the Lord of Hosts grant you success!'

By December 1941 the German forces had taken 3,350,639 prisoners in addition to the huge casualties they had inflicted on the Soviet Army. The pages of newspapers in Germany were filled with pictures of burning or wrecked vehicles and columns of tired, scruffy, starving prisoners, the *Untermenschen*, plodding westwards. Now all that remained for the German forces was a final push to capture Moscow and, in Hitler's words at the beginning of Barbarossa, to watch as 'the whole rotten structure [comes] crashing down'.

However, the thrust finally came to an exhausted halt on 5 December when Hitler ordered that operations should cease for the winter; some of the positions occupied were actually to the east of Moscow. Moscow is at 37° East, and when the 29th Motorized Infantry Division, part of Guderian's II *Panzerarmee*, reached Mikhaylov they were actually at 39° East, about 150km (93 miles) south and 30km (18 miles) east of the Soviet capital. The defences commanded by General Katukov at the city of Tula, known as 'little Moscow', held on and this prevented the tanks from rolling up the front. To the north of the city the tanks of General Erich Höppner's *Panzergruppe* 4 had reached the Volga canal at Yakhroma and at Krasnaya Polyana the tram stops for the outer suburbs of Moscow. Here they were halted by the defences manned by the Twentieth and Thirty-Third Armies of the Soviet Western Front.

Soviet soldiers had always demonstrated a talent for defence, and to their obstinacy, stamina and cunning was added the sinister threat of the NKVD security units stationed just behind the front line. Their mission was to prevent soldiers retreating or deserting and under Order No 356, promulgated in 1940, they were empowered to execute men who might be deserters.

On 2 December *Unterscharführer* Streng of the *Waffen-SS*

watched an air attack on Moscow from a forward observation post. 'Over the precincts of Moscow hung giant flash rockets like stars of Venus, and tight packs of searchlight beams hurtled around the sky, went out again, then appeared, ghost like, clawing the air again at other places, criss-crossing in giant packs of beams. Between them, the flashing pearl garlands of heavy Soviet flak. The light trails from shells sent long threads of dark red and orange into the night sky. Moscow roared, the loud thunder piercing the December night.'

Below: An MG34 machine gunner and his No 2 manage smiles for the photographer as they plod through the early snow. They are comparatively well dressed for 1941 with gloves and scarves, while helmets are slung from their equipment since the steel conducts the cold.

'GENERAL WINTER'

By 8 December, as winter gripped Russia, the German commanders realized that they must dig in to see out one of the coldest winters on record. The thermometers now registered -35ºC (-95ºF), but would go lower. The Germans had suffered 250,000 dead and twice that number of wounded. By the end of the year they would be 340,000 under strength and troop reinforcements were being transferred from France to bring formations up to strength.

A soldier in the Rifle Regiment 69, 10th Panzer Division confided ruefully to his diary, 'We are waging the winter war as if this was one of our Black Forest winters back home'. Of the 26 supply trains required daily by Army Group Centre only eight or ten were making it through the bitter weather.

Richard Sorge's warnings about Barbarossa may have

MARSHAL GEORGI ZHUKOV

Although Zhukov had modest beginnings, he would become one of the finest leaders of the Soviet Army. He was born of peasant stock near Moscow in 1896 and entered the Imperial Russian Army aged 15. Like many of Stalin's cronies, he became an NCO in the cavalry, but unlike such cavalry generals as Voroshilov and Budenny he was tough and highly competent. He joined the Communist Party in 1919. In September 1939 the then little-known General Zhukov inflicted a sharp defeat on the Japanese Kwantung Army on the Halha river at Khalkin-Gol in Outer Mongolia. For this he received the Order of Lenin.

At Leningrad he was seen as halting the German attack and so Stalin moved him to Moscow. Here poor weather, fatigue and stiffening Soviet resistance halted the German attack. Using reinforcements from the Far East, Zhukov attacked in December and remained on the offensive until March 1942. He master-minded Operation Uranus, the counter-attack at Stalingrad, followed by Operation Saturn, which forced the Germans back to the river Donets. In January 1943 he was promoted to the rank of Marshal. At Kursk, Soviet forces under his overall command halted the German attacks and then rolled on to an unstoppable offensive. He destroyed Army Group Centre during Operation Bagration in June and July 1944, and finally led the 1st Byelorussian Front to victory in Berlin in 1945.

Resentful of his popularity, Stalin banished Zhukov to command a remote military district after the war. Following Stalin's death, however, he was appointed Minister of Defence from 1955 to 1957. He died in 1974.

move these last reserves, eight tank brigades and 34 high quality Siberian divisions, from the east and employ them in the counter-attack at Moscow in the winter of 1941–2.

In Germany the gravity of the threat in the East became evident on 20 December, when the propaganda chief Dr Joseph Goebbels launched an appeal for winter clothing for troops in the East. It would yield a curious mixture of winter sports clothing and high fashion garments like fur coats and hats. Meanwhile Germans soldiers captured by Soviet forces were sometimes found wearing their drill fatigue uniforms over their issue tunics and trousers and bulking them out with waste paper, including surrender leaflets that had not been dropped over Soviet lines. Whitewash was painted onto tanks and vehicles and bed sheets used as improvised personal camouflage. Experienced soldiers from the eastern territories of the Third Reich knew that winters could be

been ignored but his most important information for Stalin was that the Japanese did not intend to capitalize on the Soviet Union's misfortunes in 1941 and invade from Manchuria. The Japanese Kwantung Army in Manchuria was an élite force and consequently the Soviet forces deployed opposite it were of an equally high standard. Sorge's intelligence allowed the *Stavka* (Soviet High Command) to

Right: At a parade in Berlin at the end of the war Marshal Zhukov takes the salute. A successful commander, he was popular with the soldiers who nicknamed him 'old vinegar face' but was tough with officers under his command who did not deliver victory.

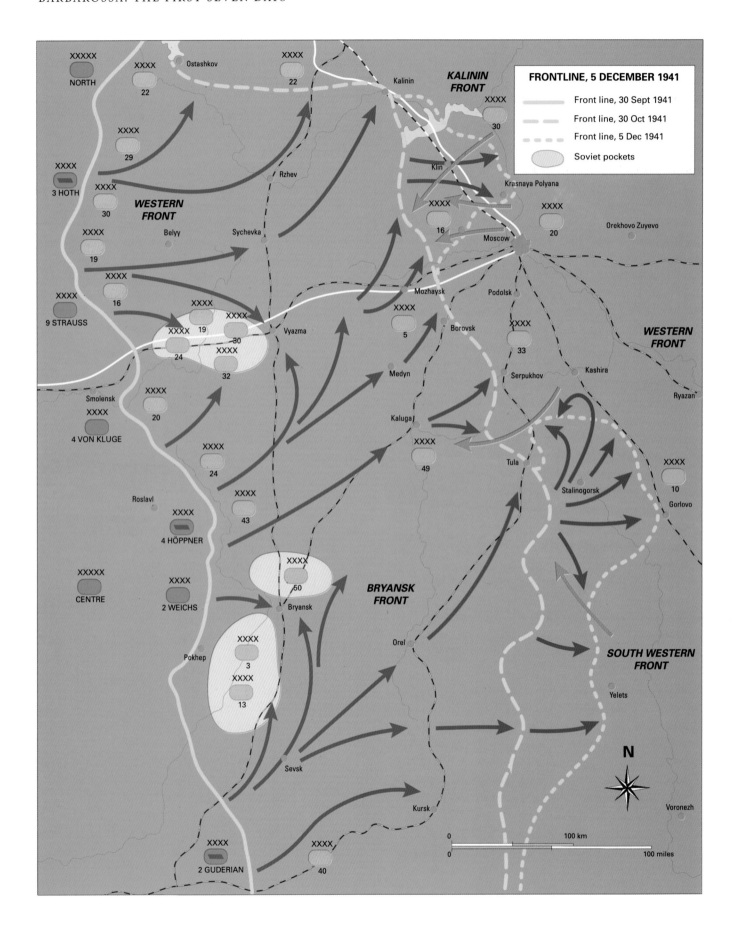

FRONTLINE, 5 DECEMBER 1941

Front line, 30 Sept 1941
Front line, 30 Oct 1941
Front line, 5 Dec 1941
Soviet pockets

XXXXX
NORTH

XXXX
22

Ostashkov

XXXX
22

Kalinin

KALININ FRONT

XXXX
30

XXXX
29

XXXX
3 HOTH

XXXX
30

Rzhev

Klin

Krasnaya Polyana

WESTERN FRONT

XXXX
19

Belyy

Sychevka

XXXX
16

XXXX
16

Moscow

XXXX
20

Orekhovo Zuyevo

XXXX
9 STRAUSS

XXXX
16

XXXX
19

XXXX
30

XXXX
24

XXXX
32

Vyazma

Mozhaysk

Podolsk

XXXX
5

Borovsk

XXXX
33

WESTERN FRONT

Smolensk

XXXX
20

Medyn

XXXX
4 VON KLUGE

XXXX
24

Kaluga

Serpukhov

Kashira

Ryazan

Roslavl

XXXX
43

XXXX
49

Tula

Stalinogorsk

XXXX
10

Gorlovo

XXXX
4 HÖPPNER

XXXXX
CENTRE

XXXX
2 WEICHS

XXXX
50

Bryansk

BRYANSK FRONT

Orel

SOUTH WESTERN FRONT

Pokhep

XXXX
3

XXXX
13

Yelets

Sevsk

Kursk

Voronezh

XXXX
2 GUDERIAN

XXXX
40

0   100 km

0   100 miles

N

Left: Theoretically the Moscow counter-attack should not have succeeded since the German forces were stronger. However, while the Soviet forces were bolstered with fresh troops from Siberia, the Germans were exhausted after six months of continuous marching and fighting.

severe and would wear slightly larger jackboots that could be padded out with insulation, but those wearing steel helmets and steel-shod boots conducted cold to their head and feet.

The cold was so severe that mineral oils became thick and ceased to lubricate weapons. The ersatz rubber of wheels and tyres, named after the Buna factory where it was developed, turned to the consistency of wood. Unprotected hands froze to exposed metal parts of weapons and vehicles and frostbite became as great a danger as the marauding Soviet forces. German soldiers took the caps, gloves, boots and quilted coats from the Soviet dead and when they robbed prisoners of their clothing effectively condemned them to death in the extreme cold.

SOVIET PREPARATIONS

In contrast to the Germans, Soviet troops were excellently equipped. Beneath their white camouflage smocks and trousers the men would be wearing a padded *telogreika* or a sheepskin jacket, padded trousers (*vatnie sharovari*), a fleece cap (*shapka-ushanka*) and sometimes compressed felt boots (*valenki*), a superior and much prized version of which had a waterproof rubber sole.

Cavalry and ski troops were also able to move freely across the snow and frozen rivers, outflanking German positions. As their resources had been stretched, the German armies were relying on mobile patrols and artillery fire to cover the gaps between their positions and it was through these gaps that Soviet troops were able to filter. Not all the Soviet soldiers who went into action in the winter of 1941 were

A mood of alarm spread in the city. The evacuation of industrial undertakings, Ministries, authorities and institutions was speeded up. There were also, at that time, sporadic cases of confusion among the public. There were people who spread panic, who left their place of work and hastened to get out of the city. There were also traitors who exploited the situation in order to steal socialist property and who tried to undermine the power of the Soviet State.

A.M. Samsonov
Soviet official historian

The icy cold, the wretched accommodation, the insufficient clothing, the heavy losses of men and matériel, and the meagre supplies of fuel are making military operations a torture, and I am getting increasingly depressed by the enormous weight of responsibility which, in spite of all fine words, no-one can take off my shoulders.

Heinz Guderian, writing to his wife

tough and experienced, since many were under or over age and had had limited training, but there were enough troops from the Siberian armies to give them backbone.

The Germans' first indication that fresh forces were being deployed around Moscow came in early December. The electronic warfare detachment of the 135th Infantry Regiment, part of the 45th Infantry Division, was fighting in the village of Yelets on the right flank of the German advance. Hooking into a Soviet telephone landline they picked up references to 'the Khabarovsk lot'. This was the city, beyond the vast expanses of Siberia, where in the early 1930s Marshal Tukhachevskiy had established the Far Eastern Army 'Special Corps'. By 1936 this force consisted of 60,000 serving soldiers and could draw on 50,000 peasant farmers as reservists.

COUNTER-ATTACK

The Red Army under General Zhukov launched its counter-attack at Moscow on 6 December. It appeared an ambitious plan, with attacks along a wide front by the North-Western Front, Kalinin Front, Western Front and South-Western Fronts beginning in December and building up into the New Year. There was

Right: General Timoshenko in the 1930s pattern Soviet Army uniform. To revive the military tradition, a new one was introduced on 6 January 1943 which had shoulder boards for officers, based on old Tsarist patterns.

even an airborne landing on 18–22 January by the 21st Parachute Brigade and Airborne Regiment 250 to the rear of Army Group Centre's forces facing Moscow.

Stavka did not realize that the German attacks had literally frozen in their tracks and still saw the threat to Moscow as extremely serious. Their attacks were prompted as much by desperation to take the pressure off the city as a move to exploit their tactical advantage in winter warfare. In fact the three Fronts were outnumbered by the forces at Army Group Centre – they had 718,800 men, 7985 guns and 720 tanks, while the Germans had 800,000 men, 14,000 guns and 1000 tanks. The German forces, however, were now operating at the end of a long logistic chain that stretched back through western Russia to Poland and bases in Germany. Although attacks by partisans had not become the threat that they would pose in 1942–3, and more so in the last two years of the war, they were beginning to disrupt the flow of supplies.

Left: Armed with a Tokarev SVT1940 automatic rifle fitted with a x 3.5 PV telescopic sight a sniper waits in ambush. He has chosen his position so that the scrub behind him breaks up his outline. His fur mitts have a single uninsulated trigger finger.

LEND-LEASE

On 24 June 1941, the British Foreign Secretary Anthony Eden announced an Anglo-Soviet aid agreement to the House of Commons in London. On 12 July in Moscow Sir Stafford Cripps, the British Ambassador to the Soviet Union, and Foreign Minister Vyacheslav Molotov signed the pact. It was the beginning of a supply of weapons and equipment that would flow from the United Kingdom via the Arctic ports of Murmansk and Archangel and later when the United States had entered the war, overland via Persia. The first convoy, codenamed 'Dervish' reached Archangel on 31 August.

American, British and Canadian Lend-Lease weapons and equipment made a very significant contribution to the Soviet Union's victory in the east. However, after the war the Soviets played down their role. It had in fact constituted about 15 per cent of the total equipment used by the Soviets. It was said that the only vehicles that moved through the mud towards Germany from 1943 onwards were the T-34 tanks with their wide tracks and the Lend-Lease American Studebaker trucks.

The USA supplied the Soviet Union with 6430 aircraft, 3734 tanks, 104 ships and boats, 210,000 motor vehicles, 3000 anti-aircraft guns, 245,000 field telephones, petrol, aluminium,

steel and five million tons of food. The Red Army depended heavily on American trucks for its mobility, since 427,000 out of its fleet of 665,000 motor vehicles at the end of the war were of Western origin. More significantly the promise to supply this aid was made to Mr Oumansky – the Soviet Ambassador in Washington on 4 August 1941 – four months before the United States was drawn into the war. On 1 October 1941 Lord Beaverbrook for Britain and Averell Harriman for the US were in Moscow to confirm the aid.

Britain supplied 5800 aircraft, 4292 tanks, and 12 minesweepers. The British tanks – though inferior to the T-34 – were critical in 1941, when Soviet tank factories in the Urals were not in full production and the Red Army had suffered huge tank losses in the opening months of Barbarossa.

Canada supplied 1188 tanks, 842 armoured cars, nearly one million shells, and 208,000 tons of wheat and flour.

A Western diplomat in Moscow pressed his Soviet counterpart about the lack of coverage of Lend-Lease in the Soviet press and, by implication, a lack of gratitude. He received the terse reply: 'We are losing millions of men fighting against the Nazis and you want us to express gratitude for Spam?'

The Red Air Force, which had been virtually eliminated in the opening months of Barbarossa, was beginning to become a real threat to the *Luftwaffe*. The obsolete slow types like the radial-engined Polikarpovs had been destroyed in the air and on the ground, but now new fighters like the Lavochkin LaGG-3, Mikoyan-Gurevich MiG-3 and the Yakovlev Yak-1, operating from airfields with heated hangars located around Moscow, were able to intercept German bombers.

The first Soviet attack in the early hours of 5 December was by General Ivan Konev's Kalinin Front, whose troops punched across the frozen waters of the Upper Volga. Despite the severe cold the German resistance was so strong that only one of the three armies, the Thirty-First under Yushkevich, enjoyed any measure of success. By the end of the second day

it had penetrated nearly 40km (25 miles) and recaptured the town of Turginovo. Zhukov's West Front attacked the overextended *Panzergruppen* 3 and 4 on 6 December. The attack was initially undertaken by the three most northerly armies, who made slow progress even when the Sixteenth Army joined in on 7 December. The Soviet tactics of frontal assaults were being held and the Germans were withdrawing in good order. At Stalin's bidding Zhukov switched to flanking attacks, focusing to the north of Moscow on the key

Below: The cooks of a Red Army field kitchen ladle out a hot meal in the winter of 1941. The food being served is probably soup or the traditional Russian dish kasha – *a filling buckwheat porridge that can be flavoured with vegetables or meat.*

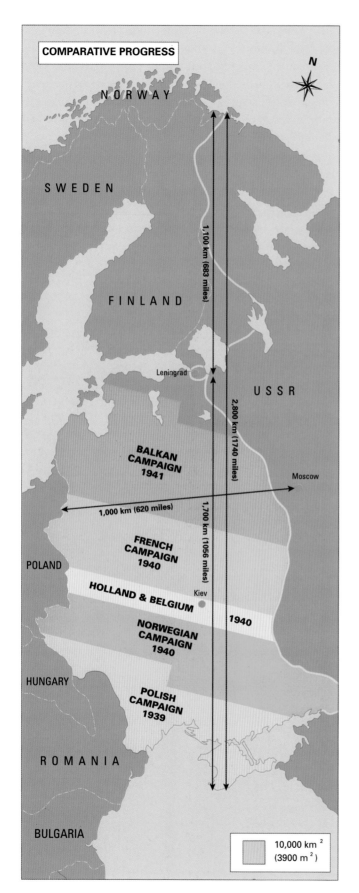

COMPARATIVE PROGRESS

NORWAY

SWEDEN

FINLAND

Leningrad

USSR

BALKAN CAMPAIGN 1941

1,100 km (683 miles)

2,800 km (1740 miles)

Moscow

1,000 km (620 miles)

1,700 km (1056 miles)

FRENCH CAMPAIGN 1940

POLAND

HOLLAND & BELGIUM

Kiev

NORWEGIAN CAMPAIGN 1940

1940

HUNGARY

POLISH CAMPAIGN 1939

ROMANIA

BULGARIA

10,000 km² (3900 m²)

town of Klin, which straddled the railway link to Leningrad. If Zhukov could capture it quickly, *Panzergruppe* 3 would be cut off and the left flank of Army Group Centre unhinged. The staff of the West and Bryansk Fronts, however, were not experienced in operational skills and the ambitious flanking attacks would prove difficult to control and coordinate. As *Generalfeldmarschall* von Leeb was receiving reports from the front lines on 7 December and adjusting the deployment of his forces to meet these threats, he was informed of new attacks directed against his right flank. On 13 December Timoshenko's South-Western Front began to attack to the northwest between Yelets and Livny. His Thirteenth Army ripped into the left flank of the German Second Army. Guderian was forced to make a hurried withdrawal as his right flank was exposed and vulnerable.

'STAND AND FIGHT'

Generalfeldmarschall Walther von Brauchitsch flew to the front to confer with Bock and decided that Army Group Centre should withdraw to a 'Winter Line' about 180km (112 miles) west of the front line. This was to follow the north–south roadway just east of Vyazma, passing through Zubtsov, Gzhatsk (now Gagarin) and Yukhnov. In the OKH General Halder pronounced the Soviet counter-attack as 'the greatest crisis in two World Wars'. But there would be greater to come.

Left: This diagram demonstrates the vast gains made by the German Army by the autumn of 1941, in comparison with the shorter campaigns that had preceded Barbarossa in Western Europe. However, while the longest of the earlier operations had lasted no more than six weeks, the Eastern campaign was to last four years and end in German defeat.

Right: A cheerful picture for the folks at home. German troops were woefully equipped for the severe Russian winter: they had no special cold weather clothing so some men packed out their uniforms with paper.

Left: A Cossack cavalry patrol at the charge. They have drawn their shashka *traditional straight-bladed sabres. They do not wear spurs but use a whip or* nagaika, *the distinctive wooden framed saddle with its leather cushion giving them a characteristic high seat.*

Above: The PzKpfw II was a good reconnaissance vehicle during the fighting in 1939–40, but by the winter of 1941 it was virtually obsolete. Its armour was too thin, the 2cm (0.8in) cannon ineffective and the narrow tracks unsuitable for snow.

Hitler was enraged by this proposal and countermanded the orders on 14 December, instigating a round of sackings. Von Bock was replaced by von Kluge on 18 December. Von Brauchitsch tendered his resignation and Hitler, the former World War I corporal, assumed command of the German Army on 19 December, ordering his troops to stand fast. Guderian, the Panzer expert, was sacked on Christmas Day, along with another exponent of armoured warfare, General Erich Höppner.

Now that the threat to Moscow had diminished, government ministers began to return to their posts from the towns to the east where they had been evacuated. The Bryansk Front under General Cherevichenko was established to the south of Moscow on 18 December, in preparation for an attack in a northwest direction to assist in a double envelopment of Army Group Centre.

Hitler's 'stand and fight' order and the successful defence of two pockets to the north at Demyansk and Kholm, which were supplied by air and later relieved by the Sixteenth Army, prevented the collapse of Army Group Centre. He came to see these measures as a panacea for all subsequent battles of encirclement and would issue similar orders to the Sixth

Army at Stalingrad in 1942. Where troops were forced back Hitler insisted that they destroy any buildings that could be used as shelter by the advancing Soviet forces. Although this scorched earth policy was followed in some withdrawals, many Germans knew that smoke would attract roving Soviet patrols and it was self-interest that prompted them to spare some of the thatched wooden or mud-brick houses.

THE PRICE OF THE FIRST WINTER

The fighting around Moscow lasted from December to March 1942, during which the German forces were pushed back by as much as 500km (310 miles) in some sectors. In just five months (22 June to 26 November 1941) the German armed forces had lost 187,000 men, killed or missing. The wounded for this period totalled 555,000, of whom two-thirds might be expected to return to duty. The killed and missing for the whole of the Eastern Front from 27 November to 31 March 1942 were put at 108,000 and the wounded at 268,000, a total of 376,000 men.

To this figure must be added 228,000 cases of frostbite and more than a quarter of a million others suffering mainly from exhaustion, exposure, typhus, scarlet fever, jaundice, diphtheria and stomach and skin complaints of various types. Most of these were the result of the terrible conditions in which front line troops were expected to live. By April the overall deficiency in manpower in the East stood at 625,000.

Below: Huddled together for warmth under empty mail bags, German prisoners await the bidding of their Soviet captors. The arrogant optimism that had fired the planning and first months of Barbarossa had become a distant memory.

Left: The Yak-1 had one 20mm (0.8in) ShVAK cannon firing through the propeller hub; two 7.62mm (0.3in) ShKAS machine guns in the upper cowling, a maximum bomb load of 200kg (440lb) or six 82mm (3.2in) RS-82 rocket projectiles. Maximum speed was 500km/h (311mph) and range 850km (528 miles).

YAKOVLEV YAK-1

Some 400 Yak-1 fighters were available in June 1941 and 8720 were built during the war. It was the first of a series of successful designs from the Yakovlev design bureau and was replaced by the Yak-3. The Yak-1 initially equipped the all woman 586th Fighter Regiment and the French volunteer 'Normandy-Niémen' fighter squadron as well as the first of four Polish volunteer units.

Men were not the only casualties of the fighting at Moscow. A quarter of a million horses, half of those that had entered the Soviet Union, perished in the cold. The Germans lost 2300 armoured vehicles, of which 1600 were PzKpfw III and IV tanks or assault guns. By April the artillery were short of 2000 guns and howitzers and 7000 anti-tank guns.

SPRING DISPOSITIONS

Stalin was now beginning to listen to the advice of his senior commanders and give them strategic objectives, what today would be called 'mission statements'. They were tasked with defence or attack, but given freedom to conduct operations in the manner they thought was most effective at a tactical level. Hitler, in contrast, was dismissing suggestions that German forces should withdraw to avoid being cut off in vulnerable salients. His tactics were described by Halder as *Flickwerk* ('patchwork'), cobbling together defences to restore breaks by deploying troops from other areas.

With the onset of the spring mud the front finally stabilized. Territory had been liberated in the north, producing a huge salient with a series of smaller salients, like the truncated fingers of a huge hand, facing southwest towards Vitebsk. To the south, a German salient had been created with Vyazma at its base and Rzhev at its northernmost point. Hitler would delude himself that this was a potential jumping off point for a renewed attack on Moscow in the summer of 1942. Thousands of young men and women from Vyazma were deported to the Reich as slave labourers during its occupation. The Germans destroyed practically the whole city before they withdrew in the spring of 1943. To the south the long salient that had hooked around Tula had been eliminated by the Bryansk Front and the front line effectively straightened out into a rough north–south line. Zhukov's West Front had pushed towards the Dniepr, north of Bryansk, to produce a small salient. As the counter-offensive liberated areas that had been under German control, the brutal character of the German occupation was revealed.

The Soviet victory at Moscow may well be described, in the words the Duke of Wellington ascribed to his own triumph at Waterloo in 1815, as 'A near run thing'. If Hitler had not switched the weight of the German attack between the different Army Groups, and if the Germans had reached the capital in September or October, would they have won the war in the East?

There are reports that Zhukov understood that Stalin was prepared to make a separate peace with Hitler in late 1941. It is unlikely, however, that Nazi Germany would have accepted this, leading to a fight for Moscow. As Stalingrad would demonstrate a year later, the troop numbers needed for a sustained fight in a city would have been huge. Dependent on reinforcements drawn from Army Group North and

Discipline began to crack. There were more and more soldiers making their own way back to the west, without any weapons, leading a calf on a rope, or drawing a sledge with potatoes behind them – just trudging westward with no one in command. Men killed by aerial bombardment were no longer buried. Supply units, frequently without officers, had the decisive way on the roads, while the fighting troops of all branches, including anti-aircraft artillery, were desperately holding out in the front line. The entire supply train – except where units were firmly led – was streaming back in wild flight.

General Schaal
Panzerdivision 10

PARTISAN HEROINE

Among the litter and detritus found on the battlefield were snapshots of the last moments of Zoia Kosmodemianskaia, a young Russian *Komsomol* member who was hanged by the Germans on 29 November 1941. The pictures showed grinning soldiers escorting the girl to the improvised gallows. Around her neck there was a sign saying 'She set fire to houses', a common practice intended to explain why the sentence had been carried out. Kosmodemianskaia had been caught while attempting to set fire to stables housing German Army horses in the village of Petrischevo. Just before her execution she turned to her executioners and said, 'You can't hang all 190 million of us'.

Two weeks later, during the Soviet counter-offensive, a *Pravda* war reporter named Lidin found the sequence of photographs on the body of a German soldier, an 'atrocity tourist', and then incredibly recovered her body in the snow. His photograph of her body and the account of her death turned Zoia into a symbol of resistance.

South, this strategy would in turn have taken the pressure off the Soviet forces to the north and south and allowed them to regroup for a counter-offensive.

The German attack on the USSR was a demonstration of hubris, and as in Greek tragedy, from which this concept of arrogant pride is derived, by the close of the play the protagonist was justly punished for his pride. The Soviet writer and propagandist Ilya Ehrenburg, writing in the Soviet Army newspaper *Red Star*, commented dryly on the successful counter-attack and the German Army's experience of the winter of 1941–2: 'The Russian winter was a surprise for the Prussian tourists.'

Right: A cross in a frontline cemetery bears the motto 'Fallen in action for Greater Germany!' The cemetery in Krasnaya Polyana was constructed close to the grave of the Russian writer Leo Tolstoy who was buried near his dacha outside Moscow.

Below: One of a number of pictures taken at the execution of Zoia Kosmodemianskaia, showing a curious and rather ghoulish group of German soldiers escorting the partisan heroine to the gallows. Around her neck hangs a sign proclaiming, 'She set fire to houses'.

Gefallen für Gross-Deutschland!

1939

Führer Headquarters

OKW/WFSt/Abt.L(I) No.33 408/40 g.K. Chiefs

Directive No. 21
Case Barbarossa

The German Wehrmacht must be prepared, even before the conclusion of the war with England, *to defeat Soviet Russia in one rapid campaign* ('Case Barbarossa.')

The Army must in this case be prepared to commit all available formations, with the proviso that the occupied territories must be secured against surprise attacks.

The Air Force will have to make available for the support of the Army in the Eastern campaign forces of adequate strength to ensure a rapid termination of land action and to give the East German territories maximum protection against enemy air raids. This making of the main effort in the east must not be carried to a point at which we can no longer adequately protect the totality of our battle and our armament zones against enemy air attacks, nor must the offensive against England, and in particular against England's supply routes, suffer in consequence.

For the Navy the point of main effort will remain consistently against England, even while the Eastern Campaign is in progress.

I shall give the order for the assembly of troops, etc., for the proposed operation against Soviet Russia, should the occasion arise, eight weeks before the operation is due to begin. Preparations that require more time than this shall – so far as they have not already been made – be begun at once and are to be completed by the 15th May, 1941. Great stress however, must be laid on disguising any offensive intentions. Preparations by the high commands are to be based on the following considerations.

I. General Intention

The mass of the Russian army stationed in Western Russia is to be destroyed in bold operations involving deep penetrations by armoured spearheads, and the withdrawals of elements capable of combat into the extensive Russian land spaces is to be prevented.

By means of a rapid pursuit a line is then to be reached from beyond which the Russian air force will no longer be capable of attacking German home territories. The final objective of the operation is to be the attainment of a line sealing off Asiatic Russia and running, in general, from the Volga River to Archangel. From such a line the one remaining Russian industrial area in the Urals can be eliminated by the Air Force should the need arise.

In the course of this operation the Russian Baltic Fleet will rapidly be deprived of its bases and thus will no longer be capable of combat.

Effective intervention by the Russian air force is to be prevented from the very beginning of the operation by means of powerful attacks against it.

II. Probable Allies and their Tasks

1. On the wings of our operations we can count on active co-operation in the war against Soviet Russia by Romania and Finland. How exactly the combat forces of those two countries will be under German control when they go into action is a matter that the *Oberkommando der Wehrmacht* will arrange and lay down at the proper time.

2. Romania's task will be to pin down the enemy's forces opposite that sector and to give assistance in rear areas.

3. Finland will cover the movement of the Northern German Group coming from Norway (elements of Group XXI) and will then operate in conjunction with this group. The elimination of Hango will also be Finland's responsibility.

4. It may be anticipated that the Swedish railways and roads will be made available for the movement of the Northern German Group, at the latest when the operation has begun.

III. Conduct of the Operations

(A) ARMY: (in approbation of the intentions submitted to me)

The area of operations is divided into southern and northern halves by the Pripet Marshes. The point of main effort will be made in the *northern* half. Here two Army Groups are to be committed.

The southern of these two Army Groups – in the centre of the whole front – will have the task of breaking out from the area around and to the north of Warsaw with exceptionally strong armour and motorized formations and of destroying the enemy forces in White Russia. This will create a situation which will enable strong formations of mobile troops to swing north; such formations will then co-operate with the northern Army

Group – advancing from East Prussia in the general direction of Leningrad – in destroying the enemy forces in the area of the Baltic states. Only after the accomplishment of these offensive operations, which must be followed by the capture of Leningrad and Kronstadt, are further offensive operations to be initiates with the objective of occupying the important centre of communications and of armaments manufacture, Moscow. Only a surprisingly rapid collapse of the Russian ability to resist could justify an attempt to achieve both objectives simultaneously.

The primary task of Group XXI, even during the Eastern operations, remains the protection of Norway. Forces available other than those needed for this task (mountain corps) will first of all be used to protect the Petsamo area and its mines together with the Arctic road, and will then advance, in conjunction with Finnish forces, against the Murmansk railway and will cut the Murmansk area's land supply routes.

Whether an operation of this nature can be carried out by *stronger* German forces (two to three divisions) coming from the area of Rovaniemi and to the south is dependent on Sweden's willingness to make the Swedish railways available for such a move.

The mass of the Finnish army will have the task, in accordance with the advance made by the northern wing of the German armies, of tying up maximum Russian strength by attacking to the west, or on both sides, of Lake Ladoga. The Finns will also capture Hango.

The army group *south of the Pripet Marshes* will make its point of main effort from the Lublin area in the general direction of Kiev, with the object of driving into the deep flank and rear of the Russian forces with strong armoured formations and of then rolling up the enemy along the Dneiper River.

The German–Romanian group on the right flank will have the task of:

(a) protecting Romanian territory and thus of covering the southern flank of the whole operation;

(b) tying up the enemy forces on its sector of the front, in co-ordination with the attack by the northern elements of the southern Army Group; then, as the situation develops, of launching a second thrust and thus, in conjunction with the air force, of preventing an orderly enemy withdrawal beyond the Dniestr River.

Once the battle south or north of the Pripet Marshes have been fought, the pursuit is to be undertaken with the following objectives:

– *In the South,* the rapid occupation of the economically important Donetz Basin;

– *In the North,* the speedy capture of Moscow.

(B) AIR FORCE:
It will be the task of the Air Force, so far as possible, to damage and destroy the effectiveness of the Russian air force, and to support the operations by the army at the points of main effort, that is to say in the sectors of the central Army Group and in the area where the southern Army Group will be making its main effort. The Russian railways will either be destroyed, or, in the case of more important objectives close to hand (i.e., railway bridges) will be captured by the bold use of parachute and airborne troops. In order that maximum forces may be available for operations against the enemy air force and for direct support of the Army, the munitions industry will not be attacked while the major operation is in progress. Only after the conclusion of the mobile operations will such attacks, and in particular attacks against the industrial area of the Urals, be considered.

(C) NAVY:
During the war with Soviet Russia it will be the task of the navy to protect the German coast line and to prevent any hostile naval force from breaking out of the Baltic. Since once Leningrad has been reached the Soviet Baltic fleet will have lost its last base and will thus be in a hopeless position, major naval operations are to be previously avoided. After the destruction of the Soviet fleet it will be the responsibility of the Navy to make the Baltic fully available to carrying sea traffic, including supplies by sea to the northern wing of the army. (The sweeping of minefields!)

IV

It is important that all commanders-in-chiefs make it plain that the taking of necessary measures in connection with this directive is being done as a *precaution* against the possibility of the Russians adopting an attitude towards us other than what it has been up to now. The number of officers engaged in the early stages on these preparations is to be kept as small as possible, and each officer is only to be given such information as is directly essential to him in the performance of his task. Otherwise the danger will arise of our preparations becoming known, when a time for the carrying out of the proposed operation has not even been decided upon. This would cause us the gravest political and military disadvantages.

V

I anticipate further conferences with the commanders-in-chief concerning their intentions as based on this directive. Reports on the progress made in the proposed preparations by all services of the armed forces will be forwarded to me through the Armed Forces High Command.

Signed
Adolf Hitler

ORDER OF BATTLE, 22 JUNE 1941

GERMAN *OBERKOMMANDO DER HEERES*
(von Brauchtisch)

Army Group North (von Leeb)

SIXTEENTH ARMY (Busch)

II CORPS (von Brockdorff-Ahlefeldt)
  12th Infantry Division
   (von Seydlitz-Kurzbach)
  32nd Infantry Division (Bohnstedt)
  121st Infantry Division (von Lancelle)

X CORPS (Hansen)
  30th Infantry Division (von Tippelskirch)
  126th Infantry Division (Laux)

XXVIII CORPS (von Wiktorin)
  122nd Infantry Division (Macholz)
  123rd Infantry Division (Lichel)

(Reserve)
  206th Infantry Division (Hofl)
  251st Infantry Division (Kratzert)
  253rd Infantry Division (Schellert)

EIGHTEENTH ARMY (von Küchler)

I CORPS (von Both)
  1st Infantry Division (Kleffel)
  11th Infantry Division (von Böckmann)
  21st Infantry Division (Sponheimer)

XXVI CORPS (Wodrig)
  61st Infantry Division (Hänicke)
  217th Infantry Division (Baltzer)
  291st Infantry Division (Herzog)

XXXVIII CORPS (von Chappuis)
  58th Infantry Division (Heunert)
  254th Infantry Division (Behschnitt)

PANZERGRUPPE **FOUR** (Höppner)

XLI CORPS (MOT) (Reinhardt)
  269th Infantry Division (von Leyser)
  1st Panzer Division (Kirchner)
  6th Panzer Division (Langraf)

LVI CORPS (MOT) (von Manstein)
  290th Infantry Division (von Werde)
  8th Panzer Division (Brandenberger)

(Reserve)
  3rd Infantry Division (mot) (Jahn)
  36th Infantry Division (mot) (Ottenbacher)
  SS-Division *Totenkopf* (Eicke)

Army Group Centre (von Bock)

FOURTH ARMY (von Kluge)

VII CORPS (Fahrmbacher)
  7th Infantry Division (von Gablenz)
  23rd Infantry Division (Hellmich)
  258th Infantry Division (Henrici)
  268th Infantry Division (Straube)

IX CORPS (Geyer)
  137th Infantry Division (Bergmann)
  263rd Infantry Division (Haeckel)
  292nd Infantry Division (Dehmel)

XIII CORPS (Felber)
  17th Infantry Division (Loch)
  87th Infantry Division (von Studnitz)
  78th Infantry Division (Gallenkamp)

LXIII CORPS (Heinrici)
  131st Infantry Division (Meyer-Bürdorf)
  134th Infantry Division (von Cochenhausen)
  252nd Infantry Division (von Böhm-Bezing)

NINTH ARMY (Strauss)

VIII CORPS (Heitz)
  8th Infantry Division (Hohne)
  28th Infantry Division (Sinnhuber)
  161st Infantry Division (Wilck)

XX CORPS (Materna)
  162nd Infantry Division (Francke)
  256th Infantry Division (Kauffmann)

LXII CORPS (Kuntze)
  102nd Infantry Division (Ansat)
  129th Infantry Division (Rittau)

PANZERGRUPPE **TWO** (Guderian)

XII CORPS (Schroth)
  31st Infantry Division (Kalmukoff)
  34th Infantry Division (Behlendorff)
  45th Infantry Division (Schlieper)

XXIV CORPS (von Schweppenburg)
  1st Cavalry Division (Feldt)
  255th Infantry Division (Wetzel)
  267th Infantry Division (von Wachter)
  10th Infantry Division (mot) (Löper)
  3rd Panzer Division (Model)
  4th Panzer Division
   (von Langermann-Erlencamp)

XLVI PANZER CORPS
(von Vietinghoff-Scheel)
  Infantry Regiment *Grossdeutschland* (mot)
   (von Stockhausen)
  10th Panzer Division (Schaal)
  SS-Division *Das Reich* (Hausser)

XLVII PANZER CORPS (Lemelsen)
  167th Infantry Division (Schönhärl)
  29th Infantry Division (mot)
   (von Boltenstern)
  17th Panzer Division (von Weber)
  18th Panzer Division (Nehring)

PANZERGRUPPE **THREE** (Hoth)

V CORPS (Ruoff)
  5th Infantry Division (Allmendinger)
  35th Infantry Division (von Weikersthal)

VI CORPS (Förster)
  6th Infantry Division (Auleb)
  26th Infantry Division (Weiss)

XXXIX CORPS (MOT) (Schmidt)
  14th Infantry Division (mot) (Wosch)
  20th Infantry Division (mot) (Zorn)
  7th Panzer Division (von Funck)
  20th Panzer Division (Stumpf)

LVII CORPS (MOT) (Kuntzen)
  18th Infantry Division (mot) (Herrlein)
  12th Panzer Division (Harpe)
  19th Panzer Division (von Knobelsdorff)

Army Group South
(von Rundstedt)

SIXTH ARMY (von Reichenau)

XVII CORPS (Kienitz)
  56th Infantry Division (von Oven)
  62nd Infantry Division (Keiner)

XLIV CORPS (Koch)
  9th Infantry Division (von Schleinitz)
  297th Infantry Division (Pfeffer)

LV CORPS (Vierow)
  168th Infantry Division (Mundt)
  213th *Sicherungs* Division (de l'Homme
  de Courbière)

ELEVENTH ARMY (von Schobert)

XI CORPS (von Kortzfleisch)
  76th Infantry Division (de Angelis)
  239th Infantry Division (Neuling)

XXX CORPS (von Salmuth)
  198th Infantry Division (Röttig)

LIV CORPS (Hansen)
  50th Infantry Division (Hollidt)
  170th Infantry Division (Wittke)

(Reserve)
  22nd Infantry Division (von Sponeck)
  72nd Infantry Division (Mattenklott)
  99th Infantry Division (von der Chevallerie)

SEVENTEENTH ARMY (von Stülpnagel)

IV CORPS (von Schwedler)
  24th Infantry Division (von Tettau)
  71st Infantry Division (von Hartmann)
  262nd Infantry Division (Theisen)
  295th Infantry Division (Geitner)
  296th Infantry Division (Stemmermann)

XLIX CORPS (MTN) (Kübler)
  68th Infantry Division (Braun)
  257th Infantry Division (Sachs)
  1st Mountain Division (Lanz)

LII CORPS (von Briesen)
  101st *Leichte* Infantry Division (Marcks)
  444th *Sicherungs* Division (Rußwurm)
  454th *Sicherungs* Division (Krantz)

(Reserve)
  97th *Leichte* Infantry Division (Fretter-Pico)
  100th *Leichte* Infantry Division (Sanne)

***PANZERGRUPPE* ONE** (von Kleist)

III CORPS (MOT) (von Mackensen)
  44th Infantry Division (Siebert)
  298th Infantry Division (Gräßner)
  14th Panzer Division (Kühn)

XIV PANZER CORPS (von Wietersheim)
  9th Panzer Division (von Hubicki)
  16th Panzer Division (Hube)
  SS Division *Wiking* (Steiner)

XXIX CORPS (von Obstfelder)
  111th Infantry Division (Stapf)
  299th Infantry Division (Moser)

XLVIII PANZER CORPS (Kempf)
  57th Infantry Division (Blümm)
  75th Infantry Division (Hammer)
  11th Panzer Division (Crüwell)

(Reserve)
  16th Infantry Division (mot) (Henrici)
  25th Infantry Division (mot) (Clößner)
  13th Panzer Division (Düvert)
  Leibstandarte SS Adolf Hitler (Dietrich)

THIRD ARMY, ROMANIA (Dumitrescu)

MOUNTAIN CORPS
  1st Mountain Brigade
  2nd Mountain Brigade
  4th Mountain Brigade

CAVALRY CORPS
  5th Cavalry Brigade
  6th Cavalry Brigade
  8th Cavalry Brigade

FOURTH ARMY (Constantinescu)

  5th Infantry Division
  6th Infantry Division
  7th Infantry Division
  Gds Infantry Division
  Frontier Brigade
  Armoured Brigade

NORWAY AND FINLAND

ARMY OF NORWAY (Dietl)

XXXVI CORPS
  SSKg *Nord*
  169th Infantry Division
  6th Infantry Division (Finnish)

MOUNTAIN CORPS
  2nd Mountain Division
  3rd Mountain Dviision

III FINNISH CORPS
  3rd Infantry Division

SOUTH EAST ARMY, FINLAND (Laatikainen)

II CORPS
  2nd Infantry Division
  10th Infantry Division
  15th Infantry Division
  18th Infantry Division

IV CORPS
  4th Infantry Division
  8th Infantry Division
  17th Infantry Division

ARMY OF KARELIA (Mannerheim)

VI CORPS
  1st Infantry Division
  5th Infantry Division
  11th Infantry Division
  163rd Infantry Division (German)

SOVIET SUPREME COMMAND
(S. Timoshenko)

Leningrad Military District
(M.M. Popov)

FOURTEENTH ARMY (V.A. Frolov)

SEVENTH ARMY (G.A. Gorelenko)

TWENTY-THIRD ARMY (P.S. Pshennikov)
  X MECH CORPS

Baltic Special Military District
(F.I. Kuznetsov [then Sobennikov])

EIGHTH ARMY (P.P. Sobennikov)

TWENTY-SEVENTH ARMY (N.E. Berzarin)

ELEVENTH ARMY (V.I. Morosov)
  III MECH CORPS
  XVIII MECH CORPS

West Special Military District
(D.G. Pavlov [then Timoshenko])

THIRD ARMY (V.I. Kuynestov)
  IV CORPS
  XI MECH CORPS

FOURTH ARMY (A.A. Korobkov)
  XXVIII CORPS
  XIV MECH CORPS

TENTH ARMY (K.D. Golubev)
  V CORPS
  I CORPS
  VI MECH CORPS
  XIII MECH CORPS

Kiev Special Military District
(M.P. Kirponos [then Budenny])

FIFTH ARMY (M.I. Potapov)
  XXII MECH CORPS

SIXTH ARMY (I.N. Muzychenko)
  IV MECH CORPS

TWELFTH ARMY (F. Yakostenko)
  XV MECH CORPS

TWENTY-SIXTH ARMY (P.D. Ponedelin)
  VIII MECH CORPS

Odessa Military District
(I.V. Tyulenev)

EIGHTEENTH ARMY (A.K. Smirnov)
  XVI MECH CORPS

NINTH ARMY (Ya. T. Cherevichenko)
  II MECH CORPS
  XVIII MECH CORPS

BIBLIOGRAPHY

ABBOT, PETER AND NIGEL THOMAS. *Germany's Eastern Front Allies 1941–45.* London: Osprey Publishing, 1982.

BEKKER, CAJUS. *The Luftwaffe War Diaries.* London: Macdonald, 1964.

CARELL, PAUL. *Hitler's War on Russia.* London: Harrap, 1964.

CHAMBERLAIN, PETER AND CHRIS ELLIS. *Soviet Combat Tanks.* London: Almark Publishing, 1970.

FUGATE, BRYAN. *Operation Barbarossa.* Novato, California: Presidio Press, 1984.

GUDERIAN, HEINZ, GENERAL. *Panzer Leader.* London: Michael Joseph, 1952.

GLANTZ, DAVID. *The Initial Period of War on the Eastern Front.* London: Frank Cass, 1993.

GRUNBERGER, RICHARD. *A Social History of the Third Reich.* London: Weidenfeld & Nicholson, 1971.

HAUPT, WERNER. *Army Group North: The Wehrmacht in Russia 1941–1945.* Atglen, Pennsylvania: Schiffer Military History, 1997.

————*Army Group Center: The Wehrmacht in Russia 1941–1945.* Atglen, Pennsylvania: Schiffer Military History, 1997.

————*Army Group South: The Wehrmacht in Russia 1941–1945.* Atglen, Pennsylvania: Schiffer Military History, 1998.

KARPOV, VLADIMIR. *Russia at War 1941–45,* London: Century Hutchinson, 1987.

KERSHAW, ROBERT. *War Without Garlands: Operation Barbarossa 1941–42.* London: Ian Allan, 2000.

KNAPPE, SIEGFRIED AND TED BRUSAW. *Soldat,* London: Airlife Publishing, 1992.

LUCAS, JAMES. *War on the Eastern Front.* London: Greenhill Books, 1979.

MANSTEIN, ERICH VON, GENERAL. *Lost Victories.* London: Methuen & Co, 1958.

MAYER, S.L. (EDITOR). *The Russian War Machine.* London: Bison Books, 1977.

METELMANN, HENRY. *Through Hell for Hitler.* London: Spellmount, 2001.

NEUMANN, PETER. *Other Men's Graves.* London: Weidenfeld and Nicholson, 1958.

REITLINGER, GERALD. *The SS: Alibi of a Nation 1922–1945.* London: Arms and Armour Press, 1981.

SEATON, ALBERT. *The Russo-German War 1941–45.* Novato, California: Presidio Press, 1971.

SHALITO, ANTON, ILYA SAVCHENKOV AND ANDREW MOLLO. *Red Army Uniforms of World War II.* London: Windrow and Greene, 1993.

ZALOGA, STEVEN. *The Red Army of the Great Patriotic War 1941–5.* London: Osprey Publishing, 1989.

INDEX